D0494834

# Clark Gable

# Clark Gable
## Tormented Star

David Bret

BOOKS

This book is dedicated to Maria da Fé, Amalia Rodrigues and *Les Enfants de Novembre*.

*N'oublie pas . . .*

*La vie sans amis c'est comme un jardin sans fleurs*

First published in Great Britain in 2007 by JR Books,
10 Greenland Street, London NW1 0ND
www.jrbooks.com

A catalogue record for this book is available from the British Library.

ISBN 978 1 906217 04 4

1 3 5 7 9 10 8 6 4 2

Typeset by SX Composing DTP, Rayleigh, Essex
Printed by MPG Books, Bodmin, Cornwall.

# Contents

# ACKNOWLEDGEMENTS

Writing this book would not have been possible had it not been for the inspiration, criticism and love of that select group of individuals whom I regard as my true *famille et autre coeur:* Barbara, Irene Bevan, René Chevalier, Marlene Dietrich, Roger Normand, *que vous dormez en paix.* Lucette Chevalier, Jacqueline Danno, Betty et Gerard Garmain, Annick Roux, Tony Griffin, Terry Sanderson, Helene Delavault, John and Anne Taylor, Francois and Madeleine Vals, Axel Dotti, Caroline Clerc, Charley Marouani, David and Sally Bolt, and those *hiboux* and *amis de foutre* who happened along the way. Very special thanks to Maria da Fé, the greatest living *fadista*, and those at Senhor Vinho, particularly Filipa and Rita, Jose-Luis Gordo, Aldina Duarte, Antonio Zambujo, Maria Dilar, Carlos Macedo and Vanessa Alves for inadvertently offering support when it was most needed. And to Amalia, always in my thoughts. Finally, a massive cloudburst of appreciation to Jeremy Robson and the magnificent team at JR Books, and to my agent, Guy Rose, and to my wife Jeanne, still the keeper of my soul.

David Bret,
June 2007

# Introduction:
# A Hunk Of Rough

Like most of the great Hollywood icons, little is known of Clark Gable's early years other than the facts that he himself wanted the world to know, together with the usual publicity-driven biography part-fabricated by the studios who stood to profit from the legend they had created and nurtured.

Clark Gable was the archetypal *supermensch*, the kind of rough-and-ready man women yearned for, while their jealous husbands longed to be him. In fact he was bisexual although he would be better described today as 'gay for pay' since this aspect of his complex persona was more for career elevation than natural inclination. In an age when such men were invariably perceived as lily-livered and effete – which Gable most definitely was not – this fact was airbrushed out of his image. Indeed, in this respect he figures among illustrious company for Rudolph Valentino, Cary Grant, Randolph Scott, Gary Cooper, Errol Flynn and Rock Hudson all possessed similar traits and in no way could any of these greats be described as effeminate. Fearful of exposure, all of these men married and had almost 20 wives between the lot of them. Fifty years from now, when they are dead and gone (and no longer able to sue), similar anecdotes concerning many modern day lothario screen heroes rarely seen in public without being in the company of beautiful women will also be revealed.

Throughout his life, Gable's father was prepossessed with the word 'sissy'. It was almost as if, at some stage, he had doubted his own sexuality at a time when homosexuality was regarded as an affliction, if not an actual disease. William Henry Gable was born around 1870 in Meadville, Pennsylvania, one of at least eight children. In 1900 the staunch Methodist married farmer's daughter Adeline Hershelman. Despite her Jewish-sounding name, Adeline was a Catholic and, like William, of German-Dutch descent. Needless to say, their respective parents strongly disapproved of the union. In Adeline's case this was not simply on grounds of William's religion, but also because he earned his crust as a 'wildcatter' (an oil-prospector) and between long shifts he spent most of his time away from home gambling and womanising. Nor was it a very profitable profession. Major prospectors such as John D. Rockefeller's Standard Oil Company had long held a monopoly on the region, leaving little chance for such small fry as William Gable to strike oil big time – not that this ever stopped them trying. The nearest free-for-all oilfield to Meadville was Titusville, 7 miles away. Most of William's workmates did not mind walking to work twice a day whereas he stayed in lodgings. It was a case of what Adeline did not see, would not hurt her.

Shortly after their marriage, and weary of family interference, William upped sticks and took his new wife to Cadiz, Ohio, where he found employment in an oilfield with better prospects and rented a small apartment. As before, Adeline saw little of him, and when she did, he was frequently drunk and abusive. But Adeline was not a healthy woman: reports state that she appeared to be suffering from epilepsy and a heart condition which would only became aggravated when, against doctors' orders, she fell pregnant in the late spring of 1900. Her son, whom she insisted should be named Clark after the family name of her maternal grandmother, came into the world on 1 February 1901. Whether or not this name was included on the baby's original birth certificate at a time when these were non-mandatory is unclear. William always maintained Clark was too sissified a name for any son of his, so it is likely – again in keeping with a tradition of the time – that he was registered *William* Clark Gable. Until he left home, his father would only address him as 'William C', or more familiarly as 'The Kid'.

For Adeline, Clark's arrival was the beginning of the end and she grew progressively weaker. By the time his birth was registered in

June of the same year, she was virtually bedridden and being cared for by a nurse. She was well enough to attend his baptism on 31 July – though for some unexplained reason William did not – at a Catholic Church in Dennison and soon afterwards she returned to live with her parents. On 14 November she died, aged thirty-one. In his notes, one of the doctors attending her suggested she might also have been suffering from a brain tumour on account of her severe headaches and general condition. The official cause of death recorded on the death certificate, however, was an epileptic fit.

In January 1902, William Gable had for some reason re-registered Clark's birth in Cadiz, at the same time as he registered Adeline's death. By now he had all but turned his back on the boy, leaving him with his grandparents – effectively a practical solution since this saved him the expense of having to pay someone else to look after his son.

In next to no time, William Gable found himself another woman. Coal miner's daughter Jennie Dunlap worked as a seamstress and lived at the Cadiz boarding house where he lodged. She was around his age – early thirties – and married him on 16 April 1903. Combining their savings, the couple deposited $150 on a 4-acre plot of land near Hopedale, Cadiz, and acquired planning permission to build a modest home. It would take them another five years to complete the project aided by Jennie's three brothers (also coal miners), one room at a time so they had somewhere to live while the house grew around them. In the meantime, William set about 'reclaiming' the son he had not seen since dumping him on his in-laws.

So far as William was concerned, little had changed in his life save that he now owned his own property and had a little cash to spare. He still spent most of his time away from home and so Clark bonded with Jennie Dunlap – he would always recall her with both names, never 'stepmother' – and it was she who encouraged and developed his interest in the arts. It was also Jennie, never William, who threw a lavish party for 'Clarkie', as she called him, every year on his birthday. Jennie taught him how to sing and play the piano, and it was she who paid for him to have music lessons. By the age of 12, he was so adept with the French horn that he was invited to join the town band.

Clark appears to have been a well-behaved youngster, requiring little discipline. He was also a tall lad – standing 5 feet 9 inches tall and tipping the scales at 150 pounds by his fourteenth birthday – when he stood shoulder to shoulder with his father, who never lost an opportunity to denounce him as effeminate on account of his artistic leanings. All the men in his family, William reminded his son, had gone in for extreme manual work and he would be no exception. To appease his father, Clark participated in every sport going at the Hopedale Grade School and swimming, sprinting, baseball and shot putting were favourites at which he excelled. Though less interested in the staple subjects – maths, English and Latin – he achieved above average grades and was encouraged by Jennie to study just that little bit harder. At this stage girls did not figure in his life – he would more than make up for this later on. He was the biggest boy at his school but because of his placid, unassuming nature, he often found himself picked on. Rather than fight, he later confessed how he had preferred to talk himself out of tricky situations because he had been saving his fists – which were enormous – should the time come, to use them on his father! At the age of 15, Clark was working part-time and earned 50 cents a week as a delivery boy – no amount at all, but enough to make him more independent of his father.

Then, in 1917, William Gable gave up prospecting, sold his house, and bought a farm at Ravenna, some 60 miles from Hopedale. For Clark, relocating was a terrible wrench. Not only did he have to give up his school, friends and pastimes, but he was now subjected to the horror of being with his father all of the time. Initially, he recalled, this was not too bad for William taught him how to hunt, shoot and fish. Such excursions were the only period in their lives when father and son got along, and they became pastimes for which Gable would develop a lifelong passion. He was enrolled at a new school – Edinburgh High – but stayed here just a few months before leaving to make his own way in the world. Oddly, instead of finding a job, he opted to help out on the farm. Later he admitted that he was desperate to prove to his father that he was a *real* man. Sadly, William Gable's 'sissy' paranoia had been passed down to his son.

Fortunately, Jennie Dunlap soon persuaded Clark to recognise the error of his ways and he found other work: water-carrying at a mine. He was paid $5 a day and lived frugally for several months until he had saved up $175 for his first car – the Ford Roadster, in which his father taught him to drive. According to Gable he mastered this in a single lesson through fear of his bullying parent. Upon his return to Hopedale, William sold it to him for what he had first paid for it – something of a cheek considering he had had it for years.

Clark stayed on at Hopedale long enough to plan his next move: accompanying a group of friends to Akron, Ohio. In the days before achieving its status as the supplier of over half the world's rubber, Akron, some 35 miles south east of Cleveland, was an industrial boomtown. B.E. Goodrich had established a rubber factory there in 1870 and production dramatically increased around 1910 with the demand for car tyres. By the time Clark arrived in 1917, the company – along with Firestone, Miller and Goodyear – was operating full-steam around the clock, producing not just tyres but other rubber goods for US forces fighting overseas in World War I.

William Gable tried to prevent Clark from leaving Hopedale. His place, he declared, was staying put and toiling in the oilfields or on the farm. Jennie, however, supported Clark's decision. By this time her health had begun to fail, but rather than keep her stepson tied to her apron strings, she wanted him to make something of himself. It was almost as if she was aware that she would never see him again. Akron was but 60 miles from Hopedale, but in those days of primitive commuting, when hardly anyone ventured beyond their neighbourhood, it might just as well have been at the other side of the world.

In Akron, Clark was employed on $100 a month as a clerk with the Miller Rubber Company – a good salary at the time. He rented a room over a pharmacy and while his buddies hit the bars and went out chasing girls after work, he was interested only in exploring the town's cinemas and theatres. None of these attractions existed in Hopedale and after his first visit to the 'flickers' he was hooked, particularly on the Westerns of Tom Mix. If the legend is to be believed, the first play he ever saw was Richard Walton Tully's *Bird of Paradise*, which first opened on Broadway in 1912. The Akron production was staged by the Pauline MacLean Players at the Music

Hall on Exchange Street. Maclean herself was in the role of the Hawaiian princess who, when spurned by her white American lover, flings herself into the crater of a volcano! Gable later said that it had been the most exciting night of his life thus far. Indeed, he was so impressed that he decided there and then to pursue a career on the stage.

Clark foisted himself on the actors, hung out with them after the show and became their unofficial mascot. Being 6 feet 1 inch tall, jug-eared and tipping the scales at almost 200 pounds, he was not the sort of man to go unnoticed. Occasionally he worked as the company errand-boy and his burly build made him ideal as a bootlegger's runner, standing him in good stead for some of the gangster-thug roles he played in his early films. Every now and then, when an actor called in sick, he was asked to tread the boards, usually with drastic results on account of his clumsiness.

Towards the end of 1919, Clark received word that Jennie Dunlap was terminally ill – it is believed with cancer or tuberculosis of the bowel. No sooner had he returned to Ravenna than there were fireworks with his father. Clark's maternal grandfather had recently died in Meadville, bequeathing him $300, which he would not be able to collect until he came of age. William had fought against him leaving home in the first place and now he attempted to use the inheritance as a bribe to keep him here but upset Clark with his persistent mocking of his involvement with the theatrical troupe. Jenny died on 11 January 1920 with Clark at her bedside and immediately after the funeral he returned to Akron. Her not-unexpected demise affected him in such a way that for years he would search for a surrogate stepmother in a number of relationships with much older women.

Shortly after Jennie's death, William Gable sold the farm and moved to an oilfield in Tulsa, Oklahoma, where the chance of a lucky strike was more likely than in Ohio. By August of the same year he was prospecting in Bigheart. From there, he contacted his son and asked him to join him, apparently promising him support with his acting aspirations if that was really what he wanted to do. William concluded his letter by saying that there was even a drama group in the town willing to take him on. By this time the Pauline MacLean Players had left Akron so Clark worked his last shift at Miller Rubber then headed for Bigheart. He cannot have been surprised to learn that his father had conned him for there was no acting job and William had already boozed away most of the money raised from the sale of the farm. At the oilfield he was living rough, sharing a six-bed tent with twelve roughnecks like himself. When one left for his shift at dawn, his bunk was immediately seconded to another coming in from the night shift. Such were the conditions that the fumigator had to be brought in once a week!

Clark was taken on as an odd-job man, mostly chopping wood and stoking the fires, and was eventually promoted to cleaning stills in the refinery. Between shifts, he was expected to let off steam with the other men in what appear to have been little more than what today's tabloids would refer to as 'dogging' sessions with whores brought in from the town, many of whom were well past their sell-by date. Often there were not enough women to go round, so the men would wait their turn, standing in line with no privacy between bunks while the action was taking place. Clark later said that the scenario had disgusted him but that he had forced himself to join the queue in order to prove himself a man in front of his father.

His experiences in Bigheart were to leave him with a mania for personal hygiene. Later on, when he could afford the luxury, he would shower a minimum of twice daily – baths were out because that would mean sitting in water that he had polluted. His stomach turned, he said, by the hirsute bodies of some of his fellow workers, he would shave almost daily and not just his face but also his arms, legs, chest and pubic area. Unlike the majority of American men, he was uncircumcised and would sometimes scrub his penis until it bled.

In February 1922, when he turned 21, Gable gave up his job and left for Meadville to collect his $300 inheritance. Suspecting he might be about to return to the stage, William Gable had called him 'sissy' just once too often and ended up flat on his back. The two would not see or speak to one another for almost a decade afterwards.

Chapter One

# GAY FOR PAY: ASCENDING THE LAVENDER LADDER

William Gable's slurs on Clark's masculinity were to rankle. When he left Meadville in 1922, he temporarily left his 'effeminate' name behind and for the next few years he would call himself Billy Gable. From Meadville, Billy headed for Kansas City – for no other reason, he later said, than 'it happened to be there for the drifter he had become'. His first job was with a *chautauqua* (travelling tent show) but not as a performer: instead he was erecting and taking down marquees. When the company folded in snowbound Montana, Billy and their pianist stowed away on a freight train to Bend, Oregon, where his fellow traveller's relatives lived.

For a while Billy found work as a lumberjack but handling logs damaged his hands. Unable to afford the proper, protective gloves he toughened his hands by soaking them in vinegar. He stuck with the 12-hour shifts until he had saved up enough cash to travel to the nearest big city – Portland – to hopefully set himself up. Tired of heavy-duty labour, Billy is reputed to have got himself a job working behind the neckties counter in Meir & Franks department store although this is unlikely for customers would almost certainly have been put off by the sight of his big cracked hands and decaying teeth. He is more likely to have been employed in the store's warehouse or loading bay.

It was here that Billy met 23-year-old Earle Larimore, an aspiring actor who worked at the store by day and with the Portland Red Lantern Players by night. Larimore was a good-looking, loquacious young man who developed a crush on the rough-and-ready Billy. His attraction was almost certainly reciprocated when Billy hit on the idea – the theatrical term was 'fucks for bucks' – that Larimore might be the one to help him achieve his goal of a career on the stage. Educated at Oregon State University, Larimore boasted a somewhat distinguished thespian connection: his aunt was Laura Hope Crews, the Broadway actress who would one day work with Clark Gable, movie star, in *Gone With The Wind*.

For a while, Billy and Earle were inseparable. As a cover for his homosexuality, though this was more or less accepted in theatrical circles, Larimore was dating Peggy Martin, one of the troupe's actresses, but if he was hoping to have his lover all to himself, he was to be disappointed. Billy, meanwhile, had fallen for one of the other actresses. Tiny, with mousy hair, Franz Dorfler (Frances Dorfler) looked considerably older than her 21 years. Initially, she fought off Billy's advances. Like Larimore, she was of ambiguous sexuality. Also, at the same time as he became enamoured of her, Billy was suffering from hepatitis, almost certainly contracted from one of the oilfield prostitutes, if not from his promiscuous new friend Earle. But very quickly, Billy won Dorfler over with his primeval charm and became doubly useful as a 'lavender foil' employed by her to convince her religious parents into believing that she was going steady. In fact, all Dorfler's serious relationships were with women and she never married.

In June 1922 the Astoria Players, a small stock company, breezed into Portland. Headed by Rex Jewell and his actress wife, Rita Cordero, they were recruiting actors for an upcoming summer tour. Franz Dorfler was hired at once, and aware that Billy Gable and Earl Larimore were more than just friends, persuaded Jewell to add them to the line-up – Larimore as one of the troupe's leading players, Billy as their stage-hand factotum. Jewell's productions would include such forgettable dross as *Polly of the Circus* and *The Villain Pursued Her* – which saw Clark, supposedly paranoid about his sexuality, blacking up his face and putting on a dress to play a maid called Eliza.

First stop on the road was Astoria, the town of the company's origin, which they reached via paddle steamer up the Columbia River. Once there, audiences were sparse and tempers permanently flared. When one of the actors left the company, Billy was asked to take his place though it upset him when he got laughs for a supposedly dramatic part because he kept colliding with the scenery.

Towards the end of her life, Franz Dorfler spoke to Gable's biographer, Lyn Tornabene, of his mood swings. Claiming Billy had 'vaulting highs and subterranean lows', she added, 'He seemed insecure because of past hardships . . . and had to be reassured that he was liked.' Whether their relationship was consummated or not is not known, but it is unlikely, bearing in mind the mix of Dorfler's lesbian tendencies and Billy's hepatitis, which might have made penetrative sex with a woman out of the question, while allowing him to have non-penetrative fun with Larimore. Besides, as will be seen, in homosexual relationships Gable is believed to have always been the passive partner. Dorfler maintained that she and Billy shared a room, but again this would almost certainly have been to cut down on expenses. Rex Jewell was paying his troupe virtually nothing and if they ate more than once daily it was often courtesy of their resident shoplifter.

After just a few weeks in Astoria, ticket sales were so bad that Rex Jewell shut shop – for a month, he told everyone – while he gathered funds for the second leg of a tour that had so far taken in one venue. Meanwhile his actors were asked to endure frugality just a little longer. Under normal circumstances, Billy might have moved on. He had, or so he claimed, asked Franz Dorfler to marry him. Her response was to ask him to give her a few months to think about the proposal, after which Dorfler claimed she had turned him down. In any case, when she left for the nearby town of Seaside with another Jewell actress, Lucille Schumann (whose parents lived here), Billy and Earle Larimore tagged along. The Schumanns – possibly suspecting their arrangement – agreed to feed them but refused them admittance to their home so Billy, Dorfler and Larimore were compelled to stay on the beach.

By the end of the month, the Astoria Players had reformed. They retraced their footsteps to Portland, again via the Columbia River, stopping off at small towns en route. Business was little better than before, however, and rather than use the paddle steamer, again the troupe hitched rides on cargo boats, sleeping on deck regardless of the weather. During this time Laura Hope Crews somehow got a message to Larimore that she had secured her nephew a place with the New York based Jessie Bonselle Stock Company. A few years later, he was to triumph opposite Tallulah Bankhead in *Dark Victory*. Later, he joined the New York Theater Guild and married one of its leading lights, Selena Royle. Following their divorce, unable to cope with his declining career and the threat of his homosexuality becoming public knowledge, Larimore hit the bottle and died in 1947, aged 48.

With Larimore gone, and taking with him most of the excitement in Billy's life, he and Franz Dorfler began to drift apart. With so little theatre work in the offing, much of it unpaid, Billy earned his living wherever he could, lumber-jacking most days so that his evenings would be free to allow him to help out with the Astoria Players. Neither his hepatitis nor his mood swings were getting any better. At the end of her tether, Dorfler returned to Portland. For a few months, she and Billy stayed in touch, exchanging letters and hoping that a temporary separation might help; to no avail. When Billy arrived in Portland in January 1923, Dorfler was gone.

Over the next few months, Billy worked for *The Oregonian* as an advertiser's runner and office factotum. In his spare time he took singing and dancing lessons, the latter in an attempt to cure him of his clumsiness. Then, around June of that year, he heard that actress-turned-teacher Josephine Dillon was in town to start up a drama group. He auditioned and against all odds, for he still could not act, he was taken on. Born in Denver in 1884, the young Josephine Dillon moved to Los Angeles with her parents and later studied at Stanford University at a time when the establishment rarely admitted female students. Rather than follow in her father's footsteps and go into law, after graduating she opted to tread the boards. Dillon claimed she had had some success on Broadway, but there is no evidence to support this. She had toured in a play with Edward Everett Horton, and said that of all the places they had visited, Portland had been her favourite, hence her decision to settle here.

Josephine Dillon was another woman of ambiguous sexuality. She always signed herself 'Joe', never Jo, and she was on the lookout for a man with whom she could engage in a lavender marriage for the sake of preserving her career. When she first met Billy, she was living with an unnamed actress. The woman in question is quite probably the character she refers to as Beaurien (good-for-nothing) in a novel she subsequently penned. Completed in 1951, untitled, and never published, the book is supposed to be a record of Josephine Dillon's Svengali-like relationship with the future Clark Gable. As such it is quite far-fetched to the point of being absurd. In her story, she – Julia Hood – falls in love with an actor named Mark Craven. It is so syrupy – if the extracts included in Lyn Tornabene's biography are to be taken as a guide – that it should not be used as a yardstick to measure Gable and Dillon's own affair other than to prove that this was ultimately a relationship of convenience for both parties.

As will be proven later in this book, in his formative years Clark Gable was an opportunist who would sleep with anyone. 'Anything that had a hole and the promise of a couple of dollars,' Marlene Dietrich once told me. Dillon, likewise, needed to be seen clinging to the arm of a handsomish, lusty gigolo some sixteen years her junior – not quite so dashing as her Mark Craven, and exercising his lust elsewhere – but sufficient to curb the gossips and prevent further scrutiny of her true persona. If nothing else, Dillon brimmed with self-confidence; she was the mentor who filled her protégé's head with palpable promises of stardom, who would ultimately deliver but at considerable expense to herself. Why she was hellbent on making Billy-Clark a star, aware that he would almost certainly seize the first opportunity to walk out on her, is not entirely clear but may have had something to do with their age difference. Dillon was a maternal figure, one who compares with the next generation mothers of Judy Garland and Elizabeth Taylor. Having failed to make the grade themselves – more through lack of talent than missed opportunity – they made up for their shortcomings by pushing their offspring into the limelight only to end up being repaid for their efforts by being shunted aside with the onset of fame.

Josephine managed to have Billy accepted by the Portland-based Forest Taylor Stock Company, which had recently signed Franz Dorfler. With them he played a Chinaman in *East Is West*, and a family friend in Sinclair Lewis's *Main Street*. Both Broadway hits, they were now riding on the backs of the movie versions. Leaving Billy and Dorfler to brave what must have been an embarrassing situation, Dillon left for Los Angeles – claiming her trip was to find Billy work with one of the studios – but her aim was actually to open a small drama school. At the time she was unknown in Hollywood, and for an inexperienced ham such as Billy at the time, his best chance of being discovered would have been to stand in line with dozens of hopefuls outside one of the studio gates.

In Hollywood, Dillon rented a small cottage not far from cowboy star Tom Mix's palatial residence for $20 a week. At least Billy would be able to boast of living in the same street as one of his idols. In November 1922 she sent him $50 to buy new clothes and join her – though if her novel is to believed he turned up dirty and dishevelled, very un-Gablelike, given his phobia for cleanliness. Next, there was the couple's 'moral situation' to contend with. During the last few years Hollywood had been rocked by one scandal after another, with the Fatty Arbuckle rape-or-manslaughter case, several high-profile drug-related suicides, the murder of director William Desmond Taylor and episodes of under-age sex, which had threatened the careers of a number of major stars, including Charlie Chaplin. While homosexuality was widely condemned, lesbianism was less so, simply because in those days most people were too naive to work out what they did in the bedroom. Also, living in sin was definitely not *de rigueur*.

Who popped the question is not known, but when Billy arrived in Hollywood in June 1923, Dillon paid for him to stay at a hotel, leaving him free to indulge in whatever sexual activities took his fancy. So that he could be seen to be supporting himself, she found him a job in a local garage and despite her lack of studio contacts, his first bit part in a movie. This was Ernst Lubitsch's sparkling comedy *Forbidden Paradise* set in the court of Catherine the Great and starring Pola Negri and Rod La Rocque, then promoted as lovers on and off the screen. But nothing could have been further from the truth. Negri (Apollonia Cahlupec, 1894–1987) – who a few years later would fabricate a story that she and Rudolph Valentino had been lovers at the time of his death – was a self-confessed 'fag-hag' as well as a liar *par excellence*. While shooting *Forbidden Paradise*, La Rocque (1896–1968), a 6-foot, 3-inch slab of beefcake, is known to have spent at least one weekend with the young Clark Gable. He was just as macho, if not more so, and the two would remain friends until the intensely homophobic Gable – despite his gay-for-advancement leanings – decided that to be seen in La Rocque's company might be detrimental to his career. La Rocque's later movies, though their titles sailed over the heads of general audiences at the time, should have been a clear giveaway: *Let Us Be Gay!*, *What's Wrong With Women?*, *The Coming Of Amos* . . . and *Hi, Gaucho!* Forced out of the closet in 1927, he submitted to an enforced lavender marriage with silents' vamp Vilma Banky. It was a successful partnership that surprised his oppressors by lasting until his death.

Billy and Josephine Dillon were married, most likely on 13 January 1923, by a Reverend Meadow – by which time he had cast caution to the wind reverting to the name Clark Gable. He added two years to his age, declaring that he was 24, while Dillon deducted six years, claiming on the register that she was 36. Though Clark moved into the cottage with her, he made no secret of the fact that he was sleeping around and so the arguments began. Before leaving the garage, Clark would sometimes rub salt into his wife's wounds by informing her that he had a date that evening with some hoofer and he would then disappear for days on end. Dillon shrugged her shoulders and allowed him to please himself, bringing him to heel only when she had secured him an audition. Another condition of her allowing him to roam around town like a tomcat was that he should attend some of her acting classes and acquire a speaking voice to match his rugged looks. All his life, Gable was to be criticised by directors on account of his unnaturally high-pitched tone. Like Rock Hudson, years later, Clark spoke with a light tenor, which some found effete. Dillon encouraged him to scream and yell, damaging his vocal cords so that what remained was a drawl which drove female fans wild, while filling their partners with envy.

Josephine Dillon may also be accredited with teaching Gable how to walk and how to control his long arms and over-sized hands without knocking everything and everyone in sight flying. But what she couldn't get him to curb was his acute narcissism. Indeed, she encouraged this by paying on the instalment plan for him to have his teeth fixed. Two front ones were rotten and rather than have them pulled, they were gold-capped, and as such would cause him grave problems later on. Dillon then provided him with a matinée idol wardrobe: silk shirts and boxer shorts, monogrammed suits and sweaters, as well as hand-made shoes that she could ill afford. The effect of this was only to add more clout to Gable's womanising. Nor did females have to be pretty and shapely to attract him: for the time being he was more interested in healthy bank accounts than hourglass figures. Male conquests, on the other hand, had to be big, butch and beefy – and of course influential in their field.

Like every other Hollywood hopeful, Clark joined the crowds of extras outside the studio gates and on account of his great height (the average American in those days stood at 5 feet 8 inches) was selected for a bit part in *White Man*. This earned him $150 for ten days' work. Not long afterwards, on the same daily rate of $15 and in mostly blink-and-miss parts, he appeared in *Déclassée, North Star, The Johnstown Flood* – and in *Ben Hur* (completed in 1925), where he can be briefly seen in a shot with Ramon Novarro. His biggest part should have been in Erich von Stroheim's *The Merry Widow*, but for some unknown reason the director, scathingly referred to as 'The Hun' by just about everyone who worked with him, demoted him to unpaid extra.

Silent movies, however, held no excitement for a young man who had shouted himself hoarse to perfect his speaking voice and in March 1925 Clark auditioned for an unspecified non-speaking part in *Romeo and Juliet*. The play was about to tour the West Coast in a production by husband-and-wife team Louis MacLoon and Lillian Albertson, then very much in vogue. The leads were Rollo Peters and actress-playwright Jane Cowl, who had recently triumphed on

Broadway with *Antony and Cleopatra*. Like Erich von Stroheim, the MacLoons initially wanted nothing to do with Gable, which suggests that he was either less talented than Josephine Dillon made him out to be, or possessed with an attitude brought about by her inflating of his ego. But they were overruled by Jane Cowl. Like her movie equivalent Mary Pickford, Cowl refused to believe she would not look ridiculous at almost 40 to be seen to be portraying the teenage heroine.

Jane Cowl (Grace Bailey, 1886–1950) made her debut in 1903, in the New York production of *Sweet Kitty Bellairs*. Best described as a cross between Tallulah Bankhead and Margaret Sullavan, with her deep, throaty voice and cool beauty, Cowl was a powerful name in Twenties theatrical circles, accustomed to getting her own way because her performances invariably packed halls to the rafters. To claim she was a nymphomaniac may have been putting it mildly: Cowl had a voracious appetite for young men, the younger the better, and insisted on 'auditioning' Clark in her dressing room. This he passed with flying colours but then the MacLoons were offered an ultimatum: unless Clark joined the cast, they would have to find themselves a new leading lady!

*Romeo and Juliet* opened in Los Angeles in May 1925, and from the West Coast took in Portland, San Francisco, Seattle and Vancouver before returning to New York whence the lovers parted company. Cowl was in search of the next young stud, while Gable was to appear for the MacLoons in Maxwell Anderson's *What Price Beauty?*. He auditioned for the sizeable role of Private Kiper but was initially rejected for not being manly enough. Warren G. Harris (*Clark Gable*, 2002) quotes Lillian Albertson as having said, 'He looked the hardy, virile type, but he sounded like a pansy when he read the tough and salty dialogue.' Albertson is thought to have told this to Gable's face – the *supreme* insult, given what he had been through with his father – and he must have made a sterling effort to convince her otherwise. Dropping his voice an octave, not only did he get the part but when the tour was reprised a few months later and one of the leads – Hale Hamilton – dropped out, he was promoted to the sought-after role of Sergeant Quirt.

The Gables' 'marriage' was already beyond repair by the beginning of 1926 when the MacLoons assigned Clark to *Madame X*. He played the attorney for the prosecution in this subsequently much filmed Alexander Bisson drama of the 'fallen woman' whose estranged husband raises their son with the belief that his mother is dead. When she is tried for murder, he turns up as her defence lawyer. In the title role was Pauline Frederick, one of the greatest tragic actresses of her generation, who had appeared in the film version of 1920.

Pauline Frederick (Pauline Beatrice Libby, 1883–1938) was possessed of all the dramatic qualities of Sarah Bernhardt and the beauty of Greta Garbo, with long brown hair that famously touched the stage when she bowed deeply during curtain calls. Like Garbo she was extremely fussy in her choice of roles and in those days working less on account of failing health. Her near-constant moribund state during her last years, however, never affected her libido – before succumbing to an asthma attack at 55 she had worked her way through five gay or bisexual husbands (one was the playwright Willard Mack, another committed suicide), and, like Jane Cowl, scores of much younger lovers. Her extramarital conquests included several similarly strong-willed women such as Jeanne Eagels, Lilyan Tashman and Joan Crawford.

She was 43, when she met Gable and was about to dispense with husband No. 3. Accustomed to her arriving at parties with her latest well-turned-out youth, her society friends must have been shocked to see this lanky, uncultured 'hick' with big ears and rotting teeth swimming in the pool at her Sunset Boulevard mansion. Not only this but he was receiving tennis lessons from the hunky coach with whom Frederick was also sleeping, and who is reputed to have joined in with threesomes and even foursomes when commanded to do so by *la patronne*. She is also thought to have been responsible for teaching him endurance in the sack – by buying him an 'Arab strap', which he would wear to ensure longer-lasting erections.

'Pauline Frederick couldn't get enough of me – she almost fucked me to death!' Gable is reputed to have said, claiming such had been Frederick's hunger for his body that he had actually been pleased when *Madame X* closed and she had taken the production to London. Even so, he would keep going back for more. Off and on, the affair with Frederick was to last another two years and though she could do nothing for his ears, she did pay for his dental work and bought him the second-hand, but nevertheless expensive Duesenberg Roamer that he was driving at the time.

Until now, Josephine Dillon had paid scant attention to her husband's philanderings. She changed her tune, though, when he hit the road with the now-forgotten Mabel Julienne Scott in Edward Knoblock's *The Lullaby*. Among the cities taken in was San Francisco, where Franz Dorfler had by chance founded a dance school across the way from the theatre where Clark was working. When Dillon learned that the pair had been seen socialising together she headed for the city, where she made such a nuisance of herself that the theatre manager barred her from entering his premises.

Gable's next part – an important one – was in Augustus Thomas's *The Copperhead*, directed by and starring Lionel Barrymore. First performed in 1918, this told of an elderly Yankee accused of spying for the Confederates, who at the end of the piece exonerates himself by reading out a letter from Abraham Lincoln proclaiming him a hero. Clark and Barrymore formed a close friendship that would last until the older actor's death in 1954. He also found time to appear in two matinée-movie serials, playing heavies in *Fighting Blood* and *The Pacemakers*. While shooting the latter he was befriended by William Haines, then Hollywood's biggest male star after Rudolph Valentino.

Born with the century on 1 January 1900 in Staunton, Virginia, Haines reached prominence in 1922 after winning a Sam Goldwyn *New Faces* contest. Six feet tall, butch and very good-looking, he was often typecast as the wisecracking, athletic, financially strapped guy-next-door that hooked up with the elusive rich girl at the end of the last reel. Haines was Joan Crawford's best friend, nicknamed her 'Cranberry', and was openly gay. He was making so much money for MGM, in-house or as a loan-out, that they were willing to turn a blind eye to his sexuality so long as he remained discreet.

Haines and his long-term lover, Jimmy Shields, stayed together until Haines' death on Boxing Day 1973, but both liked to play the field. A favourite cruising area was Pershing Square, in downtown Los Angeles, where there was an abundance of marines, labourers and rough trade. In those days Clark very definitely fitted into this last category and he was not averse to charging for his services. Haines told Joan Crawford (as quoted in Jane Ellen Wayne's *Golden Girls Of MGM*, 2002) how he recalled Gable 'hanging around' – in other words touting for sex – on the set of *The Pacemakers* while working as an extra. He admitted that he would have done absolutely anything to earn money or find work: 'Cranberry, I fucked him in the men's room at the Beverly Wilshire Hotel. He was that desperate. He was a nice guy, but not a fruitcake.' Haines' biographer, William J. Mann (*Wisecracker*, 1988) also exploded the myth not always known outside gay circles that big, macho men such as Clark Gable are not necessarily the active partners during sex. Referring to Haines' reputation for giving 'the best head' in Hollywood, Mann writes, 'It wasn't a blow-job,' a friend insisted. 'Billy fucked *him* in the mensroom. Billy was the *fucker*, never the *fuckee*.'

Haines also got him a walk-on part in *The Plastic Age*, starring Clara Bow. Doubtless to his lover's delight, he appears in an extended locker-room scene with 24 near-naked men, overtly homoerotic for its day and cut out of some prints. He reveals a pleasantly muscular torso, but is uglier than everyone else on display, and fifteen years from then, as will be seen, the incident within the Beverly Wilshire mensroom would have near-disastrous consequences for Gable, Haines, and several of their so-called 'fuck-buddies'.

Clark's next stage role, in Maurice Watkins' *Chicago*, was the first to get him noticed by the critics. Centred round the trial of murderess Roxie Hart, this ribald story – with Francine Larrimore in the lead – had just taken Broadway by storm. A few years later it was remade with Ginger Rogers, and later still, sensationally revived on both sides of the Atlantic with Catherine Zeta Jones and Richard Gere. Opposite Nancy Carroll's Roxy, Clark played Jake, the reporter who covers her trial – following a scene where Roxy shoots her lover dead while he is buttoning his flies after they have had sex, which had moralists up in arms. The *San Francisco Chronicle* applauded Clark as, 'The only three-dimensional portrayal of a newspaperman ever witnessed on the San Francisco stage.' The review was almost certainly instigated by Nancy Carroll herself, in the hope of getting Gable to stay with the production after an argument with the producer had seen him threaten to walk out and therefore leave her side. Like his previous leading ladies she too was paying for his stud services.

The baby-faced actress (1903–65) – regarded by many as the successor to Clara Bow, minus the dreadful nasal twang – was, at 22, the first high-profile lover to have been younger than Clark. She was about to sign a movie deal with Paramount and despite being married (to scriptwriter Jack Kirkland) with a small child, she was hoping Clark might accept a part in her next film. But he turned her down, declaring he would never face a movie camera again – unaware that in a few months' time the release of *The Jazz Singer* (1927) would take motion pictures to a new dimension and that the new-fangled concept of sound was no mere flash in the pan.

According to Josephine Dillon's more credible memoirs (*Modern Acting*, 1940), when *Chicago* closed, Gable was presented with two offers: a film with vamp Dorothy Davenport, or a season with the Laskin Brothers Stock Company based in Houston, Texas. Despite his aversion to the movies, unless he was watching them, he was in favour of the former. But the move was blocked by his wife and after all she was still paying the bills. Davenport, Dillon declared, was bad news. In 1923 she had been at the centre of a messy scandal when her husband – 30-year-old King of Paramount Wallace Reid – had died after being railroaded into a sanitarium. Following an accident on set, rather than send Reid to hospital, have him laid off for a few weeks then push the production over budget, the studio doctor had been instructed to administer morphine. Over the next few weeks he was injected regularly so that he could continue working, and when he had become addicted to the drug, Dorothy Davenport had signed the papers to have him sectioned. It was also widely rumoured that she had been behind Paramount's decision to have him 'put out of his misery'. Josephine Dillon's decision to keep Clark away from such a woman, particularly as he would almost certainly have ended up sleeping with her, was a wise one.

Gable therefore travelled to Houston, surprising even himself by triumphing at the Palace Theater. His starting salary was $40 a week and saw him playing bit parts until the managing director, Gene Lewis, offered him the lead in George Kelly's *Craig's Wife*. The *Houston Press* criticised his high-pitched voice, but concluded 'He has a charming stage personality'. Lewis next put Clark into Eugene O'Neill's *Anna Christie*, soon to be filmed as Greta Garbo's first talkie. Gable played burly seaman Matt Burke, who falls for the heroine (Eveta Nudsen), unaware that she is a prostitute. Such was his popularity that each evening he was mobbed at the stage door by female fans and invited to society parties. Such unprecedented adoration brought Josephine Dillon rushing into town and Clark, starting to tire of her now that she had served her purpose, gave instructions that she was not to be allowed anywhere near him.

In *The Gingham Girl*, he sang and danced for the first time – there is no record of how good or bad he was – in an undersized checked suit. In Willard Mack's *The Noose*, he played the owner of a plantation in the tropics. In *The Dark Angel*, he was an airman blinded during the war, and in *Zat So?* he played a boxer, offering fans a glimpse of his fine physique when he stripped off for the fight scenes.

It was at a society reception that Gable first encountered Ria Langham, or to give her her full list of names: Maria Franklin Prentiss Lucas Langham. She was thrice married and, at 44, seventeen years his senior. Born in Kentucky in January 1884, but raised in Macomb, Illinois, Maria married William Prentiss at 17, in the year of Clark's birth. The marriage lasted four years and produced a son, George. Ria had moved to Houston to acquire her divorce and next married wealthy industrialist Alfred Lucas, a widower twenty-two years her senior. The couple had had two children: George Anna (Jana) and Alfred Jr. But Lucas died in 1922, bequeathing Ria a fortune, and three years later she wed Denzil Langham. This marriage lasted just two years and Ria had just received notification of her final decree when she met Clark.

Josephine Dillon was more concerned about this relationship than any of the others. Ria had money! She therefore called in a favour from a producer friend, Arthur Hopkins, who was currently casting the Broadway production of *Machinal* – the idea being that if Clark went to New York, he would be out of Ria's clutches. Dillon only found out that her rival also had an apartment in New York after he had been given the part. Inevitably there was a row during which Clark ordered her to stay out of his life for good. Dillon's vitriolic response – 'You'd better become the best actor you can, because you'll *never* become a man!' – coming after his father's taunts and Lillian Albertson's 'pansy' slur were to rankle with him for the rest of his life.

*Machinal*, Sophie Treadwell's feminist drama starring Zita Johann, opened at the Plymouth Theater on 7 September 1928, following try-outs in New Haven, Connecticut. It was loosely based on a murder trial – Judd Gray and Ruth Snyder had been found guilty of killing Snyder's husband and were executed in Sing-Sing at the beginning of the year. What made the case more sensational was that a newspaper had sneaked a photographer into the prison to snap Snyder in the electric chair. The picture appeared on front pages across the country. Because of the legal implications, none of the characters in Treadwell's play were given names. Clark played The Lover who coerces The Woman into committing murder. His inclusion in the cast was also against the wishes of Zita Johann, an alumnus of Alfred Lunt and Lynne Fontanne. So much so that a clause was added to the contract stipulating that should she find him unsuitable in his role, he could be fired at a moment's notice and replaced with an understudy. The review in the *New York Times* – 'He's young, vigorous and brutally masculine!' – assured his stay with the production until the end of its 100-plus performances run. Indeed, *Machinal* was only removed from the Plymouth Theater's programme in December to make way for a previously sold-out seasonal item.

Thus far, in his twenty-seven years, Gable's more serious relationships had been with three homosexuals (Larimore, La Rocque and Haines), two lesbians (Dorfler and Dillon), two man-eaters (Cowl and Frederick), and now a society matron old enough to be his mother. Ria Langham, however, fitted into the same category as

Pauline Frederick in that she was not satisfied just to be seen on the arm of the testosterone charged stud with a reputation for sleeping with absolutely anyone of either sex – she needed his services in the bedroom too. In this respect she made sure he earned his keep and repaid her in kind for the luxuries she heaped upon his broad shoulders, ranging from silk underwear to a Ford Roadster. Like every one of her predecessors she also knew that once Clark tired of using her, he would cast her aside and move on. Why Ria bothered, when she had the wherewithal to attract someone of her own class who would have treated her better, only baffled those who knew her.

It was Ria who announced their forthcoming marriage in one of the society columns – mindless of the fact that Clark had yet to ask Josephine for a divorce. There is some confusion as to when, or if at all, the subsequent ceremony took place. Gable later claimed that he and Ria had married 'some time in 1929', after he had arranged a Mexican divorce from Dillon, then changed his mind and said that the ceremony took place on 31 March 1930. Dillon, however, is on record as doubting the legality of such a divorce, fearing one or both of them might have ended up on a bigamy charge, as had recently happened with Valentino. The truth appears to be that Dillon filed a suit against Clark on 30 March 1929, citing desertion, requesting no alimony, and with the decree to become absolute on 30 March 1930. Therefore one may assume, given Hollywood's traditional urgency with such matters, that the later date given by Gable was the correct one.

His career was edging forwards in smallish leaps and bounds, though not without the occasional stumbling block. He played a navy lieutenant opposite Lester Lonergan in a turkey called *House Unguarded*, a murder mystery which opened in Westchester in December 1928, from which he was fired for 'incompetent acting' before the production transferred to Broadway. His ego dented, Clark vowed never to set foot on another stage, but within weeks he auditioned for the lead in *Conflict*. But his pride took another bruising when this went to another relative newcomer – Spencer Tracy.

Next, Gable's agent, Chamberlain Brown, got him the lead in

George M Cohan's *Gambling*. Try-outs opened at Philadelphia's Garrick Theater on 13 May 1929, by which time – solely on Cohan's reputation – the production had been booked for Broadway. Cohan, however, only wanted a stooge to test out his new material. Weeks ahead of the Broadway première, when the company reached Atlantic City, Clark was fired.

In the run-up to the October Wall Street Crash, across America theatre productions had dwindling audiences. This was not just on account of the failing economic climate but also because of the Talkies boom. Most cinemas had lower overheads than the theatres, and this was passed on to the customer, whereas good seats for a stage performance cost upwards of $1; one could take in a double feature at the movies for as little as ten cents. The best-received of Gable's plays during this time was *Black Widow*, staged by the legendary David Belasco, in which Clark and Beth Merrill play inmates of a European prison awaiting execution. The pair falls in love, she becomes pregnant and their executions are deferred until after the birth of their child. The play opened in Baltimore the week of the Crash, transferred to Philadelphia and then, like *Machinal*, was removed from the programme to make way for a festive production.

*Love, Honour And Betray*, which did the rounds during spring 1930, was not a great success, though it enabled Gable to exact his revenge on an old enemy. With him in the very apt role of a gigolo, this was staged by leading Broadway producer of the time Albert H. Woods. The director was Lester Lonergan, the man who had fired him from *House Unguarded*, and though he would not be acting in this one, he made it clear that he did not want Clark in the production. Woods, a connoisseur of young men who had clearly set his sights on Clark, convinced him otherwise – either Gable stayed, or Lonergan left. This was to be the beginning of Lonergan's downfall and within the year he would die of alcoholism. Whether Woods succeeded in bedding Clark is unknown, but extremely likely considering he slept with just about every good-looking man, straight or gay, to cross his path, on the premise that it would be in the interests of furthering their career. Woods had a long-term relationship with female impersonator Julien Eltinge and was currently involved with his latest leading man, George Brent.

Clark certainly became enamoured of the leading lady, Alice Brady (1892–1939), a precursor of Carole Lombard (with whom she would appear in *My Man Godfrey* in 1936), who had a penchant for high life and vulgarity. *Love, Honour And Betray* had try-outs in Hartford and Atlantic City before transferring to Brooklyn's Flatbush Theater, then New York's Eltinge Theater on 12 March 1930, where it ran until the end of April. The play was almost a word-for-word translation of André-Paul Antoine's *L'Ennemie*, a massive hit on the Paris stage. The setting is a cemetery wherein the Brady character's newly opened grave is sandwiched between those of the two men she loved (Brent, Robert Williams). One at a time their ghosts appear and explain, with flashbacks, how Brady drove them to their deaths. Then her last lover (Clark) arrives at the cemetery, ahead of the funeral cortège, to tell his version of events.

What makes the play historically interesting is that Gable wore a moustache for the first time – which he hated and shaved off in his dressing room immediately after the final performance. The reviews tended to favour him, while virtually ignoring Brady, and this brought the curtain down on their affair and got him into hot water with Ria, particularly when the *New York Telegram* enthused, 'Mr Gable wins the kissing prize. He busses Miss Brady with vim, vigour and vitality and should be commended for his skill at such psychopathic endeavours!' It was Clark's penultimate theatrical venture and his last to be staged on Broadway. Some time during late spring 1930, Albert H. Woods earmarked him for a part in Ernest Hemingway's A *Farewell To Arms*, scheduled for its Broadway première in the September. Meanwhile Chamberlain Brown optioned him for what would have been his first major screen role opposite Mary Pickford in *Secrets*, to be filmed around the same time but not completed until 1933. But both were shelved when Clark was contacted by his former mentors, the MacLoons: the pair were planning a West Coast tour of *The Last Mile*, currently wowing Broadway audiences with Spencer Tracy in the role of hard-bitten convict, Killer Mears.

Clark saw the play at the Harris Theater and was so bowled over by Tracy's portrayal as the leader of a bunch of Death Row prisoners who instigates a breakout that he initially refused the part. But the MacLoons persuaded him otherwise. Then the production hit a snag when Chamberlain Brown, who had negotiated $400 a week for Gable's last few plays, demanded $500 for this one, which the Macloons could not afford to pay. Ria stepped into the breach: without his knowledge, she made up the difference in Clark's salary.

The try-outs in San Francisco were a disaster. Audiences were unmoved, critics never even bothered to put pen to paper. Clark was all for throwing in the towel, but he had signed a contract to travel with the production to Los Angeles, where it opened at the Belasco Theater on 7 June 1930. Here, there was a complete volte-face when he received a standing ovation after the première and the *Los Angeles Times'* notoriously hard-to-please drama critic Edwin Schallert enthused, 'In the role of the convict sentenced to walking that "last mile" to the electric chair, Gable knocked everyone in the audience between the eyes with the fierce, bloodthirsty, vindictive and blasphemous way he tore the part open'.

Clark so impressed top impressario Minna Wallis (sister of producer Hal) and her partner-lover Ruth Collier that they immediately poached him from Chamberlain Brown. It was Wallis who talked him into returning to the movies. Thus far his contribution to the medium had been virtually nil, so Wallis arguably set her sights too high by pushing for the role of Joe Massara in Mervyn LeRoy's *Little Caesar*, about to go into production with Edward G. Robinson in the title role. LeRoy liked what he saw, tested Clark for the part and paid $500 to keep him interested. The response from studio chief Jack Warner, who had also seen Gable in *The Last Mile*, has entered Hollywood folklore: 'You fool! You've just wasted $500 of my money on a jug-eared oaf with big feet, big hands, and the ugliest face I ever saw!' Subsequently the part went to Douglas Fairbanks Jr, then in the headlines on account of his 'fairytale' marriage to Joan Crawford. Clark would later exact his revenge on Fairbanks for nabbing his part by stealing his wife.

To compensate for Clark's loss, Minna Wallis negotiated a

somewhat shaky contract with Pathé, which would see him receiving fifth billing in a Western, *The Painted Desert*. He was offered $750 a week for a one-movie deal, with the possibility of this being extended, and spent several weeks in Arizona, where the locations were to be shot, perfecting his riding skills. He had not been near a horse since working on his father's farm. The star of the film was William Boyd (1895–1972), soon to become a household name in the *Hopalong Cassidy* series. Boyd had a pathological loathing of homosexuals, not that this had prevented him from once spending a night with Rudolph Valentino. He took an instant dislike to Gable, whose secret came out when he introduced him to Earle Larimore, who visited the Arizona location during a weekend break from his latest project, the Broadway production of *Strange Interlude*, which Clark would later film.

*The Painted Desert* is dreadful. Were it not for the fact that it introduced Clark Gable to the world, it would long since have deservedly been assigned to oblivion. The sound quality is appalling, even for an early Talkie, with the actors mumbling their lines far from the strategically placed microphones – or, alternatively, bawling so loudly while on top of them that their voices become distorted. There are lengthy gaps between snatches of dialogue too. It is as if these people, most of them relics from the silent age, have *forgotten* they have progressed to sound.

Longtime buddies Jeff and Cash (J. Farrell Macdonald, William Farnum) own neighbouring ranches in Arizona's Painted Desert, but fall out after finding a baby boy at a deserted emigrants' camp. The argument stems from which of them will raise the child, with Cash assuming the task and naming him Bill, allegedly because William Boyd insisted on this! The boy grows up, becomes a mining engineer and, after discovering tungsten ore on Jeff's land, hits on the idea of reuniting the two former pals: he decides that he and his father will mine, help Jeff to earn a fortune and all will be well. Complicating matters is Bill's love interest Mary-Ellen (a wildly over-the-top performance from weepies queen, Helen Twelvetrees), who also happens to be Jeff's daughter) and Jeff's thuggish factotum Rance Brett (Clark), who is also sweet on her. It is he who sabotages the mining operation, resulting in one of the hammiest, worst filmed shoot-outs ever seen in a Western.

The film may have been dire, but Clark's mad scene was the one that got him noticed. There is something of the handsome, androgynous Apache dancer in his movements, in the way he circles his persecutors when cornered with his crime. His hat falls off and his long, dark hair covers his ears, then flops forwards. In extreme close-up his face is almost feminine in composition, like that of a modern-day *Bel Ami* gay porn star, almost too beautiful to be true, spitting out his lines with accustomed venom. Yet the only critic who seemed to notice him was William Randolph Hearst's ace reporter, Adelas Rogers St Johns (1894–1988), who later developed a gushing, some thought unhealthy admiration for Clark Gable. Three years later she would observe in an article for *Liberty* magazine,

Clark is the same man on and off the screen, which is true of few stars. He has the same charm which no psychologist has ever explained – but which probably got Eve in the Garden of Eden when she first saw Adam.

## Chapter Two

# CLARK & RIA . . . & JOAN . . . & JOHNNY

By the time *The Painted Desert* wrapped, Ria Gable and her children had moved into two adjoining apartments in Ravenswood – one for her and Clark, she said, the other for Jana and Albert Jr so that they would not interfere with hers and Clark's extended love-making sessions. There were apparently few of these, though, when he returned from Arizona: on location difficulties with William Boyd had left him moody and depressed. Not only this but a dynamiting sequence rehearsal had gone wrong, leaving one extra dead and another maimed for life. He was in no hurry, he said, to face the cameras again.

Minna Wallis persuaded Clark to change his mind. Outraged by Jack Warner's outburst regarding her client's personal appearance, she marched into the mogul's office – career suicide in those days, though being the sister of one of the studio's top executives did give her a certain clout – and bawled him out, demanding Clark be given a chance. Warner capitulated, offering him the part of the sadistic chauffeur in William Wellman's *Night Nurse*. This featured new recruit Barbara Stanwyck as the nurse-companion of wealthy widow Joan Blondell, who the Gable character plans to marry, then murder! His hair sleeked back and wearing a dark, high-collared uniform, and with his feline features, Gable resembles a young Conrad Veidt and could easily have passed himself off as a Nazi.

Clark objected to the scene in the film where he had to smack Barbara Stanwyck in the mouth, having discovered she was on to his plan. Again, had this got back to Jack Warner, he would have been fired. Preview notices, however, dictated that for the foreseeable future he would be typecast as creeps, such as gangland killer Louis Blanco, who gets to battle with a corrupt journalist (Richard Barthelmess) in *The Finger Points*. The film was little better than *The Painted Desert*, but led to himself and Minna Wallis being invited to a party hosted by MGM's 'Boy Wonder' producer Irving Thalberg and his actress wife Norma Shearer.

New York-born Thalberg (1899–1936) started out as a secretary to Universal's Carl Laemmle and slowly worked his way through the ranks to producer status, joining forces with Louis B. Mayer in 1923, helping him to found MGM the following year. Mayer appointed him studio vice-president and, more than any of his other executives, he relied on his tact and experience though the two never really got along despite Thalberg's gift of turning everything he touched into box-office gold. Thalberg was the archetypal Mama's boy and suffered extremely delicate health on account of a heart defect. Therefore he was allowed far too much of his own way. Minna Wallis had organised with him a screen test for Clark – the re-enactment of the closing scene from *The Last Mile*. Thalberg was not overly impressed, but his sexually repressed wife was. Also, it was brought to his attention that Clark was being courted by RKO Pictures' Pandro S. Berman. His first films may have been mediocre but this had largely been down to poor direction. Both Thalberg and Berman told Wallis that, though rough around the edges and undisciplined in front of the camera, somewhere within Gable's brawny frame a half-decent actor was fighting to get out.

Thus it was that early on in his career, Clark was of insufficient importance to meet the head of MGM – the tyrannical Mayer, scathingly referred to as 'The Messiah' – but Thalberg railroaded him into offering him a twelve-month probationary contract. This would net him $650 a week, $100 a week less than he had earned with Pathé, though the potential was limitless, should he gain Mayer's approval after his debut film for MGM. Mayer, having been forewarned of Gable's reputation – though almost certainly he knew nothing of his homosexuality otherwise he would never have considered taking him on – never expected him to make the grade and added an extra clause to his contract:

> The artist agrees to conduct himself with due regard to public conventions and morals, and agrees that he will not do or commit any act that will degrade him in society, or bring him into public hatred, contempt, scorn, ridicule – or [any act] that will shock, insult, offend the community, or ridicule public morals or decency, or prejudice the Motion Picture industry in general.

Before putting him to work, MGM effected a few essential changes to the Gable bodywork. Considered scraggy should he be expected to remove his shirt, he was over his hepatitis but was not yet back to his regular weight. Clark was sent to a gymnasium and ordered to work out with weights. The studio make-up department plucked and reshaped his shaggy eyebrows and he was given a new hairstyle – the one with the kiss-curl dangling over his right eye. In the days before corrective surgery nothing could be done about his ears, so cameramen would have to work around the problem by not photographing him face on, or full on from behind. Little was done about his teeth for the time being other than to coat them with gleam paste immediately before a take – and in any case, as the villain in every film he was put into, no one expected him to smile much.

Gable's first MGM film was *The Easiest Way*, starring Constance Bennett as a working girl kept by a sneering Adolphe Menjou, who secretly loves smoothy reporter Robert Montgomery. In a bit part, Clark was Niki Feliki, the sinister laundryman, who marries Bennett's sister, played by Anita Page. It set a precedent for his being offered slightly unhinged Ordinary Joe roles, usually the tougher and cruder the better. Inasmuch as the majority of working-class female picture-goers liked their heroines to identify with them – thus Joan Crawford, as opposed to Garbo, Dietrich and Shearer, became the darling of shop and factory workers – so they liked their men hard-bitten and cynical. The likes of Robert Montgomery may have *looked* good enough to eat, but these women liked to fantasise about their movie heroes rough-handling them as a prelude to sex, as they had the previous decade while watching Rudolph Valentino preparing to 'ravage' Agnes Ayres in *The Sheik*.

*The Easiest Way* was shot early in 1931, days after the première of *The Painted Desert*. By the end of that year, 12 Clark Gable films would be on general release – some with him pronouncing a few lines, others which saw him sharing equal billing with some of the biggest names in Hollywood. A workaholic, and eager to earn as much as he could in case it all turned pear-shaped, Clark was on the set seven days a week, churning movies out at a rate of one or two a month. In February of that year, having proved his worth to MGM, he was handed over to ace publicity man Howard Strickling so that a suitable biography could be assembled for distribution among the movie magazines. Many stars hated Strickling for the way in which he reinvented their pasts. One doubts, however, Joan Crawford would have wanted fans to know that *her* first celluloid appearance had seen her fellating a Chicago plumber in a stag film. No more than José Ramon Samaniegos, the musclebound star of *Ben Hur*, would have admitted acquiring his more famous sobriquet because a male producer-lover likened his hirsute buttocks to the Novarro Valley. Over the coming years, Gable and Strickling would offer one another such extraneously sickly praise that one might be excused for not mistaking *them* as lovers. Clark would tell a press-conference, 'If it weren't for my old buddy Howard, I'd still be driving a truck some place,' – while Strickling would opine, 'If I ever loved another man, it was Mr Gable!'

Strickling (1894–1982) had been working as a newspaper runner in 1919 when he was spotted by Adela Rogers St Johns, as previously explained a connoisseur of sexually ambiguous young men, who had then been hired to find a press agent for director Rex Ingram. Strickling's first job had been handling Valentino: Adela and Ingram offered him the position, advising him to knock several years off his age, naively believing the priapic Latin lover would not attempt to seduce a young man under the age of 21. Whether or not he did has never been established though Strickling certainly carried a torch for Valentino – and Gable – for the rest of his life. 'I thought, gee whizz, what a tremendous guy, what a hell of a man!' he gushed half a century later to biographer Lyn Tornabene. Adding as an afterthought as if by way of an excuse to camouflage his true feelings should these be misconstrued: 'There was nothing effeminate about him, nothing actorish.'

Strickling's repackaging of Clark Gable was effectively his creating his own ideal man, using the key ingredients already there. Clark was presented to the gullible public – who had already been hoodwinked into believing Tasmanian rogue Errol Flynn was an Irish boxer and that the odious Wallace Beery was a 'loveable soul' – as the archetypal he-man. What he didn't have at the time were other interests away from work and sex, so Strickling invented a few. In the time that his secretary took to type out two sheets of A4, Clark was transformed into an experienced outdoors type who loved nothing more than to hunt, shoot and fish – pastimes he *had* once engaged in with his father, but ignored since arriving in Hollywood. Strickling had him photographed pretending to enjoy these hobbies, suitably clad and usually posed next to his Roadster. What is amazing is that the more Gable feigned such interests, the more interested in them he became.

Howard Strickling was one of the few studio 'big shots' with whom Clark regularly socialised. Most of his colleagues, he declared (and often to their faces), were hypocrites and not the kind of people he wanted to have in his home. His true friends were men like himself, who at least pretended to be unaffected by the *schmaltz* and artificiality of Tinseltown. They were extras, technicians, canteen staff, security guards and the like, to whom he did not have to pretend, or bow and scrape while wondering when they were going to stab him in the back as invariably happened. And Louis B. Mayer being the worst culprit of all. These buddies were, Strickling maintained in interviews, just like Gable – men's men who nurtured an innate repulsion for the homosexuals crowding the backlots, offices and smart houses in Beverly Hills and Brentwood. Clark and his cronies scathingly referred to these as 'fluffs' – lily-livered, effeminate individuals who made the flesh creep – or so they said. In those days this was how all gays were perceived: as precursors to the likes of Liberace. To Clark's way of thinking a 'fluff' was a degenerate while 'regular guys' like himself – and almost certainly Howard Strickling – had sex with other real men such as Rod La Rocque and William Haines. They did not mince, lisp or draw attention to themselves and were but extensions of their favourite sports and pastimes.

This was effectively locker-room horseplay with that little bit extra: machismo fun. Gable represented the archetypal repressed bisexual, the hallmarks of which were clearly evident in his early years: his marriages to strong, significantly older women frequently of Sapphic orientation. Like Rock Hudson, Cary Grant, Randolph Scott and a host of other 'he-men', he would quite unnecessarily overplay the machismo and take immense pains to conceal a feminine side that if brought to the fore would have made him a great actor instead of an inordinately good one.

Clark's next film – *Dance, Fools, Dance* – was his first to fall foul of the Hays Office, though one wonders today what all the fuss was about. Former Postmaster General Will Hays (1879–1954) set up his code in conjunction with the Bank of America and the Catholic Church in 1922. To clean up Hollywood, Hays prescribed a powerful censorship law prohibiting 'immoral' on-screen activities such as open-mouth kissing, violence, sexual innuendo, drinking, gambling, substance abuse and the displaying of navels and chest hair. Additionally, the Hays Code dictated how stars and studio employees should conduct themselves away from the set, including how they treated their families.

Hays – described by Kenneth Anger in his *Hollywood Babylon* as 'a prim-faced, bat-eared, mealy-mouthed political chiseler' – compiled a 'Doom Book' containing the names of 117 movie stars – Joan Crawford, Clark's co-star in the new film, coming close to the top of the list – whom he deemed guilty of 'moral turpitude'. Pretty soon Gable's name would be added to this illustrious roster. If Clark, Haines, La Rocque et al. preferred their men rough and ready, platonically or otherwise, then so did Joan Crawford, who was by now clinging to her marriage to mild-mannered Douglas Fairbanks Jr by a slender thread. She too had been playing the field to spice up what she described as a 'conventional, missionary position only' sex life. The film's title, nothing whatsoever to do with the scenario, alluded to Joan's flapper image. Unintentionally camp, as in *The Painted Desert*, the supports are remnants of the pre-Talkies era who still act as if they are in a silent movie. The fake accents, additionally, are dreadful, particularly each time someone pronounces the word 'you'. Only the dancing saves the day – Joan and Lester Vail's step-by-step emulation of the Argentinian Tango previously performed by Rudolph Valentino in *The Four Horsemen Of The Apocalypse* is spellbinding.

The action takes place in Chicago in the wake of the 1929 St Valentine's Day Massacre. Rich kids Bonnie and Roddy Jordan (Crawford, William Blakewell) have dropped out of school to engage in a hedonistic lifestyle, such as the party taking place aboard their yacht in the opening sequence. This ends with Bonnie and her millionaire lover Bob Townsend (Vail) encouraging the other Bright Young Things to cool off with a midnight dip in the ocean. With not enough costumes to go around, the lights dim and everyone strips down to their underwear – a scene that barely got past the Hays Office censor on account of 'Mr Vail's flagrant display of under-arm hair'. This idyllic life ends when the Jordans' fortune is wiped out by the Wall Street Crash. Forced to leave their mansion, Bonnie and Roddy share a tawdry apartment. She, wishing to remain independent, rejects Bob's marriage offer and gets a job as a reporter with *The Star*, while Roddy secretly works as a bootlegger and getaway driver for mobster Jake Luva. Clark looks rather silly in suits that are too small, the too-short sleeves making his hands appear even more shovel-like than usual.

Roddy is a bumbling weakling but invaluable to the churlish Jake because of his society connections – one of which is Bob Townsend, in whom Roddy develops an unhealthy interest. 'You'll come here again, won't you, Bob?' he pleads. 'I'm living here alone at the club and I'll be glad to see you *any* time!' When Jake's rival and six of his gang are mowed down by the Luva mob, Roddy gets sick at the wheel – having expected to be involved in nothing more serious than a hijacking. When he accidentally blabs to *The Star*'s ace reporter, Scranton (Cliff Edwards), he is given the task of eliminating him. Should he fail, Jake's men will kill them both.

The murder takes place and, to obtain a scoop, Bonnie infiltrates the Luva gang and becomes Jake's moll, though she finds him odious. She charms him into giving her a job dancing the shimmy at his club, where Roddy is hiding. When she answers the phone in Jake's apartment and hears Roddy's voice, she immediately susses out that he is the killer she is looking for. He goes to pieces when she confronts him, from which point *Dance, Fools, Dance* takes on some of the elements of a bad Keystone Cops dénouement, only marginally better than the one in *The Painted Desert*. Having worked out that Bonnie is a plant, Jake plans to have her and Roddy executed, but in the ham-fisted shoot-out Luva and Roddy both take the bullet, the young man expiring beautifully in his sister's arms while she kisses him on the mouth. And, rather than make up the story that *Jake* killed Scranton now that no one is alive to prove otherwise, Bonnie portrays the martyr by grassing up Roddy – so impressing Bob that he asks her to marry him again, this time bringing a positive reply.

Though Crawford had asked to work with Clark, no doubt to find out first-hand what all the fuss was about, she confessed to having some reservations during the run-up to the shooting. In the wake of the Talkies boom, when so many stars were falling by the wayside, the major critics generally regarded stage actors as being superior to movie stars. Similarly, Clark dreaded working with her, believing that she would look down on him for his lack of experience. His comments upon meeting her are not on record. Joan wrote of her first impression of him, 'He represented Man at his most primeval – virile, rough-and-ready, with the instincts of a wild beast, absolutely no airs and graces. Gable had more balls than any man I've ever known.' Exactly when the two became intimately involved is not known, though the likeliest date appears to be around May 1931, at a pre-première party for their film. Ria was fond of showing off her toy-boy husband, who at their shindigs thought nothing of excusing himself and heading for the shrubbery with whoever might have taken his fancy that night. On this particular evening, it just happened to be Joan.

Five years younger than Clark, Joan Crawford had gone round the block many times. While still in her teens she fled Kansas City and a martinet mother to work as a dancer and amateur porn star. She appeared on Broadway with Mistinguett and had dozens of lovers of both sexes – resulting in at least two abortions – before marrying the snobbish Douglas Fairbanks Jr in 1929. Most of her men had appealed to her by way of their softer side. Clark, meanwhile, constantly kept himself in check as if terrified of divulging some terrible secret *other* than his homosexual tendencies. But unlike Clark's other lovers and wives, who would not even scratch the surface to find out what kind of man he really was, Crawford already knew through her close friendship with William Haines.

During the early weeks of his relationship with Joan, Clark still saw a lot of Haines – as Joan's 'soul-sister confidante', he came as part of the package. It was courtesy of Haines that Clark was given a part in *The Secret Six* starring Johnny Mack Brown, Wallace Beery and Jean Harlow. Clark played a member of a group fighting against mob rule, who pretends to be a reporter in order to trap their leader, Slaughterhouse (Beery), and bring him and his cronies to justice. Again, there are shades of Conrad Veidt, this time deliberately engineered by director George Hill, an ardent admirer of the early German cinema. By the time the film reached the screen, however, most of the key scenes had been trimmed because the Hays Office deemed it too brutal. In some US states it was completely banned following a spate of copycat shootings involving children – a twist on the usual Cowboys and Injuns playground games when, in New Jersey, one boy used a real gun belonging to his father.

Most of those involved with the film expected Gable to make a play for Jean Harlow – the platinum bombshell who had recently caused a sensation in *Hell's Angels* – this time playing Beery's moll and Clark's girlfriend. He was more interested, however, in Johnny Mack Brown, William Haines' fuck-buddy, whose screen debut four years earlier had been in Haines' baseball movie, *Slide, Kelly, Slide*. A big hunk of a man, Alabama-born Brown (1904–75) was the former all-American halfback who scored the winning touchdown for the University of Alabama's Crimson Tide team in the 1926 NCAA Division Rose Bowl final. This led to his picture appearing on *Wheaties* cereal boxes as well as a Hollywood contract since which time he had partnered Norma Shearer, committed suicide in Garbo's *A Woman Of Affairs* and *The Single Standard* and appeared with Joan Crawford in *Our Dancing Daughters* and *Montana Moon*. Her leading men had been Nils Asther and Ricardo Cortez. Husky-voiced Brown pipped her to the post by bedding both.

Johnny Mack Brown was also a close friend of Humphrey Bogart, then starting to make his name. Indeed, unlikely as this seems, the two may even have been lovers. Bogart (1899–1957) is known to have been very gay friendly, and according to one of his biographers (Darwin Porter: *The Secret Like Of Humphrey Bogart,* The Georgia Literary Association, 2003), enjoyed oral sex with men *and* acted as some kind of benevolent pimp for the gay acting fraternity. In his book Porter claims Johnny Mack Brown also had an affair with the equally gung-ho Spencer Tracy and that Brown and former silent star George O'Brien were procured by Bogart to have sex with tycoon Howard Hughes – Brown solely for career advancement. Tyrone Power, Robert Taylor, Errol Flynn, Randolph Scott and Cary Grant would all follow suit. One assumes therefore that Clark, as had happened with Larimore, La Rocque and Haines, was hoping Brown might put in a word for him with his friends in high places.

Joan Crawford's chance to have Brown to herself for a little while at least came immediately after *The Secret Six* wrapped, when they were assigned to *Complete Surrender*. Her marriage to Douglas Fairbanks Jr was by now beyond repair and it must have given her some kind of kinky satisfaction to know both her current lovers were also sleeping with each other. Clark, meanwhile, was put into *A Free Soul* with Norma Shearer – a move that would almost destroy Johnny Mack Brown's career, while simultaneously setting Gable on the path towards Hollywood immortality.

*A Free Soul* was based on a story by Gable worshipper Adela Rogers St Johns, who clearly saw herself as Shearer's rich girl, who enjoys getting roughed up by Gable's uncompromising gangster – his interpretation of foreplay. She has fallen for this lout, breaking the heart of her wimpish fiancé (Leslie Howard), but promising her alcoholic lawyer father (Lionel Barrymore) that she will break up with him if *he* lays off the bottle. Then she goes back on her word, taunting her thug in ermine and pearls, screaming that he is a nobody until he finally snaps. 'Sit down and take it – and *like* it!' he growls, shoving her into a chair when she tries to get away. 'You're an idiot, a spoiled little brat that needs a hairbrush every now and then!' Then in a fit of rage the fiancé kills him. Realising the error of her ways, Shearer gets her father to defend him at his trial – with Barrymore delivering such an impassioned speech that he drops down dead of a heart attack!

Clearly, the fact that Norma Shearer was the boss's wife made the shooting all the more interesting from Clark's point of view. Irving Thalberg, though only two years his senior, was on account of his failing health incapable of 'rising to the occasion', a problem Gable had seemingly never encountered. Casually observing of his leading lady, 'She kisses like a whore on heat', adding that during one of their love scenes she had been 'naked down below and wet as October' under her dress, Brown repeated this to Thalberg, causing him to have an attack of the vapours. Naturally, from the Boy Wonder's point of view, it was therefore fitting that his 'rival' should die in the film, his and the Hays Office's theory that good invariably triumphs over evil – save that in this instance they were wrong. Many sexually repressed women watching A *Free Soul* only wished they could have changed places with Norma Shearer and maybe get a little of what they naively believed she was getting from Clark Gable once the cameras stopped rolling! Yet so far as the critics were concerned, the only scene in the movie worthy of mention was the final one with Lionel Barrymore, which won him an Academy Award.

By the time Clark finished the film, most of Johnny Mack Brown's scenes with Joan Crawford in *Complete Surrender* had been canned, with media visitors to the set predicting this would be her biggest hit to date and elevate Brown to major star status. Unlike many of his tough-guy contemporaries, Brown's sexy Southern drawl transcribed well to sound; he looked good and was possessed of tremendous on-screen charisma. Louis B. Mayer, however, was far less interested in loyalty than he was in making money. He had liked Crawford and Gable in *Dance, Fools, Dance* – though on a personal level he could stand neither, a feeling which was mutual, and was anxious to pair them again ahead of several other projects already in the pipeline. Inexcusably he fired Brown from the production, brought in Clark and the film began shooting from scratch. To monopolise on the rumours that he and Joan were having an affair – though so far nothing had appeared in the press – the title was changed to *Laughing Sinners*.

Of the eight films Gable and Crawford made together, *Laughing Sinners* is by far their least effective. Mayer told Clark to his face that he was 'too elephant-eared and unattractive' to play anything but the heavy. Irving Thalberg, however, had been made aware of the 'dirty thoughts' going through some female picture-goers' minds while watching Clark menacing his suitors and disagreed with Mayer's opinion of him. Unattractive or not, Clark also appealed to the men in the audience in a way that his nearest predecessor, Valentino, had not.

Supporting Thalberg was Adela Rogers St Johns, who some years later compared the two actors' cult status in Channel 4's *Hollywood* TV series, saying, 'Every American man was perfectly willing that his wife should be in love with Gable, because Gable is like what *he'd* liked to have been. But they were not willing that their wives should have been in love with this foreigner, this dago!' Thalberg himself was also a despicable hypocrite, who not so long before had proclaimed Johnny Mack Brown to be the *new* Valentino. To prove the point he had been instrumental in Brown acquiring the title role in King Vidor's *Billy The Kid*, MGM's first major Talkie Western which, years ahead of *The Robe*, had been shot in widescreen. Thalberg was very wrong to cast the uncultured Clark Gable as a supposedly sensitive Salvation Army officer, a role Johnny Mack Brown would have portrayed much more convincingly.

Ivy Stevens (Joan Crawford) is a chanteuse in a greasy-spoon who, when dumped by her lover, Howard, (Neil Hamilton) tries to drown herself. She is saved by Carl (Clark) and he sets out to transform this very rough diamond into a decent, God-fearing citizen. Under his Svengali-like influence she dons the Army uniform, preaches from street corners and is almost reformed when she encounters Howard once again in a seedy boarding house. They are about to make love when Carl storms in: very un-Salvation Army-like he socks Howard in the jaw, spouts a passage from the Bible, forgives Ivy her sins and returns their situation to the way it was.

*Laughing Sinners* caused a furore with the Hays Office. Salvation Army people did not go around punching people's lights out! Joan was also criticised for the scene where she appears on a table – banging her tambourine but still wearing her infamous 'Fuck me' ankle strap shoes that remind onlookers of what she used to be. Today one wonders what all the fuss was about – more importantly, was it worth pushing the production way over budget, re-shooting Johnny Mack Brown's scenes with an actor who, for this genre of film, was artistically inferior. *Billy The Kid* was released around the same time and whereas this was a box-office smash, *Laughing Sinners* barely recovered its costs. As for Brown, from this point on his career would amount to little more than B-Westerns, over 100 of these over the next 35 years. Clark Gable, the lover-turned-rival had, along with Mayer's and Thalberg's greed, inadvertently sabotaged his career.

No sooner had the film wrapped than Joan Crawford was offered *Possessed* and demanded Clark as her co-star. This was put on ice until he had cleared his busy schedule and Joan, having tired of Johnny Mack Brown, became amorously involved with the co-star of her next film, *This Modern Age* – Pauline Frederick – who had reputedly taught Clark the staying power for which he was renowned. Ironically, Gable's next film came courtesy of the ex-Mr Frederick – Willard Mack, who scripted *Sporting Blood* to tie in with the Gable 'biography' fabricated by Howard Strickling. This was the first movie to have his name heading the credits, and with no big name playing his love interest – Madge Evans was a former child star coming to the end of her career, though she would live on until 1981. Clark played a gambler who wins a thoroughbred in a wager and despite the attempts of sabotaging rivals trains the horse to win the Kentucky Derby.

Halfway through shooting, he was told that *Possessed* had been postponed for several months and that his next venture, *Susan Lenox, Her Rise And Fall*, would see him cast opposite not just his most prestigious co-star, but one who would never be eclipsed: Greta

Garbo. He hit the roof, knowing that as had happened with her every move, no matter how high-ranking her leading man, the world would only ever be interested in Garbo. To soften the blow, Louis B. Mayer extended Clark's contract by another year and upped his salary to $1,100 a week, but a fraction of what he was paying Garbo.

In the meantime, Clark was ordered to clean up his personal life. Unless he had been cut off from the outside world over the last few months, Mayer cannot have been unaware of Gable's involvement with Joan Crawford. He certainly must have been ignorant of his still-strong liaison with Johnny Mack Brown, otherwise both stars would have been hounded out of Hollywood. What Mayer was specifically referring to in this instance, however, was the rumour circulating that Clark and Ria Langham may not have been legally married. If this was the case, under the terms of the Hays Office Code, Clark was guilty of moral turpitude, leaving MGM with no option but to terminate his contract and officially blacklist him so no other studio would be permitted to employ him.

Mayer had had the matter thoroughly investigated. It emerged the ceremony, which had almost certainly taken place in New York in March 1931, was not recognised under California law. The press had to be told something so Howard Strickling fabricated the story that the couple *had* married, but that in his eagerness to make Ria his wife, Clark had forgotten his divorce from Josephine Dillon had not been finalised!

To rectify the situation, Strickling personally arranged a quickie ceremony to take place on 19 June of the same year at the Santa Ana Courthouse, Orange County. Clark registered under the name William C. Gable, and he and Strickling tried to hoodwink the press that this was his brother when everyone knew from Strickling's biography that he was an only child. What most people did *not* know, a fact conveniently omitted by Strickling, was that Clark had been married to begin with. Like Josephine Dillon, humiliated by his carousing, Ria always hovered in the background whenever he had made a public appearance. Therefore, instead of a quiet ceremony the couple were subjected to a media circus. The press had a field day. Louis B. Mayer had ordered for the register to be put on display to prove this marriage truly was authentic, and attention was drawn to the 17-year age gap, scandalous in those days. Though the word gigolo did not appear in the various columns, it was still hinted at. After reading what had been written about her – the snide comments about her age and wealth, not to mention that she was tying her new husband down with a ready-made family – Ria vowed never to attend another public function with her husband.

Clark then made matters infinitely worse by telling reporters that Ria's age and bank balance were, so far as he was concerned, not part of the equation. Ria, was his salvation, he declared – she alone was responsible for his success in Hollywood. Josephine Dillon, who for the last few years had been quietly concentrating on her drama school, took this badly. Claiming *she* had launched Clark Gable – that was more or less true – she petitioned the press, who very quickly sided with her as the wronged first wife. Stories appeared of how she had given Clark her last few dollars in the hope of making him a star, only to end up on the breadline herself. What the press didn't know was that Dillon was attempting to extort money not just from Clark, but from MGM too.

*Photoplay, Picturegoer* and *Modern Screen* and several lesser publications courted Dillon to dish the dirt on her marriage, and she prepared an exclusive which, she claimed, would 'blow the lid clean off the Gable myth'. Whether she was specifically referring to Clark's involvement with Earl Larimore is unclear, though she must have been aware of this – similarly, of his relationship with numerous 'baritone babes'. Rather than court the highest bidder, however, Dillon contacted Louis B. Mayer, assured him her version of The Clark Gable Story was unsparing of even the most intimate details of his personal life – and that this would wreck not just his reputation, but that of the studio as well. Then she got to the point: the only way MGM could prevent the story from being published would be to buy it from her. Additionally, Mayer was requested to issue a press release *acknowledging* Dillon's important role in Clark's rapid rise to fame.

Mayer bought the story for an unspecified sum, but only after forcing Dillon to sign a document wherein she would not be permitted to write or speak about Clark during his lifetime. The

Messiah was assuming that owing to the considerable difference in their ages, Gable would outlive her. This would not be the case, though strangely the kiss-and-tell has never surfaced. For Dillon, this was not enough. She asked Mayer for a job as a voice-coach! It emerged then that 'in silent and anonymous gratitude', Clark had been sending her a monthly cheque with whatever he could afford since signing his first contract with Pathé. Those payments now stopped.

Clark had been right about Garbo. *Susan Lenox*, directed by Robert Z Leonard, *was* her film, though he acted extremely well opposite her, holding his own most of the time, if not a little star-struck. He is more handsome in this film than in any of its predecessors, but struggles to play the tough guy. Indeed, *who* could play tough in front of Garbo, unless they were protecting her? When the film opens, Garbo is Helga, raised by her uncle following the death in childbirth of her unmarried mother. The uncle treats her like a skivvy and eventually expects her to marry his odious friend Mondstrum (Alan Hale). When he drunkenly tries to rape her, she rushes out into the storm and hides in the garage of mining engineer Rodney Spencer (Clark). Only now does she speak for the first time.

Helga and Rodney fall in love. She cooks him breakfast, he takes her on a fishing trip – a scene insisted on by Howard Strickling to tie in with Clark's new image. He then has to go away for a few days and leaves her alone in the house – cue the arrival of Mondstrum and her uncle, whose attempts to kidnap her fail when she steals their horse and trap and heads for the railway station at Lenoxville. Boarding a carriage occupied by a circus troupe, she becomes Susan Lenox. The circus is run by Burlingham (John Miljan) – an ageing pervert who agrees to protect her from the pursuing Mondstrum so long as she becomes his mistress and takes to the stage as Fatima, a phoney Sultan's ex-favourite. Secretly, she writes to Rodney, who catches up with the show, chins Burlingham and says he never wants to see Helga again. When she pleads she does not know how she will survive without him, he snarls, 'I'll tell you what'll become of you. You'll go from one man to another, just like every other woman in the gutter!' Her response is that if *this* is what he thinks, she will make it a *worthwhile* gutter!

Helga travels with the circus, finding a new man in every town and ending up the mistress of crooked New York politician Mike Kelly (Hale Hamilton), while Rodney loses his job after causing a mining accident and hits the bottle because he cannot stop thinking about Helga. When she learns this, Helga cons a friend into coercing Rodney into attending a society party she is hosting on the pretext this friend might offer him work. Their reunion is short-lived when they insult each other over the dinner table. Rodney leaves. Helga hits the road to search for him but he is now a bum working for a construction gang and it is he who finds her, working in a sleazy dancehall in Puerto Sacate.

Helga has by now hooked up with a sea captain, who wants to marry her and show her the world, though she could never love him because her heart belongs to Rodney, who treats her as he would any whore until he realises that she is sincere. 'Since I last saw you,' she purrs, 'no man has had a minute of me, not even a second,' adding that she would love nothing more than to cook, clean and slave over him in the dump they will have to live in because they are both broke. Effectively, Garbo was offering to fulfil the dream of every female Gable fan! When a genuine whore propositions him in the middle of this conversation, Rodney promptly tosses her over the balcony! Then comes the repartee, pronounced to the strains of 'La Golondrina'. While going over the heads of the general public, this caused closet gays everywhere to whoop with delight at a time when homosexuality was regarded by many – not least of all studio moguls – as an affliction:

HELGA: We're just two cripples – twisted! Only together can we ever become straight!
RODNEY: You have a queer way of looking at things . . .

In Britain, *Susan Lenox* immediately ran into trouble with the censor. David Graham Phillips (1867–1911), upon whose posthumous novel the screenplay was based, was a women's rights activist shot dead by a lunatic accusing him of promoting female moral depravity. Initially the film was banned, but following a petition from MGM's London representative, 125 feet was cut from the finished print and the film was given a new title. Irving Thalberg wanted to call it *The Stain*, but when a shocked censor argued that critics would begin speculating over what *kind* of stain this was referring to, everyone settled on *The Rise Of Helga*.

Halfway through shooting *Susan Lenox*, Clark received word that Thalberg had earmarked him for a role that in retrospect would have proved the most ridiculous of his entire career. In 1929 Thalberg dispatched director W.S. Van Dyke – the infamous 'One-Take Woody' – whose planning of scenes was so meticulous that this was usually all it took to get them in the can, and principals Duncan Renaldo and Edwina Booth into the African jungle to shoot *Trader Horn*. Booth had fallen ill with dysentery, while Van Dyke spent several months hitting the bottle and had driven everyone to distraction shooting thousands of feet of extra footage which had ended up on the cutting-room floor, though the end result proved a tremendous success.

Watching Gable and Garbo in the closing mock-tropical setting for *Susan Lenox* had given Thalberg a brainwave. Recently he had acquired the screen rights for Edgar Rice Burroughs' *Tarzan Of The Apes*, which he planned on shooting on an MGM back lot, using leftover footage from *Trader Horn*. And as the tree-swinging hero, he wanted Clark Gable!

Clark, never happy about stripping for the camera, is known to have submitted to a screen test, though any footage of him in a loincloth has long since disappeared. Tested at the same time was a 27-year-old Romanian-born, American-raised swimming champion by the name of Janos Weissmuller. Tall, powerfully built and good-looking, Weissmuller had won five gold medals at the 1924 and 1928 Olympic Games. When Thalberg screened both tests for his executives' approval, their decision was unanimous: all that was required was a little plastic surgery to Weissmuller's nose, and a slight change of first name, and the most famous Tarzan of them all was born. He went on to yodel and swing away through 12 phenomenally successful movies as popular today as they were then. Clark is said to have been immensely relieved!

By now, he and Ria had vacated the Ravenswood apartments and moved into a rented house on San Ysidro in Beverly Hills – a stone's throw from Pickfair, the palatial home of Joan Crawford's snooty in-laws, Douglas Fairbanks and Mary Pickford. The Gables were frequently invited here, along with Joan and Douglas Jr, enabling Clark to observe at close hand how strained Joan's marriage had become. Matters would intensify over the next few weeks when *Possessed* finally went into production. Adela Rogers St Johns, still obsessed with Clark, followed him everywhere – not just in the hope of an exclusive of the Gable-Crawford romance, but to get her claws into Clark himself. This caused him to remark to one friend, 'Maybe I should just fuck Adela and put her out of her misery!'

There have always been rumours that Clark did just this, and got her pregnant. When questioned about the subject in March 1975 on *The Merv Griffin Show*, Adela was giving nothing away when she told the host, 'What woman would *deny* that Clark Gable was the father of her child?' She later recalled seeing Clark and Joan 'necking behind the bandstand' at the Coconut Grove, adding that she had refrained from reporting this in her column to preserve her idol's dignity. Even so, this did not prevent her from gossiping about the pair to friends, resulting in the affair becoming, like Clark's sexuality, Hollywood's best-kept open secret.

*Possessed* is a wonderful film, largely because so much of the scenario resembles the rags-to-riches Joan Crawford story. Howard Strickling's fabricated biography tactics had been wasted on her: Joan never held back when discussing her background and her fans adored her all the more for this. Whenever they wanted to know more about her private life, much to Louis B. Mayer's chagrin, all they had to do was ask. The film was so 'torrid' in parts that, like *Susan Lenox*, it had the censors in a spin. And *because* of their affair, Clark and Joan were on equal terms in this one.

Joan played Marian Marker, a factory worker in a hick town where nothing happens. She has a sweetheart of sorts – labourer Al Manning (Wallace Ford) – but finds his attentions dull because they are so predictable: marriage, running his own business, getting rich. Until then, he says, they will have to make do with what they have. 'Buying happiness on the instalments plan,' she scoffs, 'And some day a fella comes and takes it all away! All I've got's my looks and my youth, and whatever it is the fellas like. Do you think I'm gonna trade that in for a chance that's never come?' Later she calls Al 'turnip' – Hollywood slang for a man with underdeveloped genitals. On her way home from work, Marian has been held up at the railway crossing when the train for New York pulls in. Through the carriage windows she has seen how the other half live, and has been offered her first champagne by drunken toff, Wally (Skeets Gallagher). Hearing of her aspirations, Wally tells her to look him up, should she ever visit the city. Next, we see her inside his plush Park Avenue pad – though now that he is sober, Wally does not feel obliged to help, claiming the East River is full of girls who took advice from him. Then she bumps into his friend, society lawyer Mark Whitney – Clark, looking even more striking than in his film with Garbo.

For Marian, it is love at first sight, especially when she learns of Mark's wealth and political ambitions. When he tells her that he is *very* rich, she pulls no punches by replying, 'That's nice. You see, I wouldn't waste my time with you if you weren't!' Three years pass. Mark is in politics, Marian his mistress, who in order to prevent a scandal has reinvented herself as respectable widow Mrs Moreland. Mark would like to marry her, but dare not as one wife has already taken him to the cleaners. There are echoes of Oscar Wilde when he tells a friend, 'Losing a sweetheart is a private misfortune – losing a wife is a public scandal.' While they are dressing, and she puts on jewellery he has bought her for each of their anniversaries, he asks if she has any regrets. The response comes from Crawford's autobiography: 'I left school when I was only 12 – never learned how to spell *regret*.' At the subsequent party she sits at the piano and accompanies herself to a stunning three-language version of 'How Long Will This Last?' Her answer comes when Al turns up unexpectedly. Wealthy in his own right, he is now on the verge of signing a major construction deal which he hopes will be aided by Mark's political clout.

For Al's benefit, Marian demotes Mark to a mere acquaintance and is distressed to learn that Al only wants the money so that he can marry her and keep her in the style to which she has become accustomed. Her relationship with Mark edges towards disaster when Mark announces that he is standing for Governor. Now he is obliged to choose between his kept woman and his public duties. Marian overhears a colleague asking him, 'What's a woman compared to a career?' while another levels, 'It's a sad thing to see you give up a brilliant future for a woman like *that*.' But Mark believes he can have both and asks Marian to marry him. Naturally, this being a Crawford 'martyr' movie, she turns him down, saying she has never loved him and that she is going to marry Al. What follows referred directly to Joan's own floundering marriage to Douglas Fairbanks Jr – on account of Clark Gable making her aware that she needed to be with her own kind, a man who like herself in the quest for fame had sold himself for sex, as opposed to Fairbanks, whose fame had been handed to him on a plate courtesy of his celebrity parents:

MARK: I don't believe it. No woman could have pretended to love a man as you loved me.

MARIAN: Oh yes, she could, if that was the way she earned her living. Even if I do say it myself, I think I've made a pretty good job of it. Now that I've got my little pile tucked away, I'm ready to sit back, take off my shoes and relax. It's been a strain [flicking cigarette ash on the floor] being a lady!

MARK: You can't mean what you're saying? It's unbelievable . . .

MARIAN: Unbelievable? Because of three years of your priceless schooling and guidance I'm walking out on you? Well, all the schooling you've hammered into me, all the clothes and perfume you've put on me, all the jewellery you've hung on me didn't change me. Inside, I'm exactly what I was when you found me – a factory girl, smelling of sweat and glue. Common, that's what I am! Common! And I like it!

MARK [slapping her] You little tramp! Get out! You might have given me two weeks' notice. My cook does that!

Across America fans applauded – Joan's shop girls and Clark's repressed females, who wished they could have been in her shoes as she suffered in splendour at the hands of this neanderthal before rushing outside and going to pieces! What they did not know was that the scene had been rehearsed time and time again during the 27-day shooting schedule – in hotel rooms, or in Clark's trailer as a prelude to the rough sex Joan liked, and he was not averse to delivering.

All ends well, of course, so this suffering has not been in vain. Al learns the truth, declares he does not want second-hand goods from a woman who is no better than a streetwalker. Then the scene shifts to Mark's electoral campaign, where his opponents attempt to discredit him by dropping leaflets on the audience to expose the scandal. It is therefore up to Marian to defend them both. She announces that she *was* his mistress, that their affair is over and that he now belongs to the people, and as such has no right to be judged by hypocrites when his only crime was falling in love. Then, for a second time, Marian exits tears, rushing out into the pouring rain – where Mark catches up with her. For the first time in his life he has got his priorities right. 'I don't care what they do to me back there,' he says, taking her in his arms, 'If I win it'll be with you, and if I *lose* it'll be with you!' Magnificent!

The critics compared the Gable-Crawford on-screen chemistry with that of Garbo and John Gilbert in *Flesh And The Devil* (1926). The gossip columnists hinted that the pair were no different off set. In *Portrait Of Joan*, published two years after Clark's death, Crawford observed:

> I knew that I was falling into a trap that I had warned young girls about – *not* to fall in love with leading men or take romantic scenes seriously. Leave the set and forget about it because that marvellous feeling would pass. Boy, I had to eat those words, but they tasted very sweet!

During the summer of 1931, Douglas Fairbanks Jr threatened to have Joan trailed by a private detective – anxious that *when*, rather than *if* they divorced, his wife would be perceived as the guilty party.

Well aware Fairbanks was cheating on her, she dared him so much as to try. Instead, he went to see Louis B. Mayer, who naturally hit the roof. Joan was about to be offered her most important role to date: Flaemmchen – in an all-star production of Vicki Baum's *Grand Hotel*. Mayer therefore offered her an ultimatum: Clark, or her career. Gable pleaded with Mayer on her behalf, promising to divorce Ria so that he and Joan could marry. Mayer's response was that if Clark continued seeing 'the washerwoman's tramp daughter', he would dispatch a memo to every studio in Hollywood ensuring neither of them ever worked again. Crossing their fingers behind their backs, Clark and Joan agreed to cool things.

Ria Gable also contacted Mayer and between them they formulated a plan: so long as Mayer put up the money, she would *prove* once and for all to the American public that their marriage was stronger than ever. It all sounds silly today, and with a less gullible press it would not have worked. Taking her youngest two children with her, Ria embarked on a train-trip to New York – stopping off at every station en route, where an MGM publicist assured her a riotous welcome, having announced that Clark would be with her. Each time Ria told the same story: work commitments prevented Clark from leaving Hollywood, though they spoke on the phone several times every day and he was just as heartbroken as she that they were apart. No one asked Ria *why* she was going to New York – nor why she had left Clark in the first place if it was causing them both such anguish.

Clark's work commitment was *Hell Divers*, with Wallace Beery – just signed to play Joan Crawford's creepy employer in *Grand Hotel*. Filmed on location at a naval base near San Diego, this was a tale of naval aviators, their triumphs and tragedies, and of course their romantic exploits. Clark's love interest was Marie Prevost, who was as lacklustre as the film itself. Shooting was a miserable experience. Clark's name may have been second billing, but he was on only one-eighth of Beery's salary. As for Prevost, she had only been offered the part out of pity. Very beautiful and a huge name during the silent era, her 'Bronx honk' proved disastrous with the advent of sound, and by the time she worked with Clark in this film and *Sporting Blood* she was a hopeless alcoholic. In 1937, her body would be discovered in her Cahuenga Boulevard apartment – partly devoured by her dog in one of the worst cases of malnutrition ever recorded in America.

After *Hell Divers* Clark asked Louis B. Mayer for a pay rise and this was refused. The Messiah informed him that his 'incentive' for his next film, *Polly Of The Circus* – the horror in which he had appeared with the Astoria Players – would be a $10,000 car which would be presented to him in a ceremony by Adela Rogers St Johns' boss, William Randolph Hearst. The newspaper magnate owned Cosmopolitan Pictures (released through MGM), most of whose productions showcased the now limited talents of his mistress, Marion Davies, with whom he lived at Saint Simeon, their magnificent mountain retreat between Holywood and San Francisco. Davies also owned a sumptuous 120-room beachside mansion in Santa Monica – and to ensure that she had every comfort while working, Hearst commissioned a 15-room villa-dressing room at MGM.

Because of Hearst's formidable wealth, Marion Davies (1893–1961) had always been exempted from the Hays Office moral turpitude clause. She had started out as a Ziegfeld girl and was a gifted slapstick comedienne who triumphed in King Vidor's *The Patsy*. By the time she worked with Clark, getting smacked in the face with custard pies was starting to become old hat, so Hearst, 30 years her senior, had attempted to turn her into a dramatic actress. This was an exercise akin to transforming Sarah Bernhardt into a Keystone Cop and in doing so, Hearst prevented Davies from reaching her full potential as a screwball comedienne, which might have seen her rivalling Hepburn and Lombard.

Of one thing the quaintly stuttering Davies could now rest assured. Like its predecessors, *Polly Of The Circus* would be a box-office flop, though owing to the nature of his deal with MGM, the production would lose money only for Hearst. This he did not mind. So long as his mistress was happy and playing the kind of roles *she* liked, he too was content. And MGM would be in no position to complain about the latest Marion Davies' turkey because any lost revenue would be more than compensated by their other films receiving free premium coverage in Hearst's publications. Not only this, the reviews were always favourable even if some of the films were dire!

What Hearst and Mayer did not figure on was Clark's reluctance to work with his latest leading lady, though the excuse he gave Mayer was that the script was not good enough. Mayer was furious: only Garbo was permitted to tell him he had made a mistake. Even so, he was willing to overlook Gable's indiscretion just this once and ordered a rewrite, which Clark still disliked – walking off the set after the first day's shooting.

Had Hearst not been involved with the production, eager to placate his distressed mistress by having her appear with Gable, no matter the cost, Clark would almost certainly have been suspended. Instead, Mayer applied his infamous 'Machiavellian technique'. Hearst's offer of the car was withdrawn but Mayer promised Clark an increase in salary if he went back to work – a new $1,500 contract would come into force on 22 January 1932. From this point on, Mayer secretly planned to look for the slightest excuse to fire him, something which would not happen because Clark always stayed one step ahead of the Hays Office. Not surprisingly, he also got to 'defrost' Marion Davies, as renowned as he was for sleeping with co-stars. Hearst may have had the wherewithal to provide his mistress with a regal lifestyle, but he is known not to have been upstanding in the bedroom department!

The film was an absolute stinker. Clark played a clergyman who loses his congregation when he marries a trapeze artiste – a profession regarded as common by the small-town gossips. She blames herself for this and prays she might plunge to her death while attempting a perilous triple somersault. When she fails to do this, encouraged by Clark and his bishop, his flock accept her and all ends well!

Half a century later, Clark's 'smugly gentle and saintly prelate' – so described by the *Chicago Tribune* – would still be making audiences cringe. In their celebrated tome, *The Golden Turkey Awards*, Harry and Michael Medved nominated Gable in their Worst Performance By An Actor/Actress As A Clergyman/Nun category. 'What a man of the cloth he makes,' they observed. 'He plays the minister as an overgrown altar boy. The beatific smile he affects for this part looks greasy and obsequious – as if Uriah Heep has taken Holy Orders.'

*Polly Of The Circus* bombed at the box-office – the first Gable vehicle to do so – and is thankfully mostly forgotten today.

Chapter Three

# HARLOW

Clark is said to have been over the moon when Louis B. Mayer announced that his next film was to be *Red Dust*, based on the stage play by Wilson Collison, scripted by John Lee Mahin—and co-starring Jean Harlow. The production had originally been commissioned for John Gilbert, but his career was on the slide following a botched (we now know deliberately sabotaged) test which deemed his voice unsuitable for sound.

When one reads the account of Gable's casting as Gilbert's replacement – organised by Mahin, producer Hunt Stromberg and director Victor Fleming – one might be excused thinking that Lyn Tornabene, quoting from contemporary sources in her biography, attempts to conceal the fact that every male associated with the film was a screaming queen! Stromberg, Mahin and Clark are described as 'men's men and a half', while Fleming as 'a man's man and three-quarters'. And John Lee Mahin, who *did* have a crush on Clark, recalled how he had told Stromberg, after watching one of his films, 'There's this guy – my God, he's got the eyes of a woman and the build of a bull. He is really going to be something!' Though Clark may have had the charisma and nerve to seduce even the most reluctant of men, like every other male involved with *Red Dust* he was interested only in winning the lottery – getting Jean Harlow into bed.

Without any doubt *the* sex goddess of the Thirties, she was born Harlean Carpenter on 3 March 1911 in Kansas City and brought to Hollywood in 1923 by her mother, whom everyone addressed as Mama Jean. At 16, she was already voluptuous and no longer a virgin for she had been allegedly raped by Mama Jean's second husband Marino Bello. Sicilian by birth, schizophrenic and a generally all-round unsavoury character, Bello (1883–1953) had Mafia links and was a close friend of gangster Johnny Rosselli.

On account of his passion for hunting and shooting, Bello also became friendly with Clark, who may have been unaware of either his shady connections, or his violent interference in his step-daughter's personal life after Harlow eloped with socialite Charles McGrew and set up home with him in Beverly Hills. In 1928, having adopted Mama Jean's maiden name, Harlow appeared as an extra in *Moran of the Marines*, and later worked with Laurel and Hardy. From this point, Mama Jean had begun handling her career and by the end of 1929 she and Bello had forced 'Baby', as she would be affectionately known for the rest of her short life, to have an abortion and end her marriage to McGrew.

Harlow's big break came with Howard Hughes' 1930 *Hell's Angels*, wherein she pronounced the immortal line, 'Do you mind if I slip into something more comfortable?' before donning the lowest-cut gown Hollywood had ever seen. While working with Clark in *The Secret Six* she had become involved with MGM executive Paul Bern. Known as 'Little Father Confessor' on account of his puny build and fondness for listening to other people's problems – though not always helping them to resolve them or indeed facing up to his own troubles – German-born Bern (Paul Levy, 1889–1932) was Irving Thalberg's right-hand man. It was with him that he produced *Grand Hotel*. Bern was also Joan Crawford's best friend after William Haines. A talented scriptwriter, he had worked with Ernst Lubitsch and Josef von Sternberg.

Sophisticated, intellectual but unattractive, Bern's powerful position permitted him to date some of the biggest names in Hollywood, female and male, including Clark. After his death, however, various inquests revealed that on account of grossly under-developed genitals he had been incapable of consummating any relationship and his always-younger conquests merely regarded him as a kindly father figure.

At 42, Bern was twice Harlow's age, but the two got along like a house on fire despite the efforts of friends such as Joan Crawford – who could not stand Harlow – trying to dissuade him by telling him that he would only end up making a fool of himself. On behalf of MGM, Bern bought out Harlow's contract from Howard Hughes for $60,000 and during the spring of 1932 assigned her to a $1,250 a week deal. Her first film under his tutelage had been *Red-Headed Woman* and she had shocked the entire set when, at the end of one scene when the director yelled 'Cut!' and told her to remove her coat, she was not wearing a stitch underneath!

This innate vulgarity came across well on screen. Harlow was never less than the platinum-haired, busty, fun-loving tart but everything she did was pure magic, perpetrated with such innocence that she could get away with anything. Off the screen, like Tallulah Bankhead and Carole Lombard, she was unrivalled for saucy anecdotes and killing one-liners. When reporter Ben Maddox once asked her what she saw in Paul Bern, she replied, 'We listen to music and read books together. Paul likes me for my mind. He isn't pawing me all the time and talking fuck, fuck, fuck! Our friendship goes beyond that.'

What many found astonishing, Clark included, is that such a bizarre little man should wish to *marry* this self-proclaimed nymphomaniac who never wore underwear, who bleached her pubic hair to match that on her head and who was not averse to flashing her 'clitty bush' to anyone who expressed interest. Yet marry they did on 2 July 1932, shortly before shooting began on *Red Dust*, at Bern's Benedict Canyon home. The guests of honour were the Thalbergs and the Gables, with Ria making a rare public outing at her husband's side.

In *Red Dust*, set in Indochina, Jean Harlow plays Vantine, the wise-cracking tart with a heart, who, on the run from the Saigon police, shows up at the rubber plantation managed by Denny Carson (Clark). He is ebullient, initially resentful of the siren who introduces herself as 'Pollyanna The Glad Girl', telling her she may stay only until the next boat docks. 'It's bad enough having to play around with them in Saigon, much less having one in your house,' he drawls, of the other whores he has known, adding that he has been looking at her kind since his voice changed.

Denny is grumpy because production is down because of its being the 'red dust' season; a situation he hopes will be remedied when he gets his new surveyor, Willis, (Gary Raymond). Meanwhile, his lack of hospitality and Vantine's coarse observations lead to attraction – he calls her Lily; she calls him Fred, nags about his drinking, hums 'Home Sweet Home' and never stops talking. Forever hitching up her skirt and flashing her thighs, she bathes in the outdoor vat containing the men's drinking water and is surprised when Denny objects, avowing that any red-blooded male would *want* to drink the water all the more after she has been in it. Her language (for the day) is appalling and even the parrot is berated when she cleans out his cage – 'What you been eating, cement?' And when Denny threatens to hit her, Vantine responds, 'You and what man's army?' Which of course leads to the obvious, as the scene fades.

Willis arrives, accompanied by his pretty but stand-offish wife Barbara (Mary Astor). He is mild-mannered, while she is in direct contrast to Harlow's loveable slut, though Denny wants her just the same. Naturally, the two women in his world do not get along. 'I wouldn't touch her with your best pair of rubber gloves!' Vantine tells him of her rival. When Willis takes a fever and Denny winds Barbara up the wrong way, she slaps him and this unleashes his animal instincts – when he kisses her she appears to be having an orgasm. And no sooner has Willis recovered than he is dispatched on a jungle mission so that Denny can finish what he has started.

Denny has never had a *lady*. Similarly, Barbara is not used to this sort of thing and feels she must come clean to her husband. Denny agrees then visits him in the jungle and on a tiger shoot the two bond. Hearing how much Willis loves his wife and of the plans they have made for the future, Denny cannot go through with it. He goes home and when Vantine sees him looking glum, she barks, 'Is the burial private, or didn't ya bring the body home with ya?', to which he responds in equally deadpan style, 'Where'd ya git that kimona?' Then he realises he must do the honourable thing and give Barbara up and that the woman he really wants is Vantine because they are the same class and temperament. They are getting into a spot of friendly wrestling-foreplay when Barbara walks in. Furious, she bawls out Denny and realises he has been stringing her along. To the delight of thousands of female Gable fans he levels, 'I'm not a one-woman man – I never have been, and never will be! If you want to take your turn, all right, if it makes you feel any better!'

Barbara draws a gun and plugs him – not fatally – just as Willis arrives and Vantine jumps to her defence. 'You oughta be proud of her,' she tells the upset husband. 'This bozo's been after her every minute, and tonight he breaks into her room and she shoots him. It's the only way any virtuous woman would with a beast like that!' Of course her quick thinking has assured Vantine of having Denny all to herself. Her rival and her husband eager to leave, Vantine cleans up Denny's wound and as the credits roll, we see him domesticated and lounging on his sickbed while she reads him a child's bedtime story!

Surprisingly, Gable's and Harlow's on-screen antics, even the bathing scene, bypassed the Hays Office censors. 'I never wear panties, so why should I put them on to take a bath in a barrel when nobody can see me?' she is said to have asked Victor Fleming, though he, the cameraman, Clark and every single technician ensured themselves an eyeful. Mary Astor's 'orgasm' was discussed, but left in when John Lee Mahin claimed her character's affection for Denny leaned more towards the maternal than the carnal – Astor was five years younger. The biggest fuss occurred in one scene when Clark removed his shirt and ripped it off in another, revealing not just his navel, but that he was not wearing an under vest. Whereas there is no evidence that women across America emulated Jean Harlow by shedding bras and panties – or rubbed their nipples with ice-cubes so that they would stand out under chiffon dresses – shops reported a decline in men's under vests during the winter of 1932–3. Louis B. Mayer asked for both scenes to be shot again; though Clark's navel remained covered on Howard Strickling's insistence the under vest stayed off. Gable, he argued, was an outdoors type, and therefore tough enough not to need one. And MGM ultimately realised, as had happened when they teamed Clark with Joan Crawford, that they had discovered another winning combination to a box-office jackpot. There would be four more Gable–Harlow movies, each one as successful as this.

Despite the fun everyone appears to have had making it, *Red Dust* was blighted by a singular tragedy. Shooting was in full swing when, on 5 September 1932, Paul Bern's naked body was discovered face down on his bathroom floor, drenched in Harlow's favourite Mitsouko perfume, with a gunshot wound to the head and a .38 pistol in his hand. His butler made the grim discovery and, in accordance with Hollywood's unwritten laws, he immediately contacted Louis B. Mayer's office, enabling Mayer and MGM's chief of police, Whitey Hendry, to check out the scenario and remove the suicide note. 'Dearest dear,' Bern had written, 'Unfortunately this is the only way to make good the frightful wrong I have done you and to wipe out my abject humiliation. PS. You understand that last night was only a comedy.'

Whitey Hendry – the man responsible for sorting out anything from traffic fines to sex scandals – continued the hypocrisy by conveying Harlow to her mother's house, where she had been briefed on how to react when the regular police arrived to inform her of her tragic loss. Stepfather Marino Bello, whom many believe would not have ruled out murdering Bern for taking his 'Baby' away from him, was ordered by Mayer – and doubtless paid for the privilege – to inform police he had been away on a hunting trip with Clark Gable at the time of Bern's death. Clark was suspected of intimacy with Harlow, particularly as Joan Crawford had been removed from the scene before *Red Dust* went into production. Following *Grand Hotel*, she had been assigned to Somerset Maugham's *Rain*, and pleaded with Mayer to give her Gable. Instead, she ended up with her dullest co-star ever: William Gargan.

*Rain* had been shot on Catalina Island – Mayer claimed to keep Clark at bay and allow Crawford and Douglas Fairbanks Jr to patch up their shaky marriage. Fairbanks added to the drama by embarking on a 'boys only' sailing trip and Joan had been taken ill during filming, resulting in her miscarrying a baby reputed to have been Clark's – though with her track record, it could have been anybody's. The Fairbanks, meanwhile, were reported to be in Europe enjoying a second honeymoon and happier than ever. In fact, sick of the charade, they curtailed the trip and returned to Los Angeles shortly after Paul Bern's death. On the night in question, Clark had been with Joan, not Marino Bello. What the press were also never told was that, after Bern's death, Mayer had taken Harlow off *Red Dust* – she had requested this, he planned announcing, out of respect for her late husband. In fact it was the Hayes Office, confusing the actress with the part (though in this instance they were not wrong) who deemed it inappropriate for a recently bereaved widow to be seen portraying a woman of easy virtue, who enjoys open-air bathing.

In one of the more foolish moves of his career, Mayer decided it would be prudent to shoot all of Harlow's scenes with another actress and offered the part to Tallulah Bankhead – ten times more scandalous than a dozen Harlows! Tallulah angrily informed The Messiah that even she had principles, rejected the offer and later wrote in her memoirs, 'To damn the radiant Jean for the misfortune of others would be one of the shabbiest acts of all time'. Worse was to come, for when Mayer tried to force her hand by threatening to expose her as a 'serial trollop who has seduced more Hollywood actors than most of us have had hot dinners', she called his bluff, venturing to inform the press of the names of six MGM actresses with whom she claimed she had been intimate, including Garbo and Crawford!

It subsequently emerged that Paul Bern's death had been more than a simple matter of suicide. He was unable to have sex because of the genital abnormality he hoped the sexually torrid Harlow would cure despite the fact that physically he was attracted only to men. But when he had failed to rise to the occasion he beat his bride black and blue with a walking cane on their wedding night. Additionally, it emerged during the inquest – hence the 'comedy' referred to in his suicide note – that on the evening of 4 September he had bought an ejaculating dildo, complete with testicles, which he had strapped on before walking into Harlow's bedroom. Whether Bern had attempted to use this on her is not known, only that she had shrieked with laughter and, it would appear, left him feeling acutely humiliated – enough to make him want to kill himself, the inquest concluded. In fact, the case was not quite so clear-cut. Three days after Bern's death, the body of a bit-part actress named Dorothy

Millette was fished out of the Sacramento River. It transpired that she had been Bern's common-law wife, who, after suffering a mental breakdown, had been committed by him to an asylum from which she had recently been discharged. Further evidence suggested Millette had been blackmailing him, threatening to expose him as a bigamist, and that *this* was the humiliation referred to in his suicide note, particularly as, unable to cope with her own shame, Millette had also chosen to take the easy way out.

Bern had lied to Harlow about being a wealthy man, leaving her a mountain of debts, which his creditors now expected her to honour. Joan Crawford, terrified Harlow might sink her claws into Clark now that she was bereft of her anchor – though there was little chance of this, with Marino Bello guarding her on the set – swooped on him, insisting he move into her rented cottage on Malibu beach. When Clark arrived, he learned that he would have to share her. Francis Lederer was a 26-year-old Czech actor, newly arrived in Hollywood. Though gay, but as had been the case with Clark during his 'bucks for fucks' episodes, he was eager to please if that meant furthering his career. Clark stayed but a few days and declined Joan's request that he join her, Lederer and William Haines on a weekend bender, taking in the gay bars and clubs of downtown Los Angeles. Had he accompanied them, he would have met a certain Carole Lombard, enjoying a similar sojourn with gay pals Cesar Romero and Ricardo Cortez.

His next cinematic outing was *Strange Interlude*, based on the play by Eugene O'Neill, a decidedly odd production that had bored Broadway audiences senseless on account of its sheer length. Sprawling across nine acts, it had been staged in two, two-hour sections separated by an hour-long interval which had seen many leave the theatre not to return for the second half. The film version was almost as bad and had the characters speaking their thoughts aloud in lengthy voice-overs that only confused picture-goers. Directed by Robert Z. Leonard, the film was considered shocking for its day. In England the title had to be changed to *Strange Interval* when one reviewer sarcastically referred to it as '*Strange Interlewd*'. The story tells of a young woman searching for a suitable stud –

Clark, aka her doctor – to father a child, which she will convince her impotent husband is his. Such a scenario might have been more credible with a Harlow or Crawford but not squeaky-clean Norma Shearer, who made sure the press informed her fans that she was not in the least like her character in the film. 'Young women who become intrigued by the sophisticated characterisations of Norma Shearer are advised by the actress not to follow her precept,' observed *Screen Book*'s snooty J. Eugene Chrisman, adding that no breath of scandal had ever touched the divinely whiter-than-white Mrs Thalberg. And of the role that had been earmarked for Joan Crawford until Louis B. Mayer was informed that she and Clark were still an item, Shearer scoffed: 'It's silly to contend that an actress must have *lived* and actually acquired a past before she is capable of portraying *that* type of woman. Of course, there must be *intelligent* observation, but most of all, all it requires is imagination!' The public, however, could never imagine a caveman like Gable – sporting his trademark moustache for the first time – getting involved with any woman as lah-di-dah as Norma Shearer, and the film was a flop.

Clark's next film, as a loan-out to Paramount, was *No Man Of Her Own*, a frothy, romantic drama with Dorothy Mackaill and 24-year-old Carole Lombard. He played a renegade gambler married to a small-town librarian (Lombard), who domesticates him to such an extent that he doesn't mind serving time in jail for his double-dealing so long as he has someone respectable to come home to. So far as is known, this was Gable's first meeting – despite her own close friendship with William Haines – with the woman who could out-curse any man he knew, and who was proud to call herself 'The Queen of Fag-Hags'. For the time being, theirs was just another working relationship for Clark was too busy cheating on Ria with Joan Crawford, while seeing Johnny Mack Brown, off and on, mindless of what had happened with *Laughing Sinners*, and according to press reports, Carole was happily married to William Powell. In fact, by November 1932, their 17-month marriage had hit rock bottom owing to Powell's acute megalomania.

Clark resented director Wesley Ruggles' pandering to Carole Lombard's constant demands and initially he treated her with disdain. It may well be that in those early days he was actually frightened of her. As William Haines' confidante, like Joan Crawford she almost certainly would have been told about the incident in the mensroom at the Beverly Wilshire, and with her tendency to shoot her mouth off without always thinking what she was saying, Clark may even have considered her dangerous. Not only this, there was also considerable on-set tension brought about by the forthcoming presidential elections. Inasmuch as studio contractees were instructed how to conduct their personal lives, so they were told how to vote, the theory being that fans would follow suit. Louis B. Mayer was a staunch Republican so it figured that if his stars wanted to stay in his good books, they too would openly support the Republican candidate Herbert Hoover. To make sure they kept their promise, Mayer was not averse to having their ballot papers examined.

Carole Lombard was a vociferous adherent of Franklin D. Roosevelt on account of his campaign to repeal Prohibition and his promises to alleviate the Depression. She absolutely loathed Hoover and made no secret of the fact. The first time Clark came on set wearing his Hoover badge, she tore it off his jacket in front of reporters and told him, 'You can go shove this up Louis B. Mayer's ass!' She and millions of Americans were therefore delighted when, on 1 November, Roosevelt scored a landslide victory over his opponent. When shooting wrapped on *No Man Of Her Own*, Clark presented her with a pair of oversized ballet shoes – he said to match her inflated prima donna ego. Unable to be beaten at her own game, she gave him a gift that she said represented his acting abilities – a large ham with his picture on it! Friends of both parties would later claim how this end-of-production sarcasm had set the scene for one of the great love affairs in Hollywood history.

Ria Gable was well aware that Clark was still seeing Joan Crawford, yet failed to object when, after Clark complained of being harassed by fans and the press, Howard Strickling found them a more secure rented property in Brentwood, but a stone's throw from Joan's house. Even so, the occasional reporter inveigled his way through MGM security and Clark, who knew little about discretion, let slip to a reporter questioning him about his youth how he had not seen his father since coming to Hollywood. He was blithely unaware the press would put out an alert, financed by Louis B. Mayer, a powerful advocate for family values. Within the week, William Gable was located working at a gas station in North Dakota. He turned up at the studio gates one afternoon, dirty and dishevelled, and was immediately chauffeured to the house in Brentwood. Had Clark been home, the old man would have been sent packing. He was not, so Ria took him in and called Howard Strickling, who knew the score between Clark and his father, but had to stick to MGM's family values policy. William was given a complete makeover and a new wardrobe, and Clark was ordered to take care of him. Later, he would shell out $3,500 to buy his father a bungalow in North Hollywood, besides paying him a $500 monthly allowance. Until then, he would live in Brentwood.

Within days he was up to his old tricks, telling reporters and studio personnel that *all* actors were sissies and the whole film community sucked. Clark, who had petitioned for the move to Brentwood to get away from the press, was now instructed to invite them into his home to observe him playing happy families with William, Ria and – Ria's children, Jana and Alfred Lucas. He claimed he could not have adored them more, had they been his own. Yet when he gave an interview to *Modern Screen*'s Gladys Hall, he could not remember the name of one child and got the others wrong:

> For a time the girl thought she would like to be in pictures. Louis B. Mayer saw a picture of her and offered to have a test made. I said that I'd make it with her, and I did. Clarence Brown directed us. It wasn't so good, and she gave the idea up. Allen is absolutely anti-movies, and never asks to come to the studio. He takes no interest in me whatsoever as a movie star. I think he forgets most of the time that I *am* one, so I take him on hunting trips with me. We play ball together and swim and ride . . .

Next, Clark was cast opposite his unlikeliest leading lady so far. Helen Hayes (1900–93) was the stage actress whose debut feature for MGM, *The Sin Of Madeleine Claudet*, had recently won her an

Oscar and she had just completed *A Farewell To Arms* with Gary Cooper. The studio therefore had a lot riding on *The White Sister*, her film with Clark. Directed by Victor Fleming, it was a remake of the 1923 silent starring Lillian Gish and Ronald Colman. Based on the 1909 novel by Francis Marion Crawford, and with the action moved forward to World War I, this was a sorry tale and saw both stars woefully miscast. Clark played Italian airman Giovanni Severa, who falls for the aristocratic Angela Chiaromonte. Her family have arranged for her to marry a man she does not love, so she runs off with Severa and they live in sin until he is called up to fight in the War. Two years pass then Angela receives news that her lover has died in action so she enters a convent. He has actually been captured and sent to a camp in Austria from where he escapes then steals a plane and returns home to reclaim his love. Of course he is too late. She has taken her final vows and shortly after bidding her farewell, he is shot during an air raid. The film ends with him dying in her arms. It was an excellent production, but Gable's fans stayed away in droves: the last thing they wanted was to sob into their popcorn while their idol expired in front of their eyes.

In *The White Sister*, Clark towers over the porcelain fragile Helen Hayes in every scene and she appears terrified of him. There was also speculation whether the two were involved off set, as had happened with most of his co-stars. The critic from a January 1933 issue of *Film Daily* did not think so, concluding, 'Contrast Helen Hayes' role with that of Clark Gable! Spirit warring with the flesh! Christ wins, Clark loses!'

Towards the end of shooting, MGM held its annual Christmas party, to which absolutely everyone was invited, attendance being mandatory – according to an announcement in *Modern Screen* – unless one's name 'happened to be Garbo, W C Fields, or God'. The twelve-hour bash always began with a speech from Louis B. Mayer, who left immediately afterwards. Though stingy with his employees the rest of the year, for the festive season Mayer always pushed the boat out. His bootlegger contacts provided a seemingly endless supply of booze – there was not a Hays Office spy in sight – stag-films were screened all night in backrooms where clothing was optional.

Guests could have sex with whomsoever they liked – so long as it was with a member of the opposite sex. Needless to say, most of the major stars, including Clark, left their spouses at home. That year he turned up with Marion Davies, he wearing his dog collar and she her trapeze outfit from *Polly Of The Circus*. Unusually, instead of leaving with Mayer, Irving Thalberg and Norma Shearer Clark stayed behind and got blind-drunk. The next morning Thalberg woke with a fever and three days later he suffered a near-fatal heart attack.

The news was kept from the press, who – having learned that Clark, Ria and Jean Harlow had visited their sick friend only to have the door slammed in their faces by an angry Norma – were informed that Thalberg had been laid low with 'nothing more serious than the flu'. Even so, with his increasingly fragile health, this could easily have carried him off. Later it emerged that even the all-important Boy Wonder had been compelled to supply Mayer with a doctor's certificate to prove he had not been faking his symptoms, whence Mayer announced that he would be stepping into Thalberg's shoes until he was fully recovered. By February 1933, he was strong enough to travel to Europe for a rest cure at a clinic in Bad Neuheim, Germany. Norma and a whole retinue of lackeys travelled with him and the press were told that he would be overseas for at least three months. Mayer then set about delegating Thalberg's astonishingly heavy workload among his executives. These included Harry Rapf, Hunt Stromberg, Walter Wanger and Mayer's son-in-law David O. Selznick, formerly chief of production with RKO Pictures. Handling Gable's affairs would be Eddie Mannix (1891–1963), a shady character who some years later would be accused of murdering his first wife. When the inquest re-opened, he was also accused of complicity in the death of Paul Bern besides that of *Superman* actor George Reeves, with whom his second wife would have an affair. The story, much-Hollywoodised, reached the big screen with *Hollywoodland* in 2006.

No sooner had *The White Sister* wrapped than Gable was rushed into *Hold Your Man*, his third outing with Jean Harlow, now seemingly over the Bern tragedy, not that MGM had helped by capitalising on this by assigning her to *Reckless*. In this she played a showgirl, whose husband kills himself after finding out she has been cheating on him. Harlow had taken such contract-enforced intimidation badly. In the wake of the film she had twice been picked up by Whitey Hendry's vice-squad for kerb crawling – her way of proving, she said, that she had still been a desirable woman with a normal sexual appetite, following the dildo incident with Bern. Currently she was dating her favourite cameraman, Hal Rosson, who had filmed her in *Red Dust*. They would wed in the September.

With a fine script by Anita Loos and a shooting schedule of just three weeks, Gable and Harlow were in sparkling form. He played Eddie, a conman hustler who barges into Ruby's apartment while pursued by the cops. Instantly attracted to him, she gets him to strip to the waist and hides him in her bathtub. He has kept his trousers on, and while these are drying out in the oven, he struts around in her bathrobe, examining the photographs on the wall, trophies of all the men who have been here before him. 'I got two rules,' she says. 'Keep away from couches, and stay on your feet.' Pretty soon, the two are an item. Eddie addresses Ruby as 'sweetmeat', takes her dancing and tells her he will grow on her. 'Yeah, like a carbuncle,' she responds. Then he learns he has competition – a wealthy, out-of-town client whom he flattens while pretending to be her brother. From now on, she belongs only to him, and to prove the point he intends making an honest woman out of her. Unfortunately, no sooner has he bought the marriage licence than the cops arrive to arrest him for the man he punched has died. Eddie escapes from Ruby's apartment, leaving her to take the rap. In the slammer, she discovers she is pregnant. He shows up, still intent on marrying her before their child is born – and in keeping with the morals of the time, all ends well. Eddie's lawyer gets him off the murder charge and he spends a short time inside before being reunited with his wife and baby son.

In the wake of the various Harlow scandals, Hays Office spies who had already attempted to shanghai her out of Hollywood infiltrated the set to ensure that she and Gable were behaving themselves. And, of course, with her kind of reputation, Harlow would never have been accepted in any role where her character did *not* come from the wrong side of the tracks. This was why, immediately after *Hold Your Man*, Louis B. Mayer cast her as the floosie in *Dinner At Eight*, produced by David Selznick and directed by George Cukor. Selznick at once agreed that Clark should be in the film, which followed in the *Grand Hotel* tradition that its stars were promoted as of equal status. In addition, Selznick had lined up John and Lionel Barrymore, Wallace Beery, Jean Hersholt, and 64-year-old Marie Dressler

The official story was that Clark was content with his relatively minor role as a Park Lane doctor, but that Mayer deemed it beneath him and had given the part to Edmund Lowe. The truth is that Gable refused to work with George Cukor, a close friend of William Haines, for reasons which were unclear then, but would become much more so a few years later, as will be seen. It was also during the shooting of *Dinner At Eight* that Mayer's esteem plummeted to an all-time low, not just in Clark's eyes but just about everyone in the know. Inasmuch as Mayer sabotaged the careers of John Gilbert and Johnny Mack Brown to assuage his own greed, so he now played a disgracefully dirty trick on Marie Dressler, adored by all who knew her, and famed for portraying equally loveable harridans. Currently MGM's top box-office draw after Garbo, she had won an Oscar for *Min And Bill*, and had recently completed *Tugboat Annie*, both phenomenally successful partnerships with Wallace Beery.

When Dressler was taken ill on the set, Mayer had her examined by his personal physician. Incurable cancer was diagnosed, but Mayer kept the news from her to keep her working. When Dressler found out, after collapsing again, Mayer took her into his office, sympathised with her condition and imposed a three-hour working day so as not to over-tire her. He promised her a $100,000 bonus – so long as she promised to hang on until the end of the year and complete the three films for which he had earmarked her. She completed them in tremendous pain (she would die in July 1934), only to have Mayer go back on his word and pay her just $10,000.

Clark's next film, therefore, teaming him up again with Helen Hayes, was *Night Flight*, based on the story, *Vol de nuit*, by French aviator-novelist Antoine de Saint-Exupéry (1900–44), whose most famous work, *The Little Prince*, was yet to come. Like *Dinner At Eight*, the project was handled by David Selznick, who wanted to pitch it against MGM's other recent blockbusters, *Grand Hotel*, *Queen Christina* and *Rasputin And The Empress*. Bereft of glamour and a decent script, and with virtually no chemistry between the leads, it did not work. Its failing was Selznick's inability to comprehend Saint-Exupery's unique sense of poetic philosophy, to which he added an innocent touch of whimsy that did not fit in with the brash Gable persona.

Alongside Myrna Loy, Robert Montgomery, and John and Lionel Barrymore (in their last film together), Clark played aviator Jules Fabian. He spends too much of his time up in the air, looping the loop over the Andes (actually the Canadian Rockies) – and not enough bonding with his stay-at-home wife (Hayes) to present any semblance of a romance between them. Even his hero's death while delivering serum to a typhoid-ravaged Rio de Janeiro is uninspired. Clark hated the film, but not nearly so much as he hated Selznick for putting him in it in the first place. He might have had more fun making *Dancing Lady* – his first outing with Joan Crawford since Louis B. Mayer ordered them to cool things eighteen months previously – had it not been for the new man in her life, whom she now insisted should appear in it as her leading man.

Franchot Tone (1905–68) was the well-heeled son of the president of the Carborundum Company. His mother, Gertrude Franchot Tone, was the political activist who caused a scandal by having an open relationship with the writer Dorothy Thompson. Educated at Cornell, Franchot had spent some time in Paris before taking up acting, first with the Buffalo Stock Company and then with the New Playwrights Theater in New York. With the great actress Katherine Cornell he subsequently founded the Group Theater. He was undoubtedly Joan's most sophisticated man since Douglas Fairbanks Jr, though not as snobbish. From the moment they met, introduced not by Joan but by their mutual friend, Jane Cowl, Clark hated him. Again this was hatred by way of fear. Franchot was living with a man, and as Cowl had always been aware of Clark's sexuality, he assumed she would have passed the news on to Franchot, who was not known for his discretion.

Initially, Franchot rejected a movie contract from MGM, declaring he did not want to be bossed around by the likes of Louis B. Mayer. Neither could he condone the movie hierarchy's loathing of homosexuals, who had always been tolerated in the legitimate theatre. Then in 1932 he decided to 'give it a go' for one year, with the proviso that if it didn't work out, he would return to the stage. His first film had been *The Wiser Sex,* during the shooting of which he became involved with its star, Ross Alexander, said to have been the great love of his life. Inasmuch as she had turned a blind eye to Clark's carousing with William Haines and Johnny Mack Brown, so Joan accepted the fact that Franchot and Ross Alexander (1907–37) looked like being in it for the long haul. What she could not contend with, however, was Douglas Fairbanks Jr coming across all self-righteous when his own extramarital schedule was just as hectic. When Joan learned that Fairbanks had hired a private detective to follow her around, she waited until he was away filming an overnight location before packing his belongings and sending them to the Beverly Hills Hotel. Then, setting a precedent for the future, she had the locks changed at her Brentwood home, changed her phone number – sent messages to friends that her 'lodger' had moved out – and for good measure changed all the toilet seats! Adding insult to injury, she informed the press of her impending divorce (this would be granted on 13 May 1933) *before* Fairbanks himself was given the news.

*Dancing Lady* was a big-budget musical directed by Robert Z. Leonard, shot over a gruelling 65-day schedule – Clark's longest to date. Today it is less remembered for his, Joan's and Franchot Tone's contribution than for being the first film to feature Fred Astaire (1899–1987), who, for some time, had been working the theatre-dancehall circuit with his sister, Adele. Until now he had been reluctant to tackle the movies, believing his equine features non-photogenic in close-up. In their Bavarian scene, while Joan looks fabulous in traditional costume and braided blonde wig, Astaire appears ludicrous with his long, bony legs protruding from his lederhosen – certainly not a sight for the squeamish!

Shooting was a complicated process. Franchot claimed his relationship with Joan was still platonic – he was still very much in love with Ross Alexander, albeit cheating on him with Bette Davis, his co-star in *Ex-Lady*. She herself only showed interest in him in the first place because she could not stand the thought of him being with Joan. *Ex-Lady* was the first Bette Davis film to feature her name above the credits and Warner Brothers pulled strings to ensure her maximum press coverage only to have her knocked off the front pages by the Crawford-Fairbanks divorce. This sparked off a rivalry between the two actresses to end only with Joan's death in 1977.

Clark's health problems only added to the drama of *Dancing Lady*. Shortly after shooting began during the early summer of 1933, he developed agonising abdominal pains, which he attributed to appendicitis. The actual cause was his rotting teeth: pyorrhoea had developed in his gums and entered his bloodstream. To help numb the pain, he swigged whisky, while many on the set complained to Robert Z. Leonard of how his halitosis was so acute that it made them retch to stand close to him. His malady also made him foul-tempered and he fell out with his agent – Minna Wallis – but was snapped up by the Bern-Allenberg Agency, who were used to grumpy stars: they also managed Wallace Beery. Matters were exacerbated when Josephine Dillon resurfaced, short of cash once more. When Clark refused to cough up, she attempted to rubbish him in a series of 'open letters' to him, which were published in several movie magazines. In the meantime, Howard Strickling arranged for him to be examined by MGM medic Edward B. Jones – the man known for examining menstruating actresses to ensure they were not pulling a fast one when asking for sick notes. Jones prescribed painkillers and referred him to George Hollenbach, one of Hollywood's leading dental surgeons.

Clark's teeth, Hollenbach stressed, would all have to come out and he would have to be fitted with dentures. He was further advised that the procedure would take at least a month to allow his gums to heal. While he was recuperating, there was an unpleasant incident concerning his ex-lover and supposed friend, William Haines, precipitated by Clark hitting the roof on being told that Franchot Tone's name would be appearing above his own in the credits for *Dancing Lady*. The news sent him into one of his not infrequent 'fag-hating' phases. Via Howard Strickling, he complained to Louis B. Mayer of how he was sick of seeing Joan Crawford squired around town by 'that goddamn fairy'. It was jealousy, pure and simple – spiteful and hypocritical, too, considering his own secret agenda, and wholly unforgivable for what happened next. Mayer assumed the 'goddamn fairy' could only have been Haines, and sought to rectify the situation by feeding the story to the press that Haines – still a sizeable box-office draw – had been contracted to make a film with his 'lover', Pola Negri.

Negri knew there was no such film, but was paid handsomely to go along with the charade. Mayer's spies informed him whenever Haines attended a party so that the Polish siren could gatecrash and 'surprise' him. She was photographed with tears in her eyes, kissing him goodnight after a 'date'. Haines was snapped buying a king-sized bed in a Hollywood department store, which the accompanying editorial declared would not, naturally, be delivered until after the nuptials. He actually purchased this for Joan Crawford, whose house he was helping to refurbish as part of her process of removing all traces of the departed Douglas Fairbanks Jr.

For Haines, who had never been *in* the closet, the last straw came when he read in a newspaper that he and Pola Negri were about to host their *engagement* party. Barging into Mayer's office unannounced, he told the mogul exactly what he thought of him, allegedly with more expletives than he had heard in his life. Not wishing to upset Haines further and have him walk off the set of his latest film, Mayer kept his cool. As soon as it wrapped, however, he had the actor trailed to one of his favourite haunts near Pershing Square. When he was observed entering a YMCA hostel with a 20-year-old marine he had picked up in a bar, Mayer's agent alerted the vice-squad and the pair was arrested.

This sort of thing had happened before, once when Haines and the director George Cukor hit this part of town in search of rough trade:

MGM's chief of police, Whitey Hendry, stepped into the breach. Money was handed over to the vice-squad and the matter dropped. Now, to teach Haines a lesson while still keeping the incident out of the press, Mayer had given instructions for the marine's bail to be posted, while Haines was dragged off to jail. Permitted the customary telephone call, he rang Joan Crawford and it was she who put up his bail. Haines was driven to San Simeon, where he and lover Jimmie Shields were taken in by Marion Davies. This time Mayer gave Haines an ultimatum: ditch Jimmie and marry *anyone*, or get out of the movies for good. Haines turned on Mayer with a 'Fuck you!', and walked out of his office, slamming the door behind him. MGM could not have chosen a more ironic title for his swansong: *The Marines Are Coming!*

Crawford never found out that Gable's hypocrisy, albeit inadvertently, contributed to the destruction of her best friend's career, though regarding Haines' work as an interior designer, as will be seen, he and Mayer had done him a favour. To teach Clark a lesson, Mayer put him on suspension – the official reason for this, the press were told, was that he had checked himself into a clinic without obtaining the studio's permission – a sackable offence at the time. This, Mayer hoped, would bring him to heel without his having to reveal that MGM's top male star was a 'raving fagelah', and of course without affecting the box-office. For his part, Clark was ordered to stick to women from now on – so far as is known, with one exception, this is what he did. He apologised for his 'mistake', promised to 'get well' as soon as possible and told the press he had 'atoned' for the sin of letting the studio down by joining the Freemasons! Even so, the suspension stayed, without pay, until the end of August of that year. Mayer also added Gable's name to MGM's Delinquents List, which included those of William Haines and Tallulah Bankhead.

Meanwhile, on the set of *Dancing Lady*, Robert Z. Leonard shot around Clark's scenes. Yet no sooner had he returned to work than he collapsed and had to be rushed to hospital: the infection which had started off in his gums had reached his gall-bladder and the prognosis was not good. He underwent an emergency operation, astonished the doctors by recovering quickly and within two weeks was back on the set, allowing the film to be completed just six weeks behind schedule, but $150,000 over budget on account of the delays.

In *Dancing Lady*, Joan Crawford plays Janie, a feisty burlesque queen, whose ambition is to appear in a sell-out Broadway musical. Unlike most of her contemporaries she is a decent girl and declares her intention to stay chaste until her wedding night – which had Crawford detractors *and* fans howling. When millionaire entrepreneur Tod Newton (Tone) offers her a bit part in a revue and proposes marriage, Janie proves no pushover – she accepts the part but informs Newton, whom she loathes, that she will marry him only if the show bombs. He, who welcomes losing money if such is to be his reward, sets out to sabotage his own production. What he hasn't reckoned with is dance director, Patch Gallagher (Clark), a no-nonsense, Billy Rose type, who also has his eye on Janie. As real-life Rose did with his wife Fanny Brice, Gallagher bullies her into shape, and doesn't care who is present when he lays into her. Little by little, Janie stands up to him and when she helps him through a last-minute hitch with the show, they fall in love. Janie is an instant hit with the public and Newton does the honourable thing by letting her go.

But Clark had not learned his lesson with Louis B. Mayer, and when shooting wrapped he bawled him out over the roles he was being offered. Claiming he had hated every moment of *Dancing Lady*, he *told* Mayer that after his next film – *Soviet* had been set up some time before by Irving Thalberg with Crawford as his leading lady – he would only accept roles which pleased him, otherwise he would leave Hollywood. Garbo, he added by way of argument, had been making similar threats for years and getting away with it because, like himself, she knew exactly what kind of roles suited her best. Mayer reminded him that a star like Garbo was irreplaceable whereas actors like himself were two-a-penny. Pointing through his office window, he declared he could pick any tall, good-looking man off the streets, turn him into the next Gable, then send the real one back to Ohio, from whence he came.

Mayer then announced that, with Irving Thalberg still far from well (he had returned from Europe in the August), *he* was in complete charge at MGM and that, rather than putting Clark into

*Soviet*, he would send him to 'Siberia'. This was Mayer's nickname for Columbia Pictures, the 'poverty row' studio to which contractees were frequently loaned out if they stepped out of line. Mayer believed that a spell at Columbia, with its Spartan conditions in those days, would soon have miscreants appreciating how fortunate they had been in working for him.

# Chapter Four

# BEN & LORETTA

Clark's film as a loan-out to Columbia was to be *Night Bus*, based on a *Cosmopolitan* magazine story by Samuel Hopkins Adams, and it was to be directed by Frank Capra, loathed by Louis B. Mayer as much as he loathed Clark. Because *Cosmopolitan* was owned by Mayer's ally, William Randolph Hearst, MGM had been given first refusal of the project, but turned it down. Of late there had been a glut of 'bus' movies: MGM's *Fugitive Lovers*, with Robert Montgomery in the role of an escaped convict, had only recently bombed at the box-office. The fact that Columbia's chief, Harry Cohn, paid just $5,000 for the screen rights suggested to everyone in the know that the end result would almost certainly be a flop. And to Mayer's warped way of thinking, if Gable's next film turned out to be a turkey, this would give him a legitimate excuse not to renew his contract.

The first good news Mayer received was that no one else wanted to be in the film: Margaret Sullavan, Constance Bennett, Miriam Hopkins and Myrna Loy had all rejected the female lead of the headstrong heiress who runs off with a bohemian artist. To fit in with Clark's character, his occupation had been changed to a hard-bitten reporter. The situation was saved by Paramount's Claudette Colbert. Like Clark, she had ruffled a few feathers along the route to success by declaring she would never be bossed around by studio big-wigs.

Born Claudette Cauchoin in Paris, Colbert (1905–96) had come to Hollywood as a child, worked on Broadway during the early Twenties and made her film debut in 1927. *For The Love Of Mike*, directed by Frank Capra, had flopped but four years later Colbert ascended the ladder with Ernst Lubitsch's *The Smiling Lieutenant*, alongside Maurice Chevalier, as well as appearing in Cecil B. DeMille's *The Sign Of The Cross*. She was about to go on vacation for four weeks and imperiously announced that she was not interested in working with anyone, least of all a director with whom she had already shared one miserable experience, and an actor who was unable to keep his pants buttoned. Assuming he would show her the door, she swanned into Harry Cohn's office and told him that *if* she did the film, she would work on it for exactly four weeks and not one moment more, and that she would not work for less than $50,000 – twice her regular salary. Cohn, in a fix, stunned her by agreeing to her terms.

Frank Capra (1897–1991) was another feisty European, a genius who spent his whole career championing the ordinary Joe, who through moral determination and conscience triumphs over adversity to beat the odds in feel-good movies. Born in Sicily, like Colbert he had moved to California while still young. In 1925, Mack Sennett employed him to write gags for Harry Langdon, who subsequently hired him as his personal director. Later, Capra moved to Columbia, and in 1931 he teamed up in what would prove a phenomenally successful partnership with Robert Riskin (1897–1955), already a well-known playwright and married to Fay Wray. The pair scripted *The Miracle Woman*, adapted from Riskin's play. Among other triumphs were *Mr Deeds Goes To Town* and *Lost Horizon*.

Capra always maintained that when he presented Clark with the script for *Night Bus* and offered to go through it with him, Gable's inebriated response had been, 'Buddy, I don't give a fuck *what* you do with it!' Later, after taking it home and reading it, he revised his opinion – and somewhere along the way its title changed to *It Happened One Night*. The film opens with spoiled heiress Ellie Andrews (Colbert) going berserk after her millionaire father (Walter Connelly, still only 45, but looking much older) annuls her marriage to opportunist King Wesley (Jameson Thomas), who she only married in the first place because her father told her not to. Aboard their yacht in Miami the pair argue, and when the old man slaps her, Ellie dives overboard and swims ashore. Next we see her boarding the night bus to join Wesley in New York, about to meet rebellious hot head hack, Peter Warne (Clark), who has just been fired. 'All hail the King,' his buddies chant as they walk him to the bus, using his famous nickname for the first time. This is the new-look Gable that men across America emulated: wisecracking, wearing a belted trench coat and smoking a pipe, his hat tilted at a rakish angle, still snarling like the Gable of old. And not least at the stuck-up girl who enters his life by purloining his seat while he is having a set-to with the driver – future *Wagon Train* star Ward Bond, in an uncredited role.

Ellie and Peter bond during a stopover at Jacksonville, when the suitcase containing her money is stolen, though when she sees the newspaper headline reporting her disappearance, all he is interested in is penning the exclusive he hopes will get him his job back. Initially, Ellie tries to buy his silence, promising him a hefty pay-off when they reach New York. But this gets him mad, for he hates rich folk who feel any problem can be resolved by dipping into their wallets rather than facing up to it. During the next leg of the journey he changes his tune when she is menaced by an unscrupulous shyster named Shapely (Roscoe Karns). Peter rescues her by pretending to be her husband – a ruse he continues to save on their virtually non-existent funds – when bad weather forces the bus to pull in for the night at a cheap motel. He has no intention of taking advantage of her, however, and puts up 'The Walls of Jericho' – a sheet slung over the washing-line that divides the room. 'If you're nursing any silly notion that I'm interested in you, forget it,' he drawls. 'You're just a headline to me!'

Nevertheless he taunts her, loaning her his pyjamas, then showing her how a *real* man undresses, with Gable once more stripping off his shirt to reveal he is not wearing an under vest. This causes Ellie to rush behind the sheet as he sings, 'Who's Afraid Of The Big, Bad Wolf?' while unbuttoning his trousers. Then, when he gets into his bed and she sits upon hers, we observe that she is falling for his brutish charms. Only now does she ask his name, bringing the response, 'I'm the whip-poor-will that cries in the night; I'm the soft morning breeze that caresses your lovely face!' The next morning, this virile hunk that uses women, fixes *her* breakfast – interpreted by fans as Gable 'going soft'. He teaches her the art of dunking donuts before, for the first time in her silver-spooned existence, she faces the harshness of an outdoor shower. When detectives hired by her father turn up, Peter and Ellie throw them off the scent by having their first marital tiff, yelling at each other in Deep South accents – the funniest of several hilarious scenes in this film.

The journey resumes with camaraderie as the passengers belt out 'The Man On The Flying Trapeze'. Then, when a poor woman flakes out through lack of food, Peter and Ellie give her the last of their money. Here, Gable lives up to his legend that he was suitably distanced from Hollywood's glitterati not to have been averse to giving a man the shirt off his back, according to journalist Ben Maddox. Then Shapely turns up again. The crook has read in the latest edition that Mr Andrews is offering $100,000 for Ellie's safe return and he wants to go 50:50 with Peter – either this, or he will tell all to the police. Peter scares him off by pretending to be a mobster – he will loan Shapely a machine-gun, then they will kidnap Ellie, who is worth much more than her father is offering, and maybe bump her off, should he not cough up. Shapely is then warned what will happen if he blabs: Peter will do to Shapely's kids what he did to his mobster rival. On hearing this, Shapely flees into the night and Peter spits after him. This was the only scene in the film questioned by the Hays Office, when William Haines cracked a joke that Clark was emulating him 'finishing off' after giving a blow-job, for the spittle drools down his jacket.

To be on the safe side, Peter tells Ellie they must leave the bus and find an alternative way of getting to New York. Though broke, she refuses to wire her father for help. They spend the night in a haywain and next morning set about hitching a ride. He claims to be an expert, but every passing motorist ignores him. Ellie fares better – walking to the kerb, she hoists her skirt above her thigh to an instant screeching of brakes. The driver is Alan Hale (1892–1950), Errol Flynn's regular sidekick, who for the few minutes he is on screen never lets us forget that he trained as an opera singer. Almost every line is delivered in a powerful baritone that sets the teeth on edge. He is a con man who drives off with their luggage while they are stretching their legs – no problem for Peter, who sprints after the car, knobbles Hale and returns with it, so they can resume their journey to New York.

The pair find a motel, though they cannot pay the bill – he will figure something out by the time they hit the road again. They are but hours from their destination and Ellie is upset their adventure is almost over and she may never see him again, though Peter appears to be indifferent. From his side of the new Walls of Jericho, he confides that he has never been in love because he has never found the right girl. If he did, he would take her to a Pacific island he knows, where lovers and the moon and the water become one, and where the stars are so close he could reach up and stir them around. This brings her to his side of the sheet, begging him to take her with him because she loves him and can't envisage life without him. Again, he bows to the edicts of the Hays Office, disappointing her by ordering her back to her own bed.

The next morning, leaving her sleeping, Peter drives into New York, where he pleads with his former editor: the paper will have its scoop for once she has dumped Wesley, Ellie will marry him! She, meanwhile, has been kicked out of the motel for not paying the bill and has finally wired her father for help. He and his police motorcade pass Peter on the road while he is heading back to give her the good news. Ellie thinks he has deserted her, and announces that she will remarry Wesley. Peter feels dejected, but this is a Frank Capra film where happy endings are mandatory. Cut to the eve of the wedding, where Peter and Mr Andrews discuss money: he is not interested in the reward, just the $39.60 it has cost him to sell his effects and get them back to New York. But, the old man demands, does he *love* her? The response is pure Gable, in keeping with the *übermensch* image: 'Any guy that'd fall in love with your daughter ought to have his head examined. . . . What she needs is a guy who'll take a sock at her once a day, whether it's coming to her or not!'

The wedding ceremony is underway when Ellie learns how Peter really feels, with Mr Andrews begging her to make him happy by choosing the man she loves. Seeing Peter's car, she dashes across the lawn, pursued by the guests and press. As the credits roll in this gem of a production – the first truly *great* Gable movie – we learn that the couple are married, enabling The Walls of Jericho to finally tumble.

Claudette Colbert, never an easy actress for anyone to work with, later claimed that *It Happened One Night* had been the worst experience of her career and that Clark resented her because he had only been on one-sixth of her salary. Much of his dissension stemmed from the fact that Colbert was a lesbian and therefore not interested in granting him his customary off-set fling. Such resentment does not come across on the screen and several scenes are known to be flunked on account of his practical jokes. In the motel sequence where Elllie begs Peter to take her with him to his Pacific island, Clark had grabbed Colbert's hand and placed it on his crotch. He had shoved a hammer-shaft inside his trousers and wanted to find out if she really was 'a strait-laced baritone babe who'd had a humour by-pass', as legend professed. Her reaction was to let out a piercing scream, grab the shaft and threaten to shove it 'where the sun never shone'.

Colbert was also against shooting the hitchhiking scene and flashing her thigh in front of Gable, worried that he might want to take advantage of the situation. To placate her, Frank Capra hired a stand-in, but Colbert hit the roof – the stand-in's legs were too scrawny, she yelled, and this would reflect badly on her. She swore she would never work with the director or Gable again – a few years later she was to revise her opinion about Clark and apparently enjoy the experience much more the second time around.

What was not predicted, when shooting wrapped on Christmas Eve 1933, however, was that *It Happened One Night* would prove such a monumental success – one of the classic social comedies of the 20th century, no less. So far as Clark was concerned, it had been just another loan-out exercise and he still had to face the daunting task of returning to MGM. On Christmas Day Louis B. Mayer wired him at Columbia with instructions to shave off his moustache and report to the front office *before* the end of the year. He was immediately put into *Men In White* with Myrna Loy – another 'baritone babe' he had already attempted, but failed, to seduce. Directed by Polish-born Richard Boleslawski, a former student of Stanislavsky and Max Reinhardt, this was filmed in fifteen days so that

Clark would be free to travel to New York to promote *It Happened One Night*, scheduled for a February 1934 release.

Set in a city hospital, *Men In White* was a pioneering medical drama, brave for its day, and one which spawned countless such movies, though it now comes across as rather dull. Clark played a young intern, torn between graduating and marrying his wealthy sweetheart (Loy) – a move which enabled him to set up his own Park Avenue practice. While deciding, he gets a nurse (Elizabeth Allan) pregnant. Following a botched abortion, she dies as he is operating on her, but this being Clark Gable, he not only gets away with it, but his distraught fiancée forgives him, too.

Gable's New York trip was without MGM's blessing. There he was handled not by a Columbia publicist, but by MGM's Howard Dietz, who made a point of meeting reporters beforehand and vetting their questions. He was then threatened with suspension, should he breathe so much as a word about *It Happened One Night*, the whole purpose of the trip in the first place! Additionally, he was supplied with a typed-up list of pre-prepared questions that he was asked to learn, as he would any script, and to deliver them off the cuff. But the press saw through the ruse. Remarks such as 'Parts appeal to me that offer powerful opportunities for definitive characterisation' were hardly likely to come tripping spontaneously off his tongue.

While shooting *Men In White*, he had had a fling with Elizabeth Allan, the 24-year-old English actress who trained with the Old Vic, who had recently arrived in Hollywood. The following year she was to become a household name courtesy of *David Copperfield*. No sooner had the film wrapped than he turned his attentions to a dashing young reporter named Ben Maddox, who appears to have been his very last homosexual conquest. One gets the impression, however, with Maddox's fearsome lothario reputation, that even though this was essentially little more than another 'fucks-for-bucks' exercise, Clark was not the one who did all the chasing.

Ben Maddox, 32 when he first championed Clark, was a hugely influential freelance reporter, who used sex as a means of acquiring his scoops. A brawny, good-looking six-footer, his trick was to interview subjects over lunch or dinner – *always* at their homes, where there was less danger of his coming unstuck – and once they had fallen for his seemingly limitless charms, offer himself as dessert. As a cub reporter, one of his earliest conquests had been Rudolph Valentino, back in 1923. 'I allowed him to ride my favourite Arabian steed around Falcon Lair, and afterwards he rode me,' Rudy wrote in his diary after Maddox's first visit to his home. Three years later he had been one of the eight lover-pallbearers at his funeral. Maddox also slept with Jean Harlow in the wake of a slanging match that he equated to foreplay: he had called her a sexless, phoney blonde and Harlow had slapped him and accused him of having a chip on his shoulder.

Some of Maddox's notes and 'spiked' interviews make for interesting reading. In 1933, within the space of one week he had seduced Anita Page, Sidney Fox, Marian Marsh and Sylvie Sydney – the latter in the back of his car in broad daylight – when the editor of *Silver Screen* commissioned a feature about 'Hollywood's bachelor maidens'. The general opinion was that all four were lesbians, but in the arms of the man for obvious reasons referred to by Tallulah Bankhead as 'Big Ben', they had become red-blooded tigresses. 'Every unmarried actress has her own opinions,' Maddox wrote in his feature, 'So I started to learn the facts as they appear to some of our charmers who so far have said NO to all altar calls.' Maddox refused to interview Barbara Stanwyck (but later 'brunched' with her husband, Robert Taylor), dismissing her as 'unglamorous'. Around the time he met Clark, he also spectacularly failed to seduce Marlene Dietrich in her dressing room on the set of *The Devil Is A Woman* by standing up and boldly indicating that her sultry tones had given him an erection. Marlene told him to take a cold shower! Maddox would, among dozens of others, subsequently 'get better acquainted' with Errol Flynn, Phillips Holmes, Ramon Novarro, George O'Brien and Tyrone Power.

Clark is thought to have 'loaned his meaty charms' to the incorrigible reporter in exchange for a high-profile interview and public relations exercise. Solely on account of the reporter's intervention, this would see his salary eventually upped to $3,000 a week – still less than John Gilbert and some of the other Talkies casualties were getting, but a step in the right direction all the same.

Likening Gable's appeal to the 'Valentino boom of yesteryear', Maddox penned the most glowing, unashamedly gushing appreciation of 'his man'. Reading between the lines it is blatantly obvious that he was in love with Clark. Not only this, but he was attempting to camouflage his affection by trying to con his readers into believing the Gables' marriage was unshakeable while personally aware that it would almost certainly be over before his feature hit the newsstands. This is exactly what happened, making him look rather silly.

> Meet Clark Gable today! This He-Man with dimples, this gangster who went heroic by feminine demand! This most desired of current screen lovers! Where does he go from here? Divorce? Nine out of ten great stars let Hollywood spoil their home life. Clark Gable won't! Here's one marriage I think we can depend upon. Clark is married to a cultured, charming woman who has the knack of completely satisfying him in every way. His salary is said to be $1,500 a week with bonuses on each film. It obviously isn't nearly so large as his popularity warrants in comparison with the other stars. Will he last? I think so. He isn't temperamental and high-strung like John Gilbert, nor sheikisk like Valentino nor complex like Phil Holmes. He has a depth and virility that the juveniles lack. To the woman he's brought a new brand of love – to us men, a masculine and intelligent movie hero whom we can respect.

The salary increase advocated by Ben Maddox would not come just yet. On 24 February 1934, *It Happened One Night* opened at New York's Radio City Music Hall as part of a vaudeville-movie double bill. Such events were commonplace in those days, with the programme changing weekly to avoid favouritism of a particular film or performer. Outside the venue Clark was mobbed, while within the auditorium the screaming from 6,000 fans drowned his introductory speech.

As a contractee of MGM, he was permitted just two visits to Radio City before being seconded to Broadway's Capitol Theater – not to promote his own film, but *The Mystery Of Mr X*, starring Robert Montgomery and Elizabeth Allan. This was failing at the box-office and needed a boost its stars could not provide. Clark was briefly reunited with his old flame: she stayed at the Waldorff Astoria, where he had a suite, as did Ben Maddox. Together they presented the film, sometimes as many as five times in one day. In between, Clark augmented the vaudeville programme performing a routine from *Dancing Lady* with the stage actress, Ruth Matteson.

Initially, *It Happened One Night* was virtually ignored because the critics were only interested in recording the hysterical scenes at the Capitol Theater. When *The Mystery Of Mr X* moved on – headed by the ubiquitous Ben Maddox – they picked up on it, the movie magazines plugged it to death and the all-important major studios realised Columbia, aka 'Siberia', had hotted up and was now a major force to be reckoned with. Louis B. Mayer dismissed the film's unexpected success as 'just another fluke' and, retaining Clark on the same salary, made no secret of the fact that he despised him no less by assigning him to yet another typical Gable rushed effort, *Manhattan Melodrama*. Produced by David Selznick, it was directed by W.S.Van Dyke – with 'One-take Woody' breezing through Clark's scenes in just twelve days.

Clark played mobster Blackie Gallagher, who as a child survived the 1904 SS *General Slocum* disaster, which claimed the lives of over 1,000 New York immigrants, burned alive during a picnicking trip. Blackie's closest friends, also aboard the ship, are Joe Patrick (Leo Carrillo) – now a priest – and lawyer and aspiring politician Jim Wage (William Powell), though by the time they reach adulthood, the latter is Blackie's enemy because of his underground activities. The film's love interest, played by Myrna Loy, is Eleanor – Blackie's moll, who complicates matters by marrying Jim.

There are echoes of *Possessed* when Jim hits the campaign trail and his foes try to sabotage his election prospects by digging up his wife's murky past. Blackie comes to her aid, accidentally kills one of her attackers and with Jim as the prosecuting attorney is sentenced to the electric chair. Jim's bringing to justice of this arch-criminal wins him his seat, but, when he learns how Blackie only killed the man to protect Eleanor whom he secretly loves, he tries to get the death sentence commuted to life imprisonment only to have Blackie refuse this. He prefers to sacrifice his life so he will never come between the couple again. The film ends with him walking to the execution chamber, comforted by Father Joe.

*Manhattan Melodrama* was a good film but tailored around the fading talents of 41-year-old William Powell to gain himself and Myrna Loy publicity for *The Thin Man*, which was about to be released. Recently divorced from Carole Lombard, Powell was now involved with Jean Harlow – separated from Hal Rosson – whose daily visits to the set caused mass disruption. When the extras and technicians wolf-whistled, Harlow would expose her breasts, or if she was feeling especially mischievous, hoist her skirt and flash her 'platinum snatch'. Today the film is remembered chiefly as the first major production to feature Mickey Rooney – then 12, he played Blackie Gallagher as a boy. It also received unprecedented free publicity when real-life gangster John Dillinger (1903–34) was shot dead by FBI agents while exiting Chicago's Biograph Cinema after watching it with his girlfriend. She had tipped off the police, it subsequently emerged, and they advised her to wear a red dress so that Dillinger might be recognised and more easily gunned down.

By the time the film wrapped, Louis B. Mayer was at a loss over what to do, not just with Clark, but with Joan Crawford, too. The pair were still rumoured to be an item, but were never seen publicly unless as a foursome with Ria and Franchot Tone, who apparently was still unaware that Clark had tried to out him. Indeed, some believed Franchot was better off *not* knowing. Despite his meek and mild appearance, he had a fearsome reputation for brawling and could turn nasty when provoked. Joan's reluctance to marry put Mayer in a quandary. He hit the roof when she told reporter Jimmie Fidler, when asked why she and Franchot Tone were deliberating over tying the knot, 'You *can* have your cake and eat it. If you just nibble around the edges, it lasts a little longer!' Supposing then, with her track record, MGM put Crawford and Tone in a film as love interests, only to have them split before its release? Franchot was no longer involved with Ross Alexander, who had moved on to Errol

Flynn – the two were currently shooting *Captain Blood* – but he had been seen drowning his sorrows in a bar, which suggested to Mayer that all was not well within the Crawford household. As a precaution, Franchot was put into *Lives Of A Bengal Lancer*, while Mayer played safe, making best use of a probable adulterous situation by assigning Joan and Clark to *Chained*, to be followed by the screen adaptation of Tallulah Bankhead's Broadway hit, *Forsaking All Others*.

Between these two, Clark squeezed in *After Office Hours* with Constance Bennett, who had just bagged a three-year contract with Myron Selznick for an astonishing $150,000 per picture. He played a wisecracking but unsympathetic newsman in what was supposed to be a screwball comedy – no easy task, he said, with this particular leading lady. Shooting ended with him vowing never to cross her path again. *Chained*, scripted by John Lee Mahin and directed by Clarence Brown, was just another routine steamboat-goes-to-the-tropics drama. Diane Lovering (Joan, whose character's name had fans laughing their sides sore) is having an affair with wealthy ship owner Richard Field (Otto Kruger) and would like to marry him, if only his wife would grant him a divorce. She therefore takes a trip to South America, where she embarks on a passionate on-board romance with tough guy Mike Brady – Clark, with his moustache grown back. When she returns to New York, she feels duty-bound to forget Mike and resume her relationship with Richard, whose wife has changed her mind about the divorce. He, however, realises Mike is the better man for her and nobly stands aside: in other words Joan's and Clark's fans would never have forgiven her for *not* choosing Gable to spend the rest of her life with!

By now the press were indifferent towards this genre of film now that they had seen Gable in a comedy. The *New York Herald Tribune* called it, 'An earnest treatment of a snappy serial in one of the dressier sex magazines', while the *New York Times* dismissed it as 'just another suspenseless triangle'. The fans were merely grateful to be seeing as much of their favourite top-liners as the Hays Office would allow: both appeared in one scene wearing skimpy bathing costumes and Clark even got away with not shaving his chest! But *Forsaking All Others*, MGM's attempt to cash in on the success of *It Happened One*

*Night* by casting Gable and Crawford in a frothy comedy, did not work. Joan's admirers liked to watch her *suffering* for love and hated to see her treating the subject flippantly. And it was Robert Montgomery who got to pronounce the screamer line which became that season's in-phrase among Hollywood's closeted gay community – 'I could build a fire by rubbing two boy scouts together!'

Jeff, Mary and Dill (Clark, Joan, Montgomery) are pals who have been inseparable since childhood. Jeff loves Mary; she loves Dill and the pair plan to marry while Jeff is overseas. He, however, leaves her standing at the altar and elopes with his mistress (Frances Drake), offering Jeff the opportunity to return home and comfort her, while Dill realises his terrible mistake and attempts a reunion with the fiancée he dumped. Not surprisingly, he fails. Mary, like Joan herself off screen, gives every impression of being partial to a little S & M. In one scene, she passes Jeff the hairbrush to deliver the spanking she feels she deserves, a punishment gentlemanly Jeff is loathe to carry out. Therefore Gable and Crawford end up in each other's arms once more in a vehicle always better suited to the stage than the screen.

Throughout the production of these two films, the press scrutinised the 'still torrid' Gable-Crawford situation, which was good for the box-office but disastrous news for Will Hays and his moralist cronies. In an attempt to curb gossips speculating he would divorce Ria and marry Joan – spurred on by Ben Maddox, still keeping Clark company away from home and anxious that *this* little snippet did not make the headlines – Louis B. Mayer instructed the Gables to give an exclusive to *Modern Screen*'s catty reporter, Gladys Hall. It was to be featured in the magazine's December 1934 issue. That a second writer was employed to paraphrase Clark's meticulously rehearsed replies to Hall's questions – actually scripted for her by Howard Strickling – is only too obvious when one studies the finished feature.

Hall asked Clark, 'What kind of a woman do you think an actor should marry?' To which he responded, 'The kind of woman I am married to!' He then went on to discuss various failed Hollywood marriages concluding that those where the *husband* was the breadwinner always had the better chance of success. He then shot himself in the foot by adding that the *best* unions were those where both partners were of the same age. According to the Gable-according-to-Strickling doctrine, ego also played a prominent role in marriage, as did good, old-fashioned male chauvinism:

> You can't get away from the fundamental laws separating and governing men and women. Greasepaint on the face does not alter immutable laws. Man is born with a dominant ego – offend that ego, or compete with it in the same field, and if you are a woman you will soon be a divorcee.

It was important, too, that Ria had a life of her own but equally imperative that she should know her place:

> *I* am the star! Ria is my wife, who though not in my profession *is* in it – for me, not for herself. She has her own interests . . . she doesn't seize hold of my own life with idle and therefore morbidly curious hands!

And of the rumours that he might divorce Ria and marry someone from his own profession? By telling Clark what to say, Strickling was of course hoping to dispel once and for all the rumour that he might be thinking of marching Joan Crawford up the aisle:

> I could not, *would* not, be married to an actress! In the first place, one professional ego is enough in any home. Two egos of the same stamp would blow the roof off Buckingham Palace. We would have had a bad day, each of us. We would come home with nerves frayed and teeth on edge – and we would want to talk about it. We would want peace and comfort and sympathy. We wouldn't get it, either one of us, and all hell would break loose. In the course of many times like this, one or both of us would look for comfort and sympathy elsewhere.

And, forgetting his earlier gaff that the best partners were those of one's own age, he observed of his predilection for older women, while hammering home the point that *he* did not practise what he preached:

> A younger girl could not know what *it* is all about! A younger girl would be jealous. She would be suspicious, resentful of all the limelight flattery shown me. She would crave the same flattery, the same attention for herself! Things like that *do* happen! Ria knows how to *handle* men. If I forget to phone her during the lunch hour, I do not have to spend the rest of the day with the uneasy knowledge that when I get home that night I shall be greeted with tears and reproaches, martyred looks, or suspicious sniffs. I do not have to work on half a cylinder because I fear I'll get the devil of an evening!

What Clark was effectively saying was that, with Ria, he could get away with his carousing because, as an older woman, she should have been *grateful* for what she was getting in the bedroom department, even if only occasionally, from one of Hollywood's acknowledged studs. He then concluded, in what must be the most bare-faced lie he ever told, that there was but one solution for wedded bliss:

> No actor should marry a woman to whom he cannot tell the truth, and be believed. Ria knows that I always have and always shall tell her the truth. Marriage is a see-saw. If the balance is an uneven one, one or the other crashes down! *Our* marriage balances evenly, and on one side is equally important to the other.

His next film, as a loan-out to Fox, was *Call Of The Wild*. Jack London's classic tale of one man and his dog, set during the Yukon gold rush, was shot on location at Mount Baker, Washington, during the excessively harsh winter of 1934–5. Weather conditions were so severe – but perfect for the setting – that for weeks the production company was snowed in – in sub-zero temperatures – pushing the budget sky-high. Clark was unusually belligerent towards many of the cast and almost came to blows with director William Wellman – a former World War I aviator nicknamed 'Wild Bill', himself a tetchy character. The first time Wellman bawled out Gable for bad timekeeping, following a trip to nearby Bellingham, where he had treated himself and several technicians to a night at a brothel, Clark walked off set and did not return for three days. This, it subsequently emerged, was when he began his affair with co-star Loretta Young.

Loretta Young (1913–2000), who in her later years became a clean-up campaigner, installing holy water stoups all over her Hollywood home and swear-boxes wherever she was working, casually forgot she seldom practised what she often preached to others. Mockingly referred to by colleagues as 'Saint Loretta', she castigated them over *their* lack of morals, as a supposedly devout Catholic. Gretchen Young (Joan Crawford called her 'Gretch The Wretch') first stepped out of line at 17, eloping with 26-year-old actor Grant Withers, whom she met on the set of *The Second Floor Mystery*. A few months later the marriage was annulled, citing Withers' non-Catholicism as the cause, of which Loretta had of course been well aware of before marrying him.

She was not a very talented actress: much of her success being attributed to her great beauty and fashion sense. The *New York Times* Bosley Crowther famously opined of her, 'Whatever it was that this actress never had, she still hasn't got.' Her first screen appearance had been as an extra in Valentino's *The Sheik* (1921), but she was first noticed alongside Lon Chaney in *Laugh, Clown, Laugh* in 1928. After completing her film with Clark, Loretta moved to Paramount, where she appeared in Cecil B. DeMille's *The Crusades*. Immediately afterwards, *Variety* was fed the story by Fox that she was retiring for a year, for health reasons. Her cover was almost blown by *Photoplay*'s Dorothy Manners in a Machiavellian feature which saw the journalist *defending* Loretta against those detractors she claimed were out to ruin her reputation by suggesting she had 'gone off somewhere to have a secret child'.

In fact, the only detractor was Manners herself, whom Gable somewhat ungallantly threatened to 'bash senseless', should he ever get his hands on her. Loretta *was* pregnant with Clark's baby – a daughter, Judy, who was born 6 November 1935 at her mother's Santa

Monica beach house. A mutual friend is said to have sent Clark a telegram announcing the news, which he is said to have ripped to shreds and flushed down the toilet. Later, it was claimed, the baby was put up for immediate adoption without Clark seeing her – and the matter should have ended there. On 11 May 1937 the press would report how Loretta had recently returned from a San Diego orphanage, where she had adopted a little girl named Judy, whom she claimed had been born in June 1935. This way, once the gossip columnists began doing their sums, they would realise the child could not have been conceived while Loretta and Clark had been snowed in on Mount Baker. Hedda, Louella et al. could have reminded their readers that it was *illegal* for single people in the United States to adopt, save none of them believed Judy *had* been adopted. Loretta's mother, interior designer Gladys Belzer, had been looking after her in Santa Monica. Loretta then dug herself into a much deeper hole by 'confiding' in Louella Parsons – well aware that this would end up in her column – that she had adopted *two* babies in San Diego, but that the other one had been returned to her birth mother.

Off and on, Loretta would permit Clark to see their daughter, but Judy (who became Judy Lewis when Loretta married advertising executive Tom Lewis in 1940) would not learn the truth about her parentage until 1957. Speaking in the BBC's *Living Famously* TV series in November 2002 – and looking the very spit of her father – she explained how she had been told the news by her fiancé on the eve of her wedding. The priest conducting the ceremony advised her *not* to confront her mother, declaring Loretta would only deny it. *Call Of The Wild* director William Wellman would add his own amusing, but undignified theory some years later (in Kenneth Anger's *Hollywood Babylon*) that Judy could only have been Gable's child: 'When the film was finished, Loretta disappeared for a while and later showed up with a daughter with the biggest ears I ever saw, except on an elephant.' The ears would later be corrected by surgery.

Shooting wrapped on *Call Of The Wild* on 23 February 1935, the day the Oscar nominations were announced, days before the ceremony, and the first time these had covered the January–December period – previously, they covered August of one year until July of the next. Clark's unruly behaviour at Mount Baker had been reported to Louis B. Mayer, and he was saved from suspension only because *It Happened One Night* had been nominated in a then unprecedented five categories: Best Actor, Actress, Film, Director and Screenplay.

In these pre-television coverage days, the Oscars ceremony was not as hyped and commercially motivated as today – it was not even broadcast on national radio. It was also unheard of for a minor studio, as Columbia was back then, to have been put forward for so many awards. Indeed, MGM monopolised the proceedings: the three nominees for Best Actor were 'Mayer's Boys' – Clark (though the film was not theirs), William Powell (for *The Thin Man*) and Frank Morgan (for *The Affairs Of Cellini*). Similarly, Claudette Colbert was up against Norma Shearer (*The Barretts of Wimpole Street*) and Grace Moore (*One Night Of Love*). Colbert was so convinced she had no chance of winning that she went ahead with a trip planned to New York. Frank Capra, escorted by a motorcycle cavalcade, fetched her back from the Union Station to the Biltmore Hotel, where she collected her Oscar from *wunderkind* Shirley Temple. Despite claims that she could not stand Capra, she dedicated the award to him, and he drove her back to the station, where the train had been kept waiting. According to Louella Parsons, after receiving his Oscar, Clark was heard mumbling that the accolade would not go to his head, as had happened with some recipients he could mention, adding, 'I'm still gonna be wearing the same size hat!'

His award brought Louis B. Mayer to his senses, and assured Clark the salary rise for which Ben Maddox had petitioned – though on $3,000 a week, rising to $4,500 after two years, compared to most of his contemporaries he was still underpaid. His romance with Loretta Young had begun and ended with *Call Of The Wild*. Joan Crawford had also (temporarily) slammed the door in his face, unable to tolerate his having cheated on her with the 'Gretch The Wretch', the only woman in all Hollywood she hated more than Bette Davis. Therefore, with he and Ria on the verge of separation and incapable of meeting without one or both blowing a fuse, Clark turned once more to Ben Maddox, who again covered their tracks by way of his syndicated column.

His next film was *China Seas*, an action-packed Irving Thalberg production with Jean Harlow, Rosalind Russell – and Wallace Beery, still earning more than he was. According to Ben Maddox's account to his readers, the director – Tay Garnett – would not have to worry about off-screen shenanigans with this one. Harlow, whose divorce from Hal Rosson would not become final until March 1936, was by now inseparable from William Powell, now divorced from Carole Lombard – and, Maddox reassured everyone, 'Mr and Mrs Gable could not be happier!'

*China Seas* was scripted by Jules Furthman, who had recently scripted *Shanghai Express* for Marlene Dietrich – who got away with playing a prostitute working in the Orient, who falls for a European because *she* had not been Oriental. Furthman now created a scenario black-pencilled by the Hays Office anti-mixed-race policy – and by Clark himself. Disgraceful as this might seem today, the story of a white sea captain who gets his Chinese wife pregnant was, in the Thirties, perceived as indecent. Therefore in the re-write she becomes China Doll, another Harlow floosie, who helps the captain save his ship from marauding Malaysian pirates. There are shades of the Harlow-Astor *Red Dust* scenario with the inclusion of wealthy widow Rosalind Russell, who also has her eye on Clark. To incite his jealousy and woo him back, Harlow makes a play for odious pirate leader Wallace Beery, which in real life she claimed would have been less preferable than shoving her head between the jaws of a starving lion!

It was Ben Maddox and Gable's father (who had recently married Edna, his brother's widow, the wedding and their new home paid for by Clark), who tried to talk him out of his next film, *Mutiny On The Bounty*. To be directed by Frank Lloyd, this was Irving Thalberg's latest pet project, a part of MGM's blockbusters programme aimed at competing with Warner Brothers' *Captain Blood* (Errol Flynn, Olivia de Havilland, Ross Alexander) and *A Midsummer Night's Dream* (Alexander, James Cagney). By the end of the year, MGM would have also completed Garbo's *Anna Karenina*, David Selznick's

*A Tale Of Two Cities* with Ronald Colman, The Marx Brothers' *A Night At The Opera* and *Naughty Marietta*, the first of the Jeannette MacDonald and Nelson Eddy musicals.

Maddox – whose other 'fuck-buddy', Eddie Quillan (1907–90) had been cast in *Mutiny On The Bounty* as timid mariner Jack Ellison – was convinced neither Clark nor Quillan would be capable of effecting a half-decent English accent. Also that Clark would be completely overshadowed by Charles Laughton, whose name would appear above his in the credits. He also reminded Gable that *all* the leads in the film (himself, Laughton, Quillan, Franchot Tone, Herbert Mundin, Donald Crisp, and actress Spring Byington) were gay or bisexual, and that Hays Office spies would be hovering around the location like vultures, waiting to swoop on the slightest indiscretion. Nor did it help when William Gable told a reporter that his son would look an even bigger sissy than usual, minus his 'man's man moustache' and in breeches and pigtail.

Irving Thalberg's pitching together of Gable and Laughton, two decades before the era of Method acting, was a stroke of genius. Clark was never less than loud when declaring his loathing of homosexuals, his way of trying to prevent the truth from emerging about himself. Laughton (1899–1962), on the other hand, did not care what anyone said about the 6-foot 3-inch, 200-pound muscle-bound 'masseur' who accompanied him on his travels. He was the latest in a long line of lovers who never balked at the idea of having sex with the unattractive, overweight and generally unpleasant actor because they were being paid handsomely to keep him contented.

Thalberg's theory was that if he could get Gable and Laughton to hate each other off the screen, this would make their character antagonism more authentic. This worked well. As the thoroughly odious Captain Bligh, Laughton is superb and very nearly runs away with the picture. Perpetually sneering through rubbery lips, even in jocular roles such as his definitive, Oscar-winning portrayal of Henry VIII (1933) he was without doubt the greatest English character actor of his generation. The son of a Scarborough hotelier, he had studied at RADA, entered films with *Piccadilly* in 1929, and more recently triumphed as the despotic father in *The Barretts Of Wimpole Street*.

Both Clark and Franchot Tone came to despise him to such an extent that this led to *them* forming a close friendship while making the film – much to Joan Crawford's joy.

In what is supposed to be a quintessentially English/Colonial scenario, Laughton shows up the entire cast with his impeccable diction. None of the American actors in the production – save Eddie Quinlan, who would hold the record for murdering the Cockney dialect until Dick van Dyke trounced him in *Mary Poppins* – even *try* to pronounce their lines in King's English. This particular Fletcher Christian hails from Cumberland-in-Ohio – not that it deflects from his quite exemplary performance once the viewer becomes involved in the derring-do. Scripted from the trilogy by Charles Nordhorff and James Norman Hall, the film recounts an actual historical event, much hacked about by the scriptwriter to fit in with the actors' personalities. It had first been filmed in 1933, as *In The Wake Of The Bounty*, with Errol Flynn (a descendant of Midshipman Young, who does not feature in this one) in the role of Fletcher Christian. The role would be reprised in 1962 by an irritating, positively awful Marlon Brando – and with a more passable Mel Gibson in 1984, though Anthony Hopkins was to portray a mediocre Captain Bligh.

None of these actors remotely resembled the real Fletcher Christian (1764–93), if contemporary accounts are anything to go by. Hailing from Cockermouth, Cumberand, he had sailed with Bligh prior to the ill-fated voyage on the *Bounty*. Christian is said to have stood 5-foot 9-inch tall and to have been stocky, bow-legged and tattooed with a star on his chest and buttocks. He was also reputed to have suffered from intense body odour! After the mutiny, he had founded the Pitcairn Island settlement, lived here for a while with his wife and three children and been murdered by Tahitian natives. Clark was 29 when he completed the film, playing Christian between the ages of 22 and 28. Of the other mutineers, only John Adams (aka Alexander Smith, portrayed in the film by Herbert Mundin) survived Christian – receiving a Royal pardon, he lived until 1828.

The film opens in Portsmouth in December 1787, with the *Bounty* about to set sail for Tahiti to collect a consignment of breadfruit trees to be transported to the West Indies and replanted to provide cheap sustenance for slave labour. As there is a shortage of volunteer sailors for the perilous mission, the Navy sends out a pressgang, headed by Christian, the ship's grumbling, no-nonsense second-in-command – though as we get to know him, he emerges as a decent fellow who only turns nasty when confronted with injustice. Christian bonds with the timid Ellison (Quillan) and jovial aristocrat, Roger Byam (Franchot), who augments the crew as a midshipman to compile a Tahitian dictionary for his father. Roger sees the 2-year, 10,000-mile voyage as an adventure, though Bligh only regards midshipmen as 'the lowest form of animal life in the British Navy'. He is an absolute cretin: cruel, psychotic, a despot whose credo is that only abject fear breeds respect. Even when a man dies before receiving his punishment, he has his corpse flogged. He makes an example of Roger by having him spend his first watch strapped to the top of the mast during a tempest. Others are whipped, beaten, starved and clapped in irons for trivial matters. Bligh's dictum is that if a man can walk, he can work – even if he drops dead doing so.

There is light relief when the *Bounty* reaches Tahiti, and a girl for every sailor – save one, who ends up with a boy, a scene removed from early prints of the film. Christian is not so lucky for Bligh assigns him to surveying the ship's reconditioning, which means no shore leave. 'I've never known a better sea captain,' he rants, 'but as a man he's a snake. He doesn't punish for discipline, he likes to see a man crawl. Sometimes I'd like to push his poison down his throat!'

Following the intervention of the Tahitian chief, Christian is finally permitted ashore, where he and Roger pair up with native girls and introduce us to the film's unintentionally high-camp element. Clad in loincloths, with Franchot's leaving little to the imagination in the age of the freeze-frame video, the pair frolic in the waves. Clark is no longer merely handsome and these beach-scenes with Franchot are purposely and flagrantly homoerotic – though whereas Franchot spreads his legs and proudly offers an eyeful, Gable preserves his modesty with a strategically placed thigh. This idyll ends when Bligh summons Christian back to the ship and confiscates the pearls that his girl (Movita Castenada) has given him as a parting gift, declaring these are now Crown property. The last straw occurs when the ailing ship's doctor falls dead while watching one flogging too many. 'We'll be men again, if we hang for it!' Christian explodes; he takes Bligh prisoner and seizes the ship. He, however, is not a malevolent man and he listens to Roger's pleas to spare the Captain's life so that he may be judged when they return to England. The crew are permitted to choose sides, with those supporting Bligh put into a boat with him to fend for themselves. Roger stays he has played no part in the mutiny – 'Casting me aside, thirty-five hundred miles from a port of call,' Bligh booms, 'You're sending me to my doom, eh? Well, you're wrong, Christian. I'll take this boat if she floats to England, if I must. I'll live to see all of you hanging from the highest yard-arm in the British fleet!'

The mutineers return to Tahiti, while Bligh and his crew survive against the odds. We see both sides celebrating their respective Christmases – Christian with his baby son and placating the Hays Office by pronouncing, 'Merry Christmas, Mrs Christian!' though it is not known if it was the real Christian married or not. Then there is more homoerotic bonding with Roger – the friends, stripped to the waist, gazing into each other's eyes while eating bananas, are seemingly disappointed when their wives arrive on the scene. The final drama comes when Bligh shows up again – and when Christian once more allows his men the choice of escaping with him, or returning to England, despite the risk of a court martial. Roger plumps for the latter, confident he will not be found guilty because he played no part in the mutiny – while Christian and company set sail for Pitcairn Island, where they destroy the *Bounty* so that they may never be found, or be able to leave.

Bligh, however, has one last trick up his sleeve. Under oath he lies that Roger was Christian's co-plotter and he is sentenced to hang, only to be pardoned when his father petitions the King. The film ends with Roger going back to sea, though no end credit informs us what happened to the mutineers once they reached the settlement. Hollywood had no intention of enlightening picture-goers that Clark Gable's alter-ego had ended up being butchered by the very people who had befriended him, the theory being that, as history has also proved, the Hollywood system was more than capable of similarly treating its own!

Though Oscar-nominated for their roles in the film, Clark, Laughton and Franchot did not win: the award for Best Actor went to Victor McLaglen for *The Informer*, while Paul Muni won Best Supporting Actor for *Black Fury*. Irving Thalberg collected the award for Best Film, however, and the *Mutiny On The Bounty* proved the biggest box-office draw for the 1935–6 season, MGM's biggest grossing production since *Ben Hur*, ten years previously – which, Louis B. Mayer boasted, had also featured Clark Gable . . . for all of 10 seconds.

Shooting on Catalina Island dragged on for 88 days, with Clark spending more time with Ben Maddox and Eddie Quillan than with Ria. He and Maddox were almost rumbled by Dorothy Manners, Maddox's rival, who Clark had threatened for exposing Loretta Young's pregnancy. Manners, a close friend of Joan Crawford's who had always held Clark responsible for the break-up of her marriage to Douglas Fairbanks Jr, would have been justified in getting her revenge by outing him. All she suspected initially was that he *was* involved with someone from the *Mutiny On The Bounty* cast, but that with this being a 'man's picture' with few candidates for his affection, the obvious person was Movita Castenada.

Hoping to avenge Joan by catching Clark in the act, so to speak, Manners picked her up at her home and the two set off for Catalina Island. Movita was nowhere to be seen, but they discovered Gable and Maddox lounging, shirtless, on the beach between takes. As Joan had confided in Manners about Franchot's 'other life' with Ross Alexander – and since Maddox's amorous activities were one of Holywood's best-kept open secrets, Manners must have had few doubts as to what was going on. Still, she said nothing, and for another 25 years Gable would despise her and make very caustic personal remarks about a highly respected journalist – adding her name to the growing list of people he was terrified might one day let the world in on the secret of his sexuality. Indeed, as a favour to Joan to *prevent* the truth emerging about Clark and his 'buddy', Dorothy Manners set tongues wagging by including a photograph of

Clark/Christian and Joan in her subsequent feature. It was snapped on the beach and more than suggested they were still involved – the philosophy being it was better to be suspected of adultery than of being gay.

When shooting wrapped on *Mutiny On The Bounty*, Ben Maddox accompanied Clark on a month-long 'pleasure trip' to South America. Financed by MGM, and doubling as a publicity exercise, this took in major cities in Mexico, Argentina, Bolivia, Peru and Brazil. At each stop Gable was met by a studio representative, who fixed him up with a female date to be photographed linking his arm whenever he attended a prearranged function, but far from the prying eyes of the Hollywood gossip columnists he shared a hotel suite with Maddox. Almost certainly they would have been together when he received the telegram informing him of Judy Lewis's birth.

They also shared a stateroom aboard the SS *Pan America*, which conveyed them from Rio de Janeiro back to New York for the *Mutiny On The Bounty* première. The 'shipboard romance' set up by Maddox to fool other reporters was with 'Mexican Spitfire' actress Lupe Velez, currently married to Johnny Weissmuller, but cheating on him with Gary Cooper. Clark and Lupe are thought to have spent at least one night together – and as Maddox also slept with her 'as part of the job' and since Lupe is also known to have favoured group sex, it was alleged that a threesome took place. She was also renowned for getting her men angry in the bedroom by berating them for their performances, compared with the super-hung Cooper. A few weeks after the trip, Clark called the garage that had supplied Cooper with his custom-built Duesenberg to commission one that was a foot longer.

Ben Maddox covered the première for *Screenland*, then stayed on in New York while Clark went to Los Angeles on 18 November. Ria and the children had already moved out of the Brentwood house and into a property he had leased before leaving for South America. 'Mrs Gable and I are thrilled with our new house,' Maddox reported Gable as having told him, 'We've had to shop for more to fill the house. And *that* has been fun!' Of course Maddox had been in on the ruse that Clark had taken advantage of the trip to remove Ria from his life as much as was possible without actually filing for divorce. Within twenty-four hours, Louella Parsons was on to Clark's case. Calling Howard Strickling, she threatened to spill the beans – whatever she assumed these to be –unless he gave her an exclusive as to what was transpiring within the Gable household. As usual, Clark and Maddox had covered their tracks: neither had been seen in public unless on the arm of a beautiful woman. Unfortunately, Lupe Velez was famed for blabbing even the most intimate details of her conquests – such as how she had 'ridden' Gary Cooper until he had passed out – and some of these anecdotes, if repeated to Louella, would have been sufficient to ring down the curtain on Clark's career. Strickling therefore issued a statement that he swore had come from Clark. The Gables were *not* divorcing – they were merely putting a little space between them until they had resolved any differences they might have had. More importantly, he added, no other woman was involved. In a manner of speaking, this was the truth. That same day, Clark moved into a suite at the Beverly Wilshire, where Ben Maddox would later join him.

Other changes had been effected in Brentwood during Clark's absence. On 11 October 1935, Joan Crawford and Franchot Tone finally married at Fort Lee, New Jersey, an event that led to another spat with Bette Davis. *Dangerous*, Bette's film with Franchot, had just been released and she had coerced Warner Brothers into adding flashes across the posters, saying: 'Look Out, Franchot Tone! You're In For The Toughest MUTINY You've Ever *Faced* When BETTE DAVIS Rebels in *DANGEROUS!*' Louis B. Mayer called Clark to gloat over his 'loss' only to be told by whoever it was that answered the phone (most likely Maddox) that he had moved out of the Beverly Wilshire for a few days to spend time with the newlyweds.

Clark's last film, shot in 1935, was *Wife vs Secretary*, with Jean Harlow, Myrna Loy and James Stewart in an early role. This was a sparkling comedy directed by Clarence Brown. Gable and Loy played a happily married couple – until she suspects him of having an affair with his secretary (Harlow), who pounces on him when Loy packs her bags to leave. Morality prevails, however, when Harlow dumps him for a younger lover (Stewart), so he can go back to his wife. This prompted the question: would Clark ever return to his own wife? 'Not on your life, buddy,' he told Ben Maddox.

Chapter Five

# LOMBARD

As zany as Jean Harlow and as outrageous as Tallulah Bankhead –
though nowhere near as sexually voracious – Carole Lombard was
'one of the guys'. She was a shoulder to cry on, a confidante who
teased but only when assured that her victim would take it in the
context in which it was intended; also a hyperactive matchmaker and
a party organiser par excellence. An astonishingly lovely woman,
whose looks rivalled those of Garbo and Dietrich, she out-cursed the
filthiest-mouthed male contemporary yet still bowled over the
frostiest individual with her warmth and innate charisma. Lombard
was also *the* practical joker! Gable once said that any other man
would have strangled her for some of the tricks she pulled on him –
notably the occasion when she announced to the crowd outside
Grauman's Theater that he was not there to leave his handprints in
the famous cement but instead 'an imprint of his uncircumcised
cock'! Noel Busch observed in *Life* magazine, 'When Carole
Lombard talks, her conversation, often brilliant, is punctuated by
screeches, laughs, growls, gesticulations – and the expletives of a
sailor's parrot'.

She was born Jane Alice Peters in Fort Wayne, Indiana, on
6 October 1908. Her father, Fred, was a manic depressive, resulting
from an accident which had left him lame – he died shortly before
Carole met Clark, though he had been well out of her life for some
time before then. Unable to cope with his black moods, in 1914 Bessie
Peters brought Jane and her two brothers to Los Angeles for a holiday
and they had stayed there, renting an apartment off Wilshire
Boulevard. In 1921, Jane had been playing baseball with a group of

boys in the street outside her home when spotted by Allan Dwan, a Fox director. He cast her as a tomboy in *A Perfect Crime*. This small part led to a contract with the studio and a name change to Carol Lombard – the 'e' would come later when, ignoring pleas from her superstitious mother, she decided that having thirteen letters in her name would only bring her luck.

Like Joan Crawford, while still in her teens Lombard was an accomplished dancer, competing in speakeasy Charleston contests and later featuring regularly on the bill at the Coconut Grove. Along with Crawford, by 1925 she had been recognised as a 'promising light' by the Western Association of Motion Picture Advertisers (WAMPA). With an age ceiling of 22 – which caused a great deal of fibbing – these hopefuls were known as the 'Wampas Babes' and emulated New York's infamous Algonquin Round Table by meeting regularly at Le Montmartre, one of Hollywood's plushest eateries.

Years later, *Confidential* magazine would refer to these young actresses as 'baritone babes': the group included Mary Astor, Dolores Del Rio, Janet Gaynor, Dolores Costello and Fay Wray, some of whom entered into lavender marriages to prevent their sexuality becoming public knowledge. Lombard therefore knew from an early age how to recognise these 'Gillette blades' who cut both ways – or their beaux, who 'licked the other side of the stamp', to use the parlance of the day. By the age of 17 she had already been calling herself 'fag-hag' – a derogatory term which she made respectable with her sincerity and loyalty towards her gay friends. Chief among these were William Haines, Rod La Roque, Cesar Romero and the directors Edmund Goulding and George Cukor, friends she shared with Joan Crawford. Joan only became aware of this following a Wampas Babes reunion when newcomer Carole attempted to usurp her place as head of the table one evening at Le Montmartre. On this occasion, she had made arrangements to be photographed by *Picturegoer*. When Joan bawled at her to move, Carole loudly pronounced, 'Madame, I find your manner *most* offensive. Now, will you please go and *fuck* yourself?' Rather than retaliate, Joan saw the funny side and the two became instant and lifelong friends.

Lombard's promising career almost ended as quickly as it had begun when, in 1926, she was out driving with her playboy lover, Henry Cooper, and another car hit them from behind, smashing her face into the windscreen. The injury required 14 stitches, and with typical lack of sympathy, Fox cancelled her contract. Over the next few years, she underwent extensive plastic surgery and was rescued by Mack Sennett, who had taken her on as a $50-a-week bathing belle and put her into 13 of his shorts – again, Carole had looked upon the number as a lucky omen. While working with Sennett she formed a most curious friendship with Madalynne Fields, Sennett's 6-foot, 240-pound female clown, whom she nicknamed Fieldsie. In 1928, as his slushy, slapstick comedies were starting to go out of fashion, she was signed by Pathé. Two years later, Paramount offered her a 7-year, $375 a week contract.

At Paramount, Carole had come into her own. Courted by Myron Selznick, who became her agent, and sumptuously gowned by Travis Banton, with her beauty and hourglass figure she was transformed into a homegrown Marlene Dietrich. While filming *Man Of The World* early in 1931 she had fallen for her co-star, 39-year-old William Powell, some 16 years her senior. The two lived together openly before marrying that June, a union which would end acrimoniously two years later. By this time, Carole had 'flipped her lid' over bisexual crooner Russ Columbo, a contemporary of Bing Crosby, hugely popular with his fans, but privately a disturbed, deeply unpleasant individual. Their affair ended tragically on 2 September 1934, when Columbo had a tiff with Lansing Brown, his photographer-lover, who had been showing him his collection of antique pistols. One of these had accidentally gone off and the bullet ricocheted off a table-top and entered Columbo's eye. He died a few hours later and Carole had assumed the mantle of widow to a man so vain his family thought it appropriate that he should be buried – seven weeks after his death on account of the extended police enquiry – with a mirror inside his coffin.

At the inquest a witness had come forward, testifying that he had heard Columbo and Brown arguing, but the coroner recorded a verdict of accidental death. For another ten years, news of Columbo's death would be kept from his ailing mother, with Carole forging his signature and arranging for postcards to be sent to her from wherever he was 'touring'. It was alleged that Carole's brother, Stuart, one of the pallbearers at his funeral, had also been involved with him. 'I loved Russ, not only as a man, but as a mother loves a child,' Carole told one journalist, a remark that would pretty much sum up her relationship with Clark Gable, too.

In 1934, on the rebound, she became involved with George Raft, allegedly another of Columbo's lovers and a no-less unsavoury character with mobster connections, as well as being her co-star in *Bolero*. Next, she had a fling with *It Happened One Night* scriptwriter Robert Riskin, another bisexual man she 'borrowed' from Fay Wray. He had also been seen escorted around town with Cesar Romero, so flagrantly effeminate that with her caustic humour Carole dubbed him, 'The queens' queen'. The fact that Columbo, Riskin and Romero spent much of their time chasing other men begs the question, taking into account the circles in which he frequently moved in: did she assume the same of Clark?

So far as is known, Lombard had no same-sex relationships herself, though with her anything would have been possible. After divorcing William Powell she moved Fieldsie into her house – Louella Parsons gatecrashed the welcoming party in search of a scoop, but found none. In 1934 Carole championed the tennis player Alice Marble (1913–90), who had recently been hospitalised with tuberculosis and severe acne. She had paid for her treatment and – after hearing her singing in the shower – had sent her for singing lessons. Marble's career as a café-chanteuse was short-lived, however, and she soon returned to tennis, to be crowned four-times US champion before winning Wimbledon in 1939.

It was inevitable, with the company he kept since arriving in Hollywood – Haines and Shields, Rod La Rocque, Johnny Mack Brown, Ben Maddox and Eddie Quillan – that Clark had become, whether he admitted it or not, a fully fledged member of the movie world's lavender set. As such, it was also inevitable that he should eventually become involved, platonically or otherwise, with Carole Lombard. Their relationship received a kick-start on 25 January 1936 at the Victor Hugo restaurant in Beverly Hills, the occasion being a

Mayfair Club dinner-dance organised by Carole herself. Clark and studio date Edie Adams arrived with Marion Davies and William Randolph Hearst, and were greeted in the foyer by Carole and her 'date', Cesar Romero. Her first words to him since working together on *No Man Of Her Own* were, 'Hi, baby – I'm in charge of this fucking party!'

She had instructed her guests to wear white to match the decor and flowers – and to 'compliment' the lavender gathering, which included Myrna Loy, Barbara Stanwyck and Robert Taylor, Janet Gaynor, Claudette Colbert, Dolores Del Rio and Rod La Rocque. Jeannette MacDonald – whose singing Carole likened to a cat being roasted alive on a griddle – turned up uninvited, wearing a mauve dress which Carole told her matched her face. She had not wanted Norma Shearer there either, but was overruled by David Selznick, who financed the event. Deliberately ignoring the dress code, Norma swanned into the Victor Hugo wearing a *scarlet* gown, then proceeded to look down her nose at the other guests. According to David Niven (*Bring On The Empty Horses*) this had brought the very loud and acid observation from Carole, 'Who the fuck does Norma think she is – the house madam?'

It was not her only vulgar outburst that evening. Purely out of devilment, she invited Loretta Young to the bash, in what would be her first outing since having Clark's baby, suggesting Carole may also have known the truth. And if this was not enough, she invited Ria, who turned up with her lawyer, enabling Carole to spread the rumour that they were an item because the lawyer was 'better hung' than Gable. When Clark acknowledged his estranged wife, Carole barked, 'Who's the old bag?' And if all this was not enough to humiliate him, while she and Clark were dancing, she grabbed herself a handful and pronounced, 'So, Pa's got a hard on!' The nickname – their characters had addressed each other as 'Ma' and 'Pa' in *No Man Of Her Own* – would stick. Legend persists that Gable became so turned on, dancing with Lombard, that they slipped away from the party and went for a spin in his Duesenberg – and that Carole snubbed him when he tried to get her to go back with him to his suite at the Beverly Wilshire. This seems unlikely. As hostess she would have been missed, and not even Clark would surely have taken such a risk right under the noses of his wife, Selznick, and a whole gaggle of gossip-columnists.

One guest who definitely knew what was going on was Clark's old stalker, Adela Rogers St Johns, who rushed out the news of the Gables' split – though they had not given any official announcement – in the February 1936 issue of *Photoplay*. The feature was gushing, even by Adela's standards:

> The parting of the Gables makes my heart ache a little. Why did it have to happen? Why did two such swell people, both of them real, both of them deserving of happiness, have to come to the end of what seemed to all of us who knew them well, who'd been close friends, an ideal marriage? I've been sitting here looking out at trees that are bare, but that will be green again in the Spring, at lilac bushes that today are brown twigs, but that in April will be fragrance and colour once more, and trying to figure it out. You see, it was like this with the Gables. You felt a wholeness of self when they were together. They weren't sentimental or gushing. They were too modern for that. But your heart felt a little warmer because they were joined in their own way, and the world is often a lonely place and men and women were meant to be one, so that loneliness would roll back like a wave and stand trembling at the command of love . . . So the world, and fame, and all its petty trials and tribulations caught up with them. The very virility that had won Rhea [sic] in the beginning tortured her. The very elegance and charm that had won Clark began to smother him. And beauty drifted away and left hunger on both sides, a hunger that had sent them out to begin all over again.

Carole is reputed to have shouted for someone to fetch her a bucket while reading Adela's lament. Yet she was in no hurry to see Gable again after humiliating him in full view of Hollywood's elite. When he called her a few weeks after the Mayfair Club party and asked her out on a date, she told him to get lost – or words to that effect – though later events suggest she was playing hard to get. Clark, therefore, shrugged his shoulders and made a play for another beauty with whom he had danced at the Victor Hugo – Merle Oberon.

Born in Tasmania but raised in India, Merle Oberon (Estelle Merle O'Brien Thompson, 1911–79) had been working as an extra in 1932 when Alexander Korda cast her as Anne Boleyn opposite Charles Laughton in *The Private Life Of Henry VIII*. She subsequently married Korda, but engaged in a number of highly publicised affairs with United Artists' Joseph Schenck, Maurice Chevalier and newcomer David Niven just to get herself noticed and inch her way up the Hollywood ladder. Rumour persisted (proven after her death) that she had Asian blood, which, had Clark but known, would have kept him at bay. Much as he adored black people, for some reason he detested Orientals and Asians. Nor did their affair get very far, once Carole got wind of it.

At the end of February, Clark and Oberon were guests at a party at the mansion of millionaire entrepreneur John Hay Whitney – another Who's Who of Hollywood gathering in honour of the wife of scriptwriter Donald Ogden Stewart. It was to celebrate, of all things, her recovery from a nervous breakdown brought about by his carousing. Halfway through the proceedings, an ambulance turned up, its siren screaming – with the driver claiming there had been a fatal accident down the road and that he and his paramedic assistant needed somewhere to 'park the stiff' until the police arrived. This was stretchered into Whitney's living room and promptly sat bolt upright. It was none other than Carole, wearing a shroud over her Travis Banton gown and gatecrashing the event to save Clark from a fate *worse* than death. Exit, Merle Oberon!

The zaniness continued weeks later when Carole began shooting *The Princess Comes Across*, with Fred MacMurray – she boasted to flabbergasted reporters that a sequel was on the cards: *Gable Comes Across . . . Lombard's Tits!* She had actually been assigned to *My Man Godfrey*, with ex-husband William Powell. One of the finest rich-versus-poor movies ever made, this tells of the eccentric heiress, who takes in a vagrant, makes him her butler and subsequently learns he is just as upper-crust as she is. Once this wrapped, she provided a crutch for Clark during his 'two months of purgatory' – working on *San Francisco* with Jeanette MacDonald and Spencer Tracy. Though he would always have tremendous admiration for Tracy, Gable could not stand MacDonald, and initially told Irving Thalberg the last thing he wanted to do, short of jumping off a cliff, was to 'stand there like a dummy' while MacDonald sang at him. Louis B. Mayer, for whom the feisty diva could do no wrong, stepped into the affray with the old chestnut: Clark would do the film, keep his complaints to himself, or suffer suspension without pay until the film had been completed with his replacement. His dislike of MacDonald was nothing like her loathing of him – believed to have stemmed from one of Clark's 'fag-hating' periods when he made a few cutting remarks about her singing partner, Nelson Eddy. MacDonald certainly made life very unpleasant for him on the set, chewing raw garlic every time she had to kiss him and telling director Woody Van Dyke that this was the only thing she could eat to make her breath smell worse than Clark's!

The snooty, strait-laced MacDonald also objected to Carole visiting the *San Francisco* set. To her way of thinking, decent young women did not use words like 'shit' and 'fuck' in every sentence when addressing a priest, even if this was only Spencer Tracy's alter-ego in the film. Clark's gung-ho buddies and all the technicians, on the other hand, adored her: Carole was one of them and they did not have to mind their language when she was around. For Jeanette MacDonald, the last straw came when Carole and Tallulah Bankhead – a dangerous combination if ever there was one – arrived with Clark at a post-wrap party armed with their own plates. These were steel bedpans, which they proceeded to fill at the buffet table, to the horror of MacDonald's society friends.

In *San Francisco*, Gable played his third Blackie – Blackie Norton, owner of a seedy Barbary Coast saloon, who employs up-coming opera singer Mary Blake (MacDonald). Naturally, he treats her rough and after coercing her to show her legs, he barks, allegedly not scripted, 'You're a little thin down there, but you've a fair set of pipes!' There are shades of *Manhattan Melodrama* with Blackie and the Tracy character – childhood pal Father Mullin, who in adulthood turned against him on account of his dodgy dealings. It is he who tries to stop the virginal Mary from falling into Blackie's clutches and getting corrupted. The true star of the film is the 20-minute sequence towards the end, re-creating the 1906 earthquake that devastated the city, claiming 452 lives. In the wake of this, Mary sits amid the ruins and sings the title-song. Years later this would be reprised as Judy Garland's secondary anthem and open with the line which always made audiences titter: 'I never will forget . . . Jeanette MacDonald!'

One aspect of the shooting schedule that caused Clark to blow a fuse would be repeated a few years later while he was making *Gone With The Wind*. This was when he was expected to cry during the final scene, when Blackie learns that his beloved Mary has survived the carnage. But he refused. Tears, he declared, were for women and 'fluffs' – effeminate homosexuals. Director Woody Van Dyke offered a compromise: Gable would turn his back to the camera, *pretend* to cry, and drawl the film's most camp line, 'Thanks God – I really mean it!'

Scarcely pausing to catch his breath, or so it seemed, Gable was loaned out to Warner Brothers for his second film with Marion Davies: like *Polly Of The Circus*, *Cain And Mabel* was based on another *Cosmopolitan* short story. William Randolph Hearst had transferred loyalties, along with Cosmopolitan Pictures, to the studio because Irving Thalberg had just cast Norma Shearer in *Marie Antoinette*, a coveted role pencilled in for Davies. Instead of playing the doomed queen, Davies got to hoof it up as musical comedy star Mable O'Dare – opposite Clark, hamming as prizefighter Joe Cain. The film opens with the pair playing/sparring to a half-empty auditorium and despite the fact that they cannot stand each other, they submit to a fake romance to bolster their flagging careers.

Camp does not begin to describe this mishmash of slapstick and musical mayhem. Clark's plum line comes when he rounds on Davies with, 'If the galloping you do is dancing, I've seen better ballet in a horse show!' She slaps him; he empties a bucket of ice-cubes over her head. And, of course, the loathing turns to love. Hearst, who spent $500,000 of his own money on the 10-minute wedding day finale, had wanted this to be choreographed by Busby Berkeley, but had to settle for the less illustrious Bobby Connolly, who merely emulates the great master. Having transported the cast to Venice, Camelot and Versailles, the film ends with a 100-foot high pipe organ bursting apart and releasing 150 bridesmaid chorus girls grinning like Cheshire cats and wailing, 'I'll Sing You A Thousand Love Songs'.

On 1 June 1936, Clark took time off from *Cain And Mabel* to make his radio debut in *The Legionnaire And The Lady* with Marlene Dietrich, an adaptation of *Morocco*, her first American film, in which she starred with Gary Cooper. He was paid $5,000, Dietrich thrice this amount, and a staggering 35 million listeners tuned in to the *Lux Radio Theater* production, broadcast live from Hollywood's Music Box Theater and introduced by Cecil B. DeMille. That same week, Marion Davies downed tools and, accompanied by Joan Crawford, rushed to the aid of their friend William Haines. Since his enforced 'retirement' from the movies, Haines and Jimmie Shields had gone through some kind of marriage commitment ceremony and retreated to a beach house in El Porto, south of Manhattan Beach. Clark and Carole had visited them here many times. On the evening of 3 June, Haines and Shields were entertaining a group of male friends when they were subjected to a vicious gay bashing. 'It was a perfectly harmless and peaceful pocket of poofs,' Kenneth Anger later observed in *Hollywood Babylon*, 'Nothing like the full-scale suck-and-fuck gay communities in latter day Fire Island. Children were not molested, local husbands were not seduced.'

The attacks had been organised by the White Legion, a vigilante force not unlike the Ku Klux Klan in their hatred of homosexuals. Haines called the cops, but rather than arrest or even question the guilty party – a neighbour – they made a few homophobic comments of their own and left. Terrified of these thugs showing up again, Haines had called Joan Crawford, in the midst of entertaining Hearst and Davies. They had driven to El Porto, collected Haines and Jimmie, and brought them back to San Simeon, then the most fortified home of any Hollywood star. Clark and Carole dropped by to offer moral support – publicly, however, to reassure the press that *he* was not thus inclined, Clark condemned the couple for courting trouble by being gay in the first place. His action earned him his first verbal warning from the intensely gay-friendly Joan.

The incident brought about Crawford and Gable's first film together for some time, *Love On The Run*, directed by W.S. Van Dyke. The script was another typical John Lee Mahin racy drama. Joan played socialite heiress Sally Parker, who is about to marry the dashing Prince Igor (Ivan Lebedeff) when she realises she does not love him as much as he wants her to. Drafted in to cover the story are rivals Michael Anthony and Barnaby Pells (Clark, Franchot Tone). Initially, Sally does not suspect them of working for the press, which she despises, and uses Michael as a foil-lover to get out of marrying Igor. Soon they are skydiving over Europe in a stolen plane, then travelling to the most unexpected locations – sometimes in a flashy car, sometimes by horse and cart, always with Barnaby tagging along, secretly working on another assignment to track down an international spy. The unlikely trio are menaced by enemy agents, ending up in the equally incredulous setting of the Palais de Fontainebleu – with Sally and Michael being mistaken for the ghosts of Louis XIV and Madame de Maintenon! They also fall in love, and after dealing with the crooks and despite Sally's hatred of reporters they marry.

The critics were merciless, with the *New York Times* denouncing the film as, 'A slightly daffy cinematic item of no importance'. *Motion Picture* liked it, but gave it a bad review because Franchot Tone laid into their reporter when she visited the set, demanding that he be photographed with Joan, and not Clark. 'Mr Tone was full of superiority complex,' she observed in the magazine's November 1936 issue, cautious not to give her name and sarcastically adding of Joan, 'But the Queen was very gracious.'

On 14 September, not unexpectedly, Irving Thalberg died, aged 37, and the whole of Hollywood went into shock – some genuinely grieving, many pretending. A few weeks earlier, a simple cold had developed into lobar pneumonia. Clark and Douglas Fairbanks Jr were ushers at his funeral at the B'nai B'rith Temple on Wilshire Boulevard and everyone who was anyone was there to pay their respects – or disrespects, depending on how they had got along with MGM's precocious Boy Wonder. Only the crowd-shy Greta Garbo, heavily involved with Thalberg's *Camille*, was permitted not to attend, and she sent her condolences with a huge wreath. Joan Crawford showed up against her will – she had hated Thalberg for always giving the choicest roles to Norma Shearer.

Clark too had fought against going to the circus, as he called it. At the time of Thalberg's death, the two had not been on speaking terms because Clark had bawled him out for wanting to cast him in what would be his last big budget production, *Romeo And Juliet*. Rightly pointing out that he was way too old to play the teenage Romeo, he had added, 'Besides, I don't do that Shakespeare shit!' Thalberg cast Norma Shearer and Leslie Howard, 36 and 43 respectively, as the tragic lovers and tried to compensate for his ridiculous choice by ageing up the rest of the cast. The film was lampooned by critics.

Thalberg exited the world at a time when his powers had started to diminish. Rumour persisted that he had been planning to leave MGM to found his own production company and there had been talk of some stars breaking contract to follow him: Norma Shearer, without any doubt; Garbo almost certainly; Gable perhaps with a different attitude towards Thalberg once Louis B. Mayer was no longer part of the equation. Thalberg would serve as a model for F. Scott Fitzgerald's *The Last Tycoon* and from 1937 onwards the Motion Picture Industry (MPI) would present a Best Producer award in his memory.

Thalberg's was Clark and Joan's second major funeral that year. On 9 January John Gilbert had died of a heart attack, aged 40. Since having his voice sabotaged by Mayer, his career had nose-dived – his one moment of Talkies glory occurred in 1933 when he had starred with Greta Garbo in *Queen Christina*. 1936 was also the year of the exhaustive search for Scarlett O'Hara – setting in motion a ludicrously costly, confusing machinery of hopes, shattered dreams, ego trips and double-dealing which would involve just about every major Hollywood actress under the age of 40. In the July, David Selznick paid $50,000 for the screen rights to Margaret Mitchell's only recently completed blockbuster *Gone With The Wind*. Atlanta born and raised Mitchell (1900–49) had studied for a career in medicine, turned to journalism, and in 1925 started writing her only book. Selznick read the 1,000-pages plus work in galley proofs. After publication it went on to sell over 25 million copies in 30 languages and won Mitchell the Pulitzer Prize. Later, surprised by the fuss her book had caused, she would demand and receive another $50,000 from Selznick.

Selznick (1902–65), married to Louis B. Mayer's daughter, Irene, had approached Irving Thalberg with the project but his response had been that Civil War pictures had gone out of fashion. This contributed to an almighty bust-up with MGM. Selznick accused Mayer of supporting Thalberg's persistent favouritism of some stars (chiefly Norma Shearer), directors and scriptwriters over others, but rather than have it out with him personally, Selznick complained to Nicholas Schenck, head of Loew's Inc, MGM's parent company. When Schenck refused to support him, Selznick had taken the unusual step of tendering his resignation, announcing that he would only stay on with MGM until he had finished his current schedule (*Anna Karenina* and *A Tale Of Two Cities*). Following this he would start up his own production company. His first major film would be *A Star Is Born* with Janet Gaynor and Fredric March, but his biggest production ever would be *Gone With The Wind*.

Even before Clark was consulted over the role – and Mayer asked for his permission to loan him out – Selznick had decided that *only* Gable would be playing Rhett Butler, his decision based upon the thousands of letters he had received from fans. Clark's initial response was that he did not *want* the part, declaring he would never live up to the general public's expectations of him, as opposed to those of the fans who would, of course, have accepted him in almost any part. 'Give it to Ronald Colman,' he is alleged to have told Selznick. He was, of course, but a pawn in the machinations, being a humble contract player expected to do Mayer's bidding. Mayer therefore came back to Selznick with *his* conditions. *If* Selznick borrowed Clark, then *he* would be expected to pay his salary, currently fixed at $4,500 a week.

Unhappy with this, Selznick approached Warner Brothers with a view to pairing Clark with their biggest female star, Bette Davis, the fan magazines' second choice after Tallulah Bankhead. Initially Jack

Warner made Selznick an offer that he assumed would be turned down – Bette would only be released from her contract provided Errol Flynn was to play Rhett. Much to everyone's surprise Selznick favoured the proposal and Bette, never less than a law unto herself, was consulted even though she too was only a contract player – such was the power she wielded, like Garbo she could demand almost anything. Her response was, 'I will not be working with a man who's been in every cathouse between here and Timbuktu!' Not to be outdone, Warner subsequently got his own back on her by casting her opposite Flynn in *The Sisters*, completed in 1938.

In the meantime, Warner tried to bully Bette by telling her that *unless* she agreed to play Scarlett O'Hara, she might soon be joining the dole queue. They stirred things up by letting slip what Clark had said about her to Selznick: 'If *you* were Rhett Butler, would *you* want to kiss a mug like hers?' Yet even he must have been stunned by Bette's response. Carole Lombard had apparently shared the confidence with her that Clark suffered not just from premature ejaculation, but from acute phimosis – an inability to retract his foreskin that, despite his mania for personal cleanliness, left him with odour problems down below. According to Bette's biographer, Lawrence J. Quirk (*Fasten Your Seatbelts*), she hit back *literally* below the belt by pronouncing, 'I can't stand a man who has fake store teeth and doesn't keep his uncircumcised cock clean under the foreskin. I hear he shoots too soon and messes himself all the time. Great lover? Great fake!' Quirk also recounts an anecdote relayed to him by the writer Jerry Asher, of how director George Cukor sent Clark a 'special gift' in February 1939 for his 38th birthday – a cake of Lifebuoy anti-deodorant soap and a bottle of Listerine. Quirk observed, 'The accompanying note, according to Jerry, read, "Clark dear – the soap is to clean out the cheese beneath your foreskin and the Listerine is to take away the smell."'

Which of course begs the question – how *did* Cukor know this? One doubts that he could have been so enlightened by Carole. Though fond of cracking jokes about Clark's short-comings in the bedroom (almost certainly untrue, otherwise there would not have been an endless queue of lovers eager not just to test his libido, but also for a repeat performance), she would never have overstepped the mark by divulging such a hugely personal matter. One must therefore assume that Cukor was merely acting with untold bitterness – or speaking from first-hand experience.

Humphrey Bogart's biographer Darwin Porter also cites an incident around this time when Bogart was standing next to Clark at a men'sroom urinal in a Hollywood club. 'After doing some pecker-checking,' Porter observed, 'Bogie suggested a helpful surgical alteration for Gable's penis. Gable was so outraged that he punched Bogart'.

With Bette Davis no longer in the running for the so-called Scarlett Stakes, in near desperation Selznick had gone running back to Louis B. Mayer, no doubt chewing on a sizeable chunk of humble pie. Once more he was told that if he borrowed Gable, he would still have to pay his salary, and MGM would own one-half of the film. Next to step into the affray was Clark's agent, Phil Berg. If shooting was expected to take 16 weeks, as Selznick forecast, Clark's total salary would be $72,000 – far less than most of the major stars were receiving when working independently of their studio contracts, and less than half of what RKO were currently paying Carole Lombard. Very reluctantly, Mayer agreed to pay him a $50,000 bonus – a third of which would come from Selznick International.

Mayer also promised to pay Selznick a minimum of $1,250,000 – half of the film's estimated production costs. MGM and Selznick International would share the profits and Loew's Inc would receive 15 per cent of the gross for distribution. Because he distrusted his father-in-law, Selznick also drew up a contingency plan: unless Mayer appointed him producer of *Gone With The Wind* and welcomed him back at MGM as a vice-president, he would strike a similar deal with one of the other studios. When Mayer learned that Warner Brothers were still waiting in the wings with Errol Flynn, just as popular with cinema audiences as Gable, he very quickly capitulated. With Hollywood still reeling from the shock of Irving Thalberg's death, most people were of the opinion that Norma Shearer had a divine right to play Scarlett O'Hara – for no other reason than they felt sorry for her. Selznick would not even suffer having her name mentioned in his company for *she* had been a contributory factor to his leaving MGM in the first place!

Next in line for the part was Tallulah Bankhead – Alabama-born and therefore an authentic Southern belle. Reputations and the Hays Office's moral turpitude clause did not count so far as the search for Scarlett was concerned, otherwise the audition list might not have been so exhaustive. Selznick had been knocked sideways by Tallulah's performance in the Broadway production of *Reflected Glory*, and when the news hit the press, he received thousands of letters supporting his choice: the Governor of Alabama's telegram read: WHY DON'T YOU GIVE TALLULAH THE PART AND HAVE DONE WITH IT? On 21 December 1936, Tallulah would make two Technicolor screen tests, wearing one of Garbo's costumes from *Camille*. These would be filed with tests of other hopefuls – an amazing archive comprising 13,000 feet of colour and 120,000 feet of monochrome which, some years later, would be edited to form the documentary, *Search For Scarlett*.

Tallulah Bankhead boasted that she was ahead of all the other Scarlett contenders, aside from Joan Crawford and Carole Lombard, in that she had *slept* with Rhett Butler. Her chances were scuppered, however, when Clark let slip at a reception that he had been the one behind William Haines' sacking by Louis B. Mayer back in 1933. Tallulah laid into Clark, accusing him of hypocrisy, and she would later suspect him of being behind Louella Parsons' unnecessary and unprovoked attack in her column. Reminding her readers that one of Tallulah's closest friends, John Hay Whitney, was part-financing the film while another, George Cukor, would be directing it, Louella concluded, 'So, I'm afraid she will get the part. If she does, I personally will go home and weep because she is NOT Scarlett O'Hara in any language, and if David Selznick gives her the part he will have to answer to every man, woman and child in America.'

The other Scarlett hopefuls now heading Selznick's pared-down but still 40-strong list included Joan Crawford, Margaret Sullavan, Paulette Goddard, Claudette Colbert, Katharine Hepburn and Carole Lombard. Clark shrugged his shoulders and declared he did not care *who* Selznick chose for the role but he did voice his opinions concerning George Cukor. He never referred to him by name but as 'that goddam faggot' – conveniently forgetting that he himself had not been averse to accompanying Cukor and the Haines-Crawford gang on their trips to Pershing Square. As will be seen, Clark's hypocrisy and homophobic rantings condemned by Tallulah Bankhead would have far-reaching effects.

In the meantime, he pushed for Joan Crawford to appear opposite him in *Parnell*. This would represent Hollywood's reading of the last years of Irish Prime Minister Charles Stewart Parnell (1846–91), who had become a thorn in the side of British politics with his campaign for home rule. In 1879, Parnell formed the National Land League to reduce rents and secure for tenants the ownership of their lands from their mostly English landlords – an action that had made him the people's hero but also landed him in jail. The film, for the better part, concerned itself with Parnell's involvement with Katie O'Shea, the wife of one of his opponents, which resulted in a messy public divorce, followed by marriage to O'Shea just five months before his death. Three years earlier, Crawford had been panned by the critics for her dreadful English accent in *Today We Live* and she now declared she would not risk the same fate by attempting an Irish one. Instead the part went to Myrna Loy.

The real Parnell had been described by contemporary sources as 'frail, shy, sensitive and dull' – portrayed by Clark, only the latter adjective applied. 'Gable as the Irish patriot orating for home rule in the House of Commons looked as though he would rather be dodging debris in the 'Frisco earthquake,' was how John Douglas Eames later summed up this abhorrent mishmash in *The MGM Story*. There was a display of the now regular Gable histrionics during shooting – this time not because director John Stahl wanted him to weep but because he wanted Clark to don a false beard and at least slightly resemble the real Parnell. He refused, declaring whiskers were dirty, though he had *insisted* on wearing designer stubble for *Call Of The Wild*. Stahl got him to compromise by wearing fake sideburns, which made him look rather fetching but did nothing to prevent the film from bombing at the box-office.

On 9 January 1937, exactly one year after John Gilbert's death,

Clark attended the funeral of 29-year-old Ross Alexander, whom he had befriended by way of Franchot Tone. Yet again another fine actor's demise brought about by Hollywood's double standards, hypocrisy and greed. Alexander's body was discovered at his ranch – in a fit of despair, he had shot himself. As had happened with Paul Bern, Jack Warner and the studio police had been first at the scene to search for a suicide note. This time there had been none, so Warner Brothers fabricated the story that Alexander, deeply in debt, had never recovered from the suicide two years earlier of his actress wife, Aleta Freel – additionally, that he had been having problems with his second wife and frequent co-star, Anne Nagel.

The reason for these tall tales was that Jack Warner had unearthed Alexander's diary, full of his indiscretions and containing a blackmail letter from a young drifter he had picked up for sex during the Christmas holidays. On top of this, the actor had been publicly branded a 'dirty queer' by Bette Davis, on learning he had been pencilled in as her next leading man. As a final insult to one of his most gifted stars, Warner had given orders for Alexander's ranch to be ransacked, to make it appear that he had 'gone nuts' before killing himself. His death came as a tremendous shock to the closeted Hollywood gay community and, in the wake of the William Haines débâcle, still fresh in everyone's minds, Clark was summoned to Louis B. Mayer's office and issued with the stern warning, 'There but for the grace of God go you!'

But there was light relief a few weeks later, on 1 February, Clark's thirty-sixth birthday. Judy Garland, then 15 and two years away from *The Wizard Of Oz*, was Louis B. Mayer's 'golden child', it is reputed in more ways than one. It is a well-chronicled fact that stardom and perennial protection beckoned for any pubescent girl willing to hop onto The Messiah's casting couch – and failure for the ones who did not. Under contract to MGM, Judy had had bit parts in just three films, but Mayer was hoping for her to hit the big time with *Broadway Melody of* 1938, filmed in 1936 but scheduled for release before the end of 1937 to give it longer box-office life. In the meantime, she was compelled to sing at parties thrown for MGM stars and executives. 'Mayer treated me like the hired help,' she recalled in a 1963

'Where d'ya git that kimona?' With Jean Harlow in *Red Dust*, 1932.

1933, in the Beverly Wilshire with Ria, one of the rare occasions she smiled for the camera. Sitting behind Ria, Clark's lover Ben Maddox.

'All the nice girls love a sailor!' Clark with Jean Harlow and Wallace Beery in *China Seas*, 1935.

1935, with Movita in *Mutiny On The Bounty*. The press were fooled into believing thay may have been having a relationship to cover Clark's affair with Ben Maddox.

1936, with Joan Crawford, the great love of his life after Lombard. 'Balls, he had 'em,'
Crawford said after he died.

January 1941, at the Greek War Relief Show with Carole. One year later, she was dead.

1953, with Gene Tierney at the premiere of *Never Let Me Go*.

1955, two rare shots with Kay. Below, with Jane Russell and husband Bob Waterfield at the premiere of *The Tall Men*.

1957, with Yvonne de Carlo in *Band Of Angels*.

television interview. 'I even had to eat in the kitchen with the rest of the staff. The man was a louse.'

For Gable's birthday, Judy climbed out of a giant cake and sang 'You Made Me Love You', the McCarthy-Monaco standard prefaced by Roger Edens' now legendary 'Dear Mr Gable' sequence, which recounts the plight of the teenager with the crush on the movie star that will never be reciprocated. Mayer was so moved to tears that he recalled Judy to the set and had it added to the film. Each year, for the next three years, she was brought in to perform the same routine, with Clark faking a delighted grin but privately cringing and denouncing her 'a precocious brat'. That was until he learned that Judy had only been doing Mayer's bidding, and that to have refused him would have caused her more grief than her frail persona could have safely handled, whence they became friends.

Four weeks later Clark, Carole Lombard, Jean Harlow and William Powell all attended the Oscars ceremony at the Bilton Hotel. There were no nominations for Clark or Harlow, though Lombard and Powell had been nominated for *My Man Godfrey*. Clark's admiration for Spencer Tracy took a temporary nosedive when he was nominated for Best Supporting Actor in *San Francisco*, but none of the quintet won. Powell's other film that year, *The Great Ziegfeld*, won Best Film and its leading lady, Luise Rainer, Best Actress. Best Actor award went to Paul Muni for *The Story Of Louis Pasteur*. In the meantime, the Ross Alexander tragedy put the fear of God into the Hollywood gay community as news of his 'secret diary' spread amongst them. Almost certainly this had been confiscated and destroyed by Jack Warner, but it did not stop the panic: Alexander had been promiscuous and there was no knowing what information he had passed on to lovers in post-coital murmurings. Franchot Tone, more affected than most, hit the bottle with a vengeance and this told on his relationship with Joan Crawford – she started showing up for work wearing more make-up than usual to conceal the bruises inflicted during their latest fight. Had Clark been aware of this, with his track record of providing a strong shoulder to lean on, he would almost certainly have been hammering on the Crawford door. Joan, however, persevered as her marriage careered out of control. She had far too much respect for Clark and Carole, she said, to even think of coming between them.

Hot on the heels of the Alexander tragedy, and immediately preceding an even greater one, a scandal was meticulously orchestrated to reassure anyone who nurtured doubts regarding Clark's masculinity (in pre-Kinsey days when bisexuality was largely unrecognised) that he was very definitely a ladies' man. He might have been a disreputable cad perhaps, but unquestionably he was red-blooded. The paternity suit lodged against him in the spring of 1937 was a publicity stunt organised by Louis B. Mayer to kill off the 'fagelah' rumours once and for all. Again, the naivety of the general public was such in those days that it was considered inconceivable, if not physically impossible, for a homosexual to father a child. Of course Mayer could have gone to the press with Loretta Young's baby, currently awaiting collection from the San Diego orphanage, but this would have ruined two financially lucrative careers. Far better then, from his point of view, to fabricate a story and generously reward the parties roped into his nonsensical charade.

The willing and handsomely recompensed scapegoat was Violet Norton, claimed by Howard Strickling to be a 47-year-old Essex woman, who had turned up at MGM, 'out of the blue', with a private detective. It was he who demanded $150,000 to prevent his client going to the press with the revelation that, in September 1922, Clark – using the alias Frank Billings – had seduced her in England, resulting in the birth of a daughter, Gwendoline, the following June. Initially, Strickling's ruse failed when the magistrate he approached decided that if Norton and her lawyer were to be charged with blackmail, the matter would be best settled out of court, as had happened with Josephine Dillon. It took the likes of Hedda, Louella and Ben Maddox all of five minutes – the time it took to call the US Passport Agency – to ascertain that Clark had not been issued with a passport until 1930. MGM had no option but to reconfirm this, additionally that he had *never* been to England, an admission that should have destroyed the case, had this been a genuine blackmail threat – Norton had already furnished the prosecution with Gwendoline's birth certificate, dated June 1923. Almost certainly this was a forgery which was supposed to have been dated June 1933. Realising his faux pas, Mayer payed to have the charge amended, resulting in the US Post Office indicting Norton for sending letters of extortion to MGM. None of these were submitted as evidence, quite simply because they did not exist, and there was *still* the question of preventing Clark from being outed.

Therefore the case was now referred to the US Attorney General, who called for a trial with an all-male jury 'to avoid female blushes'. Witnesses were subpoenaed to testify to Clark's manliness. Not only this but his movements at the time he was supposed to have been overseas impregnating Violet Norton. Among them were Franz Dorfler – now reported to have been Clark's lover back in 1922–3 – and William Gable. The former could have rewarded Clark for dumping her by enlightening the court about his involvement with Earl Larimore, while the latter usually could not open his mouth without casting doubts on his son's masculinity. Both were therefore briefed over what to say at the trial and suitably recompensed.

The trial, presided over by Judge George Cosgrove, opened on 20 April and not unexpectedly turned out to be a media circus. Hundreds of Gable fans camped out overnight outside the court-house to ensure places in the gallery: they mingled with hot-dog vendors and 'screechers' hired by Howard Strickling, who ensured an hysterical atmosphere was maintained throughout the proceedings. Franz Dorfler had been discovered working in a kitchen – by sheer coincidence at the mansion owned by Bert Allenberg, partner of Clark's agent, Phil Berg. The official line was that Clark had found her the position, an action arising out of gratitude for all she had done for him. In actual fact, Howard Strickling tracked her down and told her to say that she had been working for Allenberg for a number of years. Mayer objected to this. A former lover of Clark Gable could not be seen in such a lowly profession so he offered Dorfler a 10-year contract with MGM. That way she could be introduced to the court as a successful actress then greeted by Clark with a peck on the cheek and personally escorted by him to the witness stand. Dorfler told the truth, of how Clark had been lodging at her parents' farm when

Gwendoline Norton had been conceived. Then she added an invention of her own – that she and Clark had discussed marriage at this time when they had been so very much in love! To Mayer's way of thinking, fagelahs did not go around asking women to marry them.

To make her appear more glamorous, MGM had given Dorfler a complete makeover – in direct contrast to Violet Norton, who was plump, dowdily dressed and, the press reported, so nervous that her dentures clicked all the way through her testimony. The farce continued when the ersatz Cockney announced that later in the trial she would be producing a vital character witness – Mae West, who had befriended her and subsequently offered to be Gwendoline's godmother. Naturally, Mae never showed up, Clark emerged from the mess with a whiter-than-white reputation and Violet Norton received her comeuppance. The paid jury found her guilty as charged and she was sentenced to six months in jail. A few days later, this was commuted and Norton was subsequently deported – not back not to England, but to Canada, whence she had originally come from.

Ben Maddox's editor had been paid to ensure his star reporter was out of Hollywood while the trial took place, as had Adela Rogers St Johns and others who would have exposed the scam. Exclusive coverage of the whole silly scenario had been assigned to Otto Winkler, a reporter with the Los Angeles *Herald Examiner*, who, like Franz Dorfler, had been added to the MGM payroll. From now on, Winkler would take over from Howard Strickling as Clark's 'personal public relations officer' – in other words, cover for him whenever he stepped out of line. If the whole purpose of the trial had been to prove to the world that Clark Gable was the most virile he-man in recent history, no lessons had been learned so far as he himself was concerned. When not on a hunting or fishing trip, he still hung around with the same crowd: Eddie Quillan, Ben Maddox, William Haines, Cesar Romero – though always with Carole. She saw no reason to dispense with her dearest friends just because they were regarded as 'abnormal' by their bigoted peers, not least of all Clark himself. There was a concise difference between Carole mocking him over his virility – telling all and sundry about his 'tiny meat' and 'shortcomings in the sack' – and Clark's persistent use of terms such as 'fairy' and 'faggot'. She mocked him to his face because she was convinced he could take it – while he was all buddy-buddy to his gay friends' faces, pulling them to pieces behind their backs when they were unable to defend themselves.

In 1934, Carole bought a house in Lincoln Heights (at the time of writing occupied by British singer Morrissey), and she now brought in William Haines to turn it into a very un-Gable-like miniature fun palace. With time on his hands now that his movie career was over, and championed by three close friends – Carole, Marion Davies and Joan Crawford – Haines was about to become one of the most requested interior designers in Hollywood. Carole wanted a house to match her zany, unpredictable humour, and as few had experienced this first-hand more than Haines, he was perfect for the job. Inasmuch as she mocked Clark's virility and dragged his ego down a peg or two, so she teased Haines by parading around the house naked while he was working. Haines' biographer, William J. Mann (*Wisecracker*), quotes Carole as saying to her friend, 'I wouldn't do this, Billy, if I thought I could arouse you!' Haines refused to charge her one cent for refurbishing her home, knowing that with her 'gift of the gab' she would soon spread the news of his other talent away from the screen. And he was right. Within a month the commissions came flooding in: Joan Crawford, John and Lionel Barrymore, Claudette Colbert – and even Jack Warner, the arch hypocrite who had joined forces with Louis B. Mayer to rid Hollywood of its 'fagelah epidemic'.

The Lombard house – it will never be known by any other name, no matter who lives there – today bears little evidence of her presence, but Haines' sublime craftsmanship – subsequently replaced by such items as the hideous fireplace from San Simeon and portraits of punk outfit The New York Dolls – was described by Kenneth Anger in *Hollywood Babylon II*:

> For Lombard's home decor, Haines went against the grain of the 'Hollywoodmodern' style with its accent on white . . . He made her house a riot of colour, against which her blonde loveliness

stood out. The drawing room was a sea of velvet, in six shades of blue, with French Empire furniture. He plunked a bed down in her bedroom and covered it with plum satin, with a mirror screen on each side. Soon everyone in Hollywood was chatting about the Lombard house . . . Every rising starlet wanted a mirror screen on each side of her overworked bed.

Clark was by now living with Carole, so it was inevitable that he saw a great deal of William Haines. Off and on he was still enjoying Ben Maddox's company, otherwise he appears to have left his practising gay past behind: these men had served their purpose and would soon be entirely dispensed with. Now there was absolutely no doubt that he would be playing Rhett Butler, Clark Gable was on his way towards becoming the biggest male movie star in Christendom – and there would be no room in that world for the slightest whiff of scandal.

Chapter Six

# Southern Belles & Sinners

In May 1937 Clark was assigned to *Saratoga*, part-scripted by Anita Loos, and co-starring Jean Harlow (Louis B. Mayer had initially wanted Joan Crawford). The movie and fan magazines, who had adored Clark's pairings with Harlow *and* Crawford believed Carole Lombard should have another chance to work with him – they were, after all, an undisputed item. Mayer was all for the idea until the Hays Office warned him that this would be unacceptable while Ria Gable was still around. He therefore offered to 'help' by way of subbing Clark from future earnings so that he could divorce Ria and pay her off. For the time being, however, he refused to cooperate.

While shooting *Saratoga*, Clark and Carole saw little of each other. Lombard the actress was far removed from Lombard the party animal: when working it was a strict regime of early to bed, early to rise, and no nights out. Her latest project, David Selznick's *Nothing Sacred*, was of paramount importance being her first Technicolor film. Also, she was trying to keep on side with the tetchy producer in the hope of him casting her as Scarlett O'Hara. Her hopes spiralled when Selznick signed her for two more films – upon her insistence, dramatic roles to 'get her in the mood' for the big one.

In his spare time, Clark hung out with Jean Harlow and William Powell, now unofficially engaged to be married. For months Harlow had been looking peaky: she had piled on the pounds, her features were bloated, she had begun to have blackouts; she was also suffering from the shakes and her hair had started to fall out. At least one studio doctor attributed her hair loss to over-use of peroxide to retain its platinum sheen. Initially, Clark suspected her health problems may have been due to drinking – she had hit the bottle after Paul Bern's suicide and Hal Rosson proved more of a boozing companion than the deterring influence Louis B. Mayer had hoped for.

During the afternoon of 29 May, Harlow was taken ill on the set with what the studio doctor at first suspected might have been a gall-bladder infection on account of her breath smelling of urine. Mama Jean – with her at the time – could have saved her, but as a devout Christian Scientist she refused to allow medical intervention – even from Louis B. Mayer's personal physician. Clark stepped in, personally arranging for her to be admitted to the Good Samaritan Hospital, by which time it was too late to save her. Uremic poisoning had set in, hence the odour of urine, and this was almost certainly a delayed reaction to the severe beating Bern had administered on their wedding night. On the morning of 7 June 1937, the woman affectionately known as 'Baby' passed away in her sleep. She was just 26.

Louis B. Mayer's grief for his favourite star after Garbo was profound and genuine. Indeed, all Hollywood went into mourning, with the shock all the harder to take because within hours of Howard Strickling announcing news of her illness to the press, he had to tell them she was dead. All the major studios closed for the day: cinemas and theatres across America dimmed their lights and held two-minute silences. Even the moralists had admired this 'tart with a heart' because they believed that, deep down inside, she had been a good, sincere person. It was only after her death that it was to be revealed how promiscuous she had actually been.

Clark was one of the pallbearers at her funeral, two days later. Though advised not to do so, Carole accompanied him to the ceremony at Forest Lawn's Wee Kirk O'The Heather Chapel, their first official outing as a couple. Like Irving Thalberg's funeral, it was tantamount to a royal occasion, albeit one lasting less than thirty minutes and, unlike Thalberg's, one where all those invited *wanted* to be there because they had genuinely adored her. The exceptions were Nelson Eddy, who sang 'Oh, Sweet Mystery Of Life', and Jeanette MacDonald, who warbled 'Indian Love Call' – both charged for their services. Genevieve Smith – the Christian Science practitioner who, by advising Mama Jean not to seek medical intervention had contributed to Harlow's death, if not actually caused it – read several passages from the Bible, along with an extract from Mary Baker Eddy's *Science & Health With A Key To The Scriptures*. Then 'Baby', wearing her pink negligee from *Saratoga* and reposing in a $5,000 bronze and silver casket, was laid to rest in a $25,000 vault within the Sanctuary of Benediction Mausoleum, paid for by William Powell. Over the entrance is the simple inscription, 'Our Baby'.

Initially, Louis B. Mayer announced that *Saratoga* would be scrapped, because he owed it to Harlow to respect her memory – a seemingly benevolent gesture coming from the man who had more or less fleeced Marie Dressler on her deathbed. But the press saw through the ruse. The film had cost his studio $850,000, which he would now be able to recover from their insurers. Then Mayer changed his mind. He would complete the film and release it as a *tribute* to the dead star, an announcement that attracted still more criticism. As had happened 11 years earlier in the wake of Valentino's sudden demise, MGM were accused of taking advantage of a tragedy to fill their coffers.

Shooting was resumed at once. Lookalike Mary Dees was hired for the scenes Harlow had not lived to complete but because her voice was unlike Harlow's, her lines were overdubbed by radio actress Paula Winslow. The film wrapped on 29 June, was edited quickly, and released to near mass hysteria on 23 July. In many cinemas, *Parnell* was taken off the bill to accommodate it.

The film opens at Brookvale Farm stud, once the finest in Saratoga, where feisty Grandpa Clayton (Lionel Barrymore) is about to lose his last stallion to the creditors. He runs the place with his son Frank (Jonathan Hale), who has gambled away practically everything they ever had. Enter disreputable bookmaker Duke Bradley (Clark), who rescues the situation by buying the horse for the old man because he loves him. Indeed, Duke loves everyone, including the chubby black maid Rosetta (an inspired performance from Hattie McDaniel), who says, 'Ah'd fix up for him any time. If only he was the right colour, ah'd marry him!'

When Clayton's granddaughter Carol (Harlow) arrives from England with her stuffy millionaire fiancé Hartley (Walter Pidgeon), Duke devises a scheme to get the stud farm back in the red. She is hoity-toity with a phoney King's English accent, while he is 'the perfect chump with a bankroll the size of the US Treasury'. At first, Frank is in with the plan, giving Duke the deeds to the farm to cover the gambling debt he owes him, so that it will be in safe keeping for Carol to inherit some day. When Frank dies suddenly at the racetrack, however, Carol says she will get Hartley to cover the debt so that she will not be beholden to Duke, who she suspects only wants the farm for himself. To ensure Hartley pays up, she agrees to marry him sooner than anticipated, bringing the strangled response from Duke, 'A gal that put the bite on a bridegroom for 60,000 smackers before she even gets him to the altar is awfully full of larceny!'

A battle of wits ensues between Duke and Clayton – and between Hartley and Carol when Clayton puts his only decent racehorse, Moonray, up for sale. Pitched against the rough-and-ready auction crowd, Harlow is a vision of brassy loveliness with her platinum locks and Dolly Tree gold-lamé gown. Hartley is fleeced into buying the horse for way over the odds so that Clayton can train him and keep the farm going until Duke has duped him into parting with even more cash. He does this by giving Hartley good odds on a horse that wins, gaining his confidence until Hartley starts to lose money hand over fist on worthless nags.

While Hartley cannot bear to kiss Carol (Walter Pidgeon ungallantly protested that Harlow's breath smelled of urine, which we now know to have been a symptom of her final illness), Carol pretends to dislike Duke, though she is secretly in love with him. Finally, she comes clean on the Race Special express train after a scene reminiscent of the one in *It Happened One Night* when all the passengers engage in a lively sing-song. She makes an effort to impress him, putting on her best *kimonah* (sic, a longstanding Gable-Harlow in-joke), before admitting him to her sleeping compartment *and* letting him rub embrocation on her chest and back. Then she is back to hating him again when, on learning that her 'chump' is about to be sent packing, Duke offers her a percentage if she can keep stringing Hartley along. She declares she will have her revenge: by the time *she* has finished with him, Duke will have been reduced to begging on a street corner with a tin cup!

The film's ending is disappointing, but at the time of its release of tremendous curiosity value. Picture-goers and critics alike tried to work out which was the real Harlow in some scenes, and which was her stand-in. Hartley bets a fortune on his own horse, which Carol convinces him will win the race and thus bankrupt Duke. In a photo finish, the horse loses, Clayton gets to keep his stud-farm and fate throws Carol and Duke together during another singalong on the express train – actually a scene saved over from the *first* singalong.

Between these two train scenes there have been no others with Jean Harlow. This explains why, in the first one where Carol feigns illness to gain Duke's attention, her violent coughing fit was regarded as distasteful by those believing that the film was shot in sequence and that Louis B. Mayer had left Harlow's final (sic) scene in to acquire maximum publicity. But this was not the case: her *final* scenes were at the racetrack, where Carol is first introduced to Duke (Harlow's features are bloated due to the medication she was on). There was also a scene at the very end of the film where Clark was supposed to carry her across a room and unceremoniously drop her on to a chaise longue. This was abandoned when she went limp in his arms shortly before collapsing on the set. During the last four racing scenes, Carol's features are partly obscured by her binoculars, or she is shot from behind. Similarly, in the sequence where everyone dances the Saratoga, when Harlow dances through the French windows and on to the patio, it is the less buxom Mary Dees emerging from the other side. Worse still is the scene with Hattie McDaniel, where she takes delivery of a consignment of tin cups sent by Duke as a prank – her entire head and shoulders are hidden by a ridiculously large picture hat which all but fills the screen.

Jean Harlow's death had a sobering effect of Clark. Though Carole remained her zany self – publicly deriding him for wearing dentures and for being uncircumcised, though why this should have been a touchy subject is not known – he withdrew into his shell. There were fewer parties and visits to friends' houses, more hunting-shooting-fishing trips, which enabled him to meditate in peace. What surprised his 'outdoor buddies' is that Carole tagged along, not just for the ride or to augment the scenery, but to muck in with everybody else. Clark's friends were initially horrified by her crude language, the way she pronounced when she and Clark were about to slope off for a little romance, 'Excuse us, guys, we're off to fuck in the duck-bind!' The Travis Banton gowns still hung in her closet, but these days the fan magazines photographed her most frequently in hacking jacket and corduroy trousers.

One such shot appeared in Chicago's *Herald Tribune* in November 1937 when, in conjunction with columnist (later legendary show host) Ed Sullivan, the paper ran a nationwide poll, syndicated with 50 other publications, to find the King and Queen of Hollywood. For most readers, glamour was all that counted, so Carole in her new get-up stood little chance against the likes of the no-less sophisticated Constance Bennett and Claudette Colbert. Sullivan later claimed the idea for the competition stemmed from a comment made by Spencer Tracy while driving his car through a throng of autograph hunters on the set of *Test Pilot*. He is supposed to have leaned out of his car and bawled, 'All hail the King!' The film had yet to begin shooting – the utterance actually occurred in *It Happened One Night*, when Peter Warne had been ushered on to the night bus by his reporter pals.

Clear favourites Clark and Myrna Loy romped past the winning post – allegedly by way of rigged voting and a cash injection from MGM – and were presented with their crowns by Sullivan on 8 September at the El Capitano Theater. Clark tried to play down his 'regal' role, dismissing it as 'bullshit' and telling Ben Maddox, 'I eat, sleep and go to the bathroom like the next guy. So why treat me different to anybody else?' He *was*, of course, different from everyone else, and he knew it. For the rest of his life, Clark would be known as the King – a title relinquished only after his death and passed on to Elvis Presley.

His next film, *Test Pilot*, would prove one of his most successful to date, though at the time few would cotton on to its allegorical message. Directed by Victor Fleming, now a close friend, it costarred Spencer Tracy, Lionel Barrymore – and 'Queen' Myrna Loy, who since Jean Harlow's death had been elevated to MGM's top female star. The locations were filmed at the Air Corps base at March Field, Riverside, permitting Clark to escape the artificiality of Hollywood for a while and spend quality time in the company he preferred. He began what would prove a lifelong friendship with an engineer named Al Menasco, a former World War I test pilot hired by Fleming to put him through his paces for the film's aerial sequences.

Ben Maddox compared Clark's Jim Lane and Tracy's Gunner Morris with Don Quixote and his loyal servant, Sancho Panza: the daredevil aviator and the cloying grease monkey who fusses over him like an over-anxious mother. Maddox was, of course, as one in the know, accurately interpreting the film's homosexual subtext. Modern-day audiences might perceive the pair as 'fuck-buddies' – the theory being that if, during their exploits, no suitable females could be found to alleviate the tension, then each other's company would suffice. This is displayed in a scene which would have gone over the heads of Thirties heterosexual audiences when Jim takes a prostitute back to the hotel room he shares with Gunner, only to have him send her away. The claim is that Jim needs his rest for the next day's aerial manoeuvres, though cynics might argue that Gunner wants him all to himself. This was clearly the intention of gay scriptwriter Waldemar Young, with whom Clark had a ferocious argument over some of the 'faggish' dialogue between him and Tracy that he wanted toned down. To his way of thinking, red-blooded pilots did not recite poetry or quote from the classics! Even his love interest in the film, Myrna Loy, is one of the guys, knowing more about baseball than he does. And, as invariably happens in Hollywood gay-themed dramas (*Philadelphia*, *Brokeback Mountain*, etc.), one of the protagonists has to die so that the one remaining might hopefully achieve so-called 'normality' after the credits have rolled. Gunner Morris is crushed to death, expiring heroically while his buddy, as close to tears as his over-enforced machismo will permit, risks pronouncing, 'I love you, Gunner!'

Clark's biographer, Warren G. Harris, also makes the unforgivable error of adhering to Gable's own perturbing theory that gay translates only as effete when he observes, 'Gable and Tracy both had such masculine images that there was no chance of their *Test Pilot* relationship being interpreted as homosexual'. Clark had already dispelled this theory with the half-dozen or so man-to-man liaisons he had more than willingly entered into.

While making the film, he began a rare, entirely platonic relationship with a woman – his first since Josephine Dillon. Carole had just completed *Fools For Scandal*, which had been so savaged by the critics that she announced a temporary retirement from the movies, she said, to play nursemaid to friends who needed her more than the 'shitty studios'. Madalynne Fields was about to marry the director Walter Lang, too, and Carole wanted to handle the arrangements. She had also just taken in the scriptwriter Donald Ogden Stewart, recently separated from his wife and suffering the after-effects of a serious accident. Living with her too was ex-husband William Powell, still in shock after losing Jean Harlow, and recovering from cancer treatment. She was therefore too pre-occupied to worry about what Clark might have been getting up to with 21-year-old former child star Virginia Grey (1917–2004) – who never wed, she claimed towards the end of her life, because if she could not have Gable, no other man would do!

Clark wanted Virginia to co-star in his next film, *Too Hot To Handle*, but she had already been assigned to another project – and in any case, MGM did not yet consider her leading lady material. Therefore he was once more teamed up with Myrna Loy. This time *she* was the famous aviatress who crash lands her plane and falls for the newsreel photographer (Clark), who rescues her. What she does not know is that he is the one responsible for almost killing her, forcing her to land in a field where his rivals can't get to her.

In May 1938, the Gable-Lombard affair was finally regarded as official by the press when *Photoplay* published a lengthy feature: 'Can The Gable-Lombard Love Story Have A Happy Ending?' Its writer, Edward Doherty, drew comparisons between the roles the couple played on the screen and what was happening in real life.

Though he tried not to be judgmental – he was obviously a huge fan of both – it did not take him long to get to the point:

> A beautiful blonde girl, witty and winsome and wise, in love with a debonair actor who has been married a number of years and whose wife is unwilling to divorce him. What will happen? How will the characters react? How will the story end? Will the wife step gracefully aside, someday, and allow her husband to marry the younger woman? Will she wait in patience, knowing that time oft withers infatuation . . . or will the girl, tired of waiting, give the man up? Will there be tragedy? Or will the last reel of the drama be played to the chime of wedding bells?

Hollywood, Doherty added, had always been eager to promote synthetic on-screen romances between its stars, but when it came to the real thing, it did its utmost to protect them from the world outside the confines of the studio. Everyone in America knew, courtesy of the Hollywood press, that the Gables had separated and that Clark sometimes escorted Carole here and there. But the press had been reluctant to tell the truth about Gable and Lombard, until now:

> [Hollywood] has given no hint of the heartaches that must exist deep below the surface of the story: the anguish, the yearning, the bitterness, the tears. This isn't a Springtime love affair, but it has poignancy and beauty for all that. Here are two people in the full splendid summer of their lives, with the sun of fame and fortune shining brightly on them – and autumn coming on apace. Here is the wife, the charming, cultured, sophisticated Mrs Rhea [sic] Gable, watching the two with emotions no one knows. What will the autumn bring her – restored serenity, or gray despair, loneliness or peace? Perhaps if Carole and Clark had met in the Springtime of their lives they would have been merely infatuated with each other. But it is not so now. They have experienced too much of life to trifle with anything so endearing as real love. They have suffered too much, learned too much to take love lightly . . . Stories in every newspaper every day

indicate that love dies many deaths. Carole's love for William Powell died. Clark's love for Josephine died. His love for Rhea is dying, if it be not dead.

While Clark and Carole regarded Doherty's feature as mere gossip, Louis B. Mayer was furious, but terrified of taking any action against Clark just yet on account of the discussions still taking place about *Gone With The Wind.* Mayer knew that, with his decidedly short fuse and despite the cost to himself, financially and career-wise, Gable would not think twice about walking out on the picture. He had threatened this already, for any number of reasons; therefore it was imperative that the studio get his signature on the contract. Yet it took until 25 August for MGM to officially announce that he would be playing Rhett Butler. He was photographed signing the contract with David Selznick and Louis B. Mayer – forcibly smiling and cursing from the corner of his mouth. He had just been told that if he rejected the part, in view of the *Photoplay* feature he would be suspended indefinitely without pay and would probably never work in Hollywood again. The starting date for *Gone With The Wind* had been set for 5 January 1939. Meanwhile, he was put into *Idiot's Delight* with Norma Shearer.

Since last working together, Gable and Shearer had seen a reversal of fortune. He was at the peak of his popularity, while she was no longer a massive name – her last film, *Marie Antoinette,* had bombed. But as a major shareholder with MGM she still held tremendous sway over the parts she was offered, even if this meant riding roughshod over colleagues. According to a story fabricated by Howard Strickling, Margaret Mitchell declared Shearer too ladylike to portray her flighty heroine – this resulted in MGM receiving hundreds of letter from Shearer fans, pleading with her to turn the role down. In fact, the woman mockingly referred to by Carole Lombard as 'Scarlett Goldberg' had never been offered the part in the first place. The further announcement that she had begged Louis B. Mayer to let her do *Idiot's Delight* with Clark was another fib – and one that would lead to his first serious quarrel with Carole. He made the mistake of telling Carole how Shearer often turned up on set wearing no panties under her clinging gowns while shooting *Strange Interlude*. And when Carole made one crack too many in front of friends about his 'lack of staying power' and his 'small appendage', he shot back that he had not received any complaints from Norma the last time around, and doubtless there would be none now!

Robert Sherwood's Pulitzer Prize-winning prophetic, anti-Fascist drama had taken Broadway by storm two years earlier, with Alfred Lunt and Lynn Fontanne as the two principal tourists stranded at an Italian ski resort on the eve of the outbreak of an unspecified war. By the time the movie version was released in January 1939 this looked like becoming reality. Lunt played song-and-dance man Harry Van and Fontanne was the Russian countess who is actually a meagre trapeze artiste with whom he enjoyed a one-night stand some years ago, a casual affair she has completely forgotten about.

Sherwood was roped in to write the screenplay, which had to be vetted by the Hays Office to ensure every trace of political content and innuendo had been removed – this meant any references to Italy and Mussolini, including the snatches of Italian dialogue pronounced by soldiers and bit parts. Foolishly, these were now delivered in Esperanto – and to completely ruin the piece, the setting was moved to Switzerland.

To perfect Clark's interpretation of Harry Van, director Clarence Brown sent him on a two-week song-and-dance course – his big moment in the film comes when he performs a pretty zappy 'Puttin' On The Ritz'. Clark tried to get out of the routine, but Brown persisted, and on his first day of rehearsals – in front of the other students – he received a package from Carole. It contained his costume – a ballet dancer's tutu, a pair of size 11 slippers and a sequinned jockstrap with his initials which, had he been brave enough to wear them, would have proved no less camp than the film's scenario. In the original play, Robert Sherwood intimates that the tourists are about to be annihilated by enemy bombs – they laugh and sing while fearlessly awaiting their fate. In the film version it would have been considered unthinkable to allow A-list stars to perish in a holocaust, so the enemy planes are made to go away while the former lovers sing hymns! Hugely entertaining, but clap-trap nonetheless.

Joan Crawford visited the set, furious that 'No-Tits Norma', as she called her, could have been offered such a role when she could neither dance nor sing. Nor, declared Joan, did she have any experience playing loose women – the part should have gone to herself, or Carole Lombard. Louis B. Mayer calmed her down by casting her as superbitch Crystal Allen in *The Women* – another Shearer picture to be directed by George Cukor, which would prove the top-grossing film of 1939 after *Gone With The Wind*. The production would more or less herald the end of Shearer's illustrious career. Shortly after completing it, she cast discretion to the winds by having a very public affair with 'two-way blade' George Raft. Her swan song in 1942, *Her Cardboard Lover*, would see her woefully miscast opposite Robert Taylor. Reputedly out of respect for Irving Thalberg, she never married again. She died in June 1983, aged 80, and was interred by his side.

Carole soon learned that Shearer posed much less of a threat than an extra hired to play one of Harry Van's chorines. Lana Turner (1921–95) had been discovered at 15, sitting at the counter in the Top Hat Cafe, by the *Hollywood Reporter*'s Billy Wilkerson, who was famed for bedding under-age girls. Wilkerson had introduced her to fellow lust-merchant Zeppo Marx, then out of the movies and working as an agent. He found her work as an extra in *A Star Is Born*, released in 1937. That same year – and though anything but – she had answered the call from Mervyn LeRoy, who was on the lookout for a 'sexy but virginal' murder victim for *They Won't Forget*. LeRoy put Lana in a tight skirt that exaggerated her narrow hips and a tight-fitting sweater under which she had worn a silk-lined non-uplifting bra, which encouraged her ample breasts to bounce as she walked.

Henceforth labelled 'The Sweater Girl', Turner became an overnight sensation, entering Hollywood folklore as one of the film capital's most-slept-with stars. Eventually she would work her way through eight husbands. Almost certainly she was fired from *Idiot's Delight* because Carole suspected her of getting too close to Clark. And once again the old 'appendicitis' chestnut was used as an excuse for dropping out of the production voluntarily – or rather the alleged removal of scar tissue from a botched appendectomy of 1935. Even so, in the not-too-distant future she would re-enter Gable's life with a vengeance.

So far as is known, Carole Lombard remained faithful to Clark until the very end, whereas he cheated on her whenever the opportunity arose. If anything, their first bust-up brought them closer, and they kept on addressing each other as 'Ma' and 'Pa'. Tired of trying to persuade Clark to divorce Ria, Carole set about finding them a house in the country, where they would be able to hunt, fish and live in sin to their hearts' content, far from the prying eyes of the Hays Office and studio spies.

Carole's house-hunting, and the fact that Joan Crawford was 'seeking comfort' from Clark following her separation from Franchot Tone, was picked up on by Kirtley Baskette, a reporter from *Photoplay*. Joan had ordered him out of her house four years earlier when the questions had become too personal and Joan's expletives had turned the air blue. Baskette's *Knack*, which made him one of the most despised hacks in Hollywood, was delving deeply into the private lives of stars and jumping to career-threatening conclusions, which were usually spot on. He had recently bumped into Joan at a party, asked her outright if she and Clark were having an affair, and been told, 'Oh, I can assure you, Mr Baskette, Mr Gable and I are very definitely just good friends!'. Of course this brought him to the conclusion that they *were* lovers and led to his writing a nasty exposé in the January 1939 issue of *Photoplay*, which hit the newsstands earlier than usual, on 11 December – just in time to ruin his victims' festive period. For the time being, however, Clark and Carole did not see it for that same morning they embarked on a skiing holiday to Sun Valley, Idaho.

In his uncensored feature, 'Hollywood's Unmarried Husbands And Wives', Baskette singled out five 'living-in-sin' couples who had been thrust under the Hollywood spotlight. Joan Crawford and Franchot Tone *should* have been included, but Baskette was saving them for a special 'exclusive' that, in the wake of this one, would never see the light of day. Baskette sarcastically observed how Virginia Pine always ensured that George Raft had his favourite meal waiting on the table when he arrived home and *assumed* that Barbara Stanwyck and Robert Taylor must have been cohabiting because they lived on adjoining ranches. Also how there was absolutely no proof that Charlie Chaplin and the much younger Paulette Goddard had tied the knot; how Gilbert Roland had been Constance Bennett's devoted slave for years – and how Clark Gable and Carole Lombard might as *well* have been married, the way they were carrying on:

> Unwed couples they might be termed, but they go everywhere together, do everything in pairs. No hostess would think of inviting them separately, or pairing them with another. They solve one another's problems, handle each other's business affairs. They build houses near each other, buy land in bunches, take up each other's hobbies, father or mother each other's children – even correct each other's clothes, each other's personalities. Yet to the world, their official status is 'just friends', no more.

Of Gable and Lombard, he further opined:

> Carole Lombard is not Clark Gable's wife, either. Still, she has remodelled her whole Hollywood life for him. She calls him 'Pappy', goes hunting with him, makes his interests dominate hers. Whoever heard of a woman in love with a man giving him a gun for Christmas? Or a man, crazy about one of the most glamorous, sophisticated and clever women in the land hanging a gasoline scooter on her Christmas tree? For Clark, Carole stopped almost overnight being a Hollywood playgirl. People are expected to change when they get *married*. All Clark and Carole did was strike up a Hollywood twosome. Nobody said, 'I do!' Clark Gable doesn't like nightspots or parties, social chit-chat or the frothy pretensions of society. He has endured plenty of it, but it makes him fidget. Carole, quite frankly, used to eat it up. She hosted the most charming and clever parties in town. These things were the caviar and cocktails of Carole Lombard's life – before she started going with Gable. But look what happened!

Clark didn't like it! Carole has practically abandoned all her Hollywood social contacts. She doesn't keep up with the girls in gossip as she used to. She doesn't throw parties that hit the headlines and the picture magazines. She and Clark are all wrapped up in each other's interests . . . Yes, Carole Lombard is a changed woman since she tied up with Clark Gable, but her name is *still* Carole Lombard.

Baskette summed up his findings by offering his own self-righteous dictum, particularly as *he* had never practised what he preached:

Never has domesticity outside the marital state reached such a full flower as in Hollywood. Nowhere are there so many famous unmarried husbands and wives . . . The altar record among Hollywood's popular twosomes is surprisingly slim. Usually something formidable stands in the way of a marriage certificate when Hollywood stars pair up minus a preacher. In Clark and Carole's case, of course, there is a very sound barrier. Clark is still officially a married man. Every now and then negotiations for a divorce are started but, until something happens in court, Ria Gable is still the only wife the law of this land allows Clark Gable. Yet nobody, not even Hollywood's miracle men, has ever improved on the good old-fashioned, satisfying institution of holy matrimony. And, until something better comes along, the *best* was to hunt happiness when you're in Hollywood or anywhere else is with a preacher, a marriage license and a bagful of rice.

Louis B. Mayer's reaction to Kirtley Baskette's feature – though he must have been relieved that the Gable 'fagelah' rumour had been dispensed with once and for all – was to demand a retraction. Otherwise, he declared, no *Photoplay* reporter would ever set foot on an MGM lot again. All the major studios supported him and their sponsors threatened to withdraw their advertising contracts from the magazine, then the biggest-selling in America. The editor's response was to call their bluff: if this happened, Baskette, already the victim of several death-threats, would be offered police protection while penning a no-holds barred exposé of Hollywood adultery – something virtually every major star had been culpable of at some time or other. *Photoplay* further vowed to publish a story about the saintly Norma Shearer and the 'little scenarios' which had recently taken place in her trailer-dressing-room with 19-year-old Mickey Rooney – who boasted (as he would again in his autobiography, *Life Is Too Short*) of how, 'MGM's grand lady loved nothing more than copulating, French-style, with Andy Hardy'.

Kirtley Baskette had written of how Virginia Pine had made a man of George Raft by taking him to Watson, one of Hollywood's most exclusive tailors, who rid him of his flamboyant wardrobe and dressed him more conservatively – in other words, less effete. Louis B. Mayer was distressed about a piece that almost made it to *Screenland* (bought off by Raft's studio), accusing Raft and Robert Taylor of 'impartiality towards intimacy' with a male producer for career advancement.

Within an hour of Baskette's feature hitting newsstands the Hays Office went into overdrive. On its day of issue the magazine sold out and within the week, as various stories were explored and enlarged upon by the tabloids and gossip columns, mostly wildly exaggerated though founded on fact, copies of the original were fetching up to $50 on the black market. Will Hays issued a statement claiming he had received over 5,000 letters of complaint from moral-majority organisations such as the General Federation of Women's Clubs (GFWC), the National Catholic League of Decency (NCLD) and the Daughters of the American Revolution (DAR). As a result of this correspondence Hays said that the general consensus was, 'Get these people to the altar, or we start picketing the theatres!'

George Raft absolved himself in this age of extreme naivety by threatening to 'rip apart' any man brave enough to say to his face what they were saying behind his back – to prove the point, he posed for photographs with his fists bunched. Robert Taylor, in a move which would today make him a laughing stock, proved he was 'a regular guy' – acquiring permission from the Hays Office, who normally forbade such things – by posing shirtless and displaying his hairy chest, the theory being that nature decreed only heterosexual men could be hirsute! What the press did not know was that Taylor's chest was hairier than it should have been on account of the hormone injections administered by the studio doctor to cure him of his 'affliction'. When this failed to curb the gossips, in an extreme measure – one which persists to this day – in the May, Taylor and the equally 'suspect' Barbara Stanwyck were given substantial salary increases to marry and keep up the pretence of married bliss. And finally, just in case Baskette *did* have a follow-up feature in mind, Louis B. Mayer – less interested in Carole Lombard than in his own stars – ordered Joan Crawford to stay away from Clark. About to file for divorce from Franchot Tone, Joan was reputed to be 'on the prowl' in search of her next husband.

Mayer and David Selznick were particularly aggrieved over the rumours concerning Charlie Chaplin and Paulette Goddard – she was now the main contender for Scarlett O'Hara. There is no clear evidence as to when, or indeed if, the couple ever married, and Mayer knew he was encroaching on dangerous territory by having Chaplin investigated. Like himself, Chaplin was a connoisseur of under-age girls, who had seduced his second wife, Lita Grey, when she had been just 12, and got her pregnant at 16. Mayer interviewed several journalists who claimed to have been present at a ceremony in April 1934 aboard Chaplin's yacht. Chaplin confused matters by declaring he had married Goddard 'some time in 1936', while she backed him up, adding that the ceremony had been conducted by the Mayor of Catalina – no such person existed. With the shooting of *Gone With The Wind* just around the corner, the moguls decided to play safe. Paulette Goddard, like everyone else screen-tested for Scarlett, was informed that she was 'not quite suitable' – and Selznick resumed his search.

As for Gable and Lombard, Louis B. Mayer dipped into the MGM coffers when Ria refused to grant Clark a divorce unless he coughed up $300,000 – this, her lawyer calculated, equated to half his estimated MGM pension fund. Mayer agreed to loan him the money as an advance on his contract: his current contract had two years to run but Mayer drew up a new one, upping his salary to $7,500 a week. On 14 December 1938, three days after the damning *Photoplay* feature, Clark interrupted his skiing trip to announce to the press that he was divorcing Ria. She, however, had changed her mind since her original statement. Her demands were exactly the same, but as *she* was the wronged party, she announced that it was only fair that *she* should be divorcing Gable, and not the other way around. For the time being, their respected lawyers agreed to a stalemate.

In the meantime, Carole forked out $50,000 for a two-storey house set in 20 acres of land at 4525 Petit Avenue, in Elcino, San Fernando Valley. The property had formerly belonged to director Raoul Walsh and though just 10 miles out of Hollywood it was then such an undeveloped location that it might have been in another world. Walsh's predecessor had had it partially landscaped, but for the better part this was an uncultured, totally private haven of citrus, plum and eucalyptus groves and alfalfa fields. And within a week of Carole moving in, Clark gave a press statement composed by Howard Strickling and delivered from Louis B. Mayer's office so no mistakes would be made in getting the message across to Ria, should she still have genuine cause for grievance:

> Mrs Gable and I had a fine life together until the time came that we both realised we could no longer make a go of it. I bitterly regret that a short time ago a story was printed to the effect that *I* would be seeking a divorce. After years of separation, it is only natural that *Mrs Gable* should institute proceedings that will assure her freedom.

Ria accepted 'Clark's' apology and announced her intention to leave for Nevada immediately after the Christmas holidays.

On 13 January 1939, less than two weeks before shooting with the major actors began (several of the locations were already underway), David Selznick announced that he had at last found his Scarlett O'Hara: a relatively unknown 25-year-old English actress named Vivien Leigh. One of the most beautiful but fragile women ever to grace the screen, Leigh (Vivian Hartley, 1913–67) had attended RADA and made her film debut in 1934 with *Things Are Looking Up*. The following year she appeared with Gracie Fields in *Look Up And*

*Laugh*, but her biggest break occurred in 1937 when, under contract to Alexander Korda, she had made *Fire Over England* with Laurence Olivier, whom she would later marry.

Leigh was currently visiting Olivier in Hollywood, where he was shooting *Wuthering Heights*, and her out-of-the-blue acquisition of the most sought-after role in movie history brought resentment from just about every top-liner on Selznick's long list of Scarlett contenders – none more so than Carole Lombard. She hit the roof on learning Leigh was also represented by *her* agent, Myron Selznick, David's younger brother. The official story was that Myron had taken Leigh to the set where David had been filming the burning of Atlanta, and told him, 'I'd like you to meet Scarlett O'Hara!' Carole and many others were of the opinion that she had slept with the producer, though there is no evidence to suggest this.

For the rest of her life, Carole would refer to Vivien Leigh as 'that fucking English bitch!' Tallulah Bankhead, on the other hand, was surprisingly muted when asked for her opinion, telling Ben Maddox, 'I'll go to my grave convinced that I could have drawn the cheers of Beauregard and Robert E. Lee, had I been permitted to wrestle with Rhett Butler.' Until her early death, Leigh would search in vain to recapture the most glorious moment of her career, coming close only in 1951 with her definitive portrayal of Blanche Dubois in *A Streetcar Named Desire* – a quest dogged by physical and mental illness.

Though lined up for some time, Selznick signed up the other leads on the same day as Leigh. British star Leslie Howard (Laszlow Horvarth, 1893–1943) had most recently triumphed in *The Scarlet Pimpernel*, but flopped opposite Norma Shearer in Irving Thalberg's *Romeo And Juliet*. Howard, whose plane would be shot down four years later during a wartime flight over the English Channel, initially turned down the role of Ashley Wilkes. Tired of acting, he wanted to direct. He capitulated when Selznick promised he would be able to direct *and* star in his next film, *Intermezzo*, with Ingrid Bergman. Olivia de Havilland, Joan Fontaine's sister, was Errol Flynn's favourite leading lady (8 times). Hattie McDaniel (1895–1952) was the much-loved black actress, almost always typecast as the lady's maid and apparently content with such roles. 'I would rather play a maid than be one,' she famously said at the time. Thomas Mitchell (1892–1962) would win an Oscar for Best Supporting Actor in that year's *Stagecoach*. Ann Rutherford was best known as the kid's girlfriend in the *Andy Hardy* series.

Gone With The Wind began shooting on 23 January 1939, and wrapped on 27 June – $2 million over budget. Though Vivien Leigh complained persistently to Selznick about her co-star's halitosis, Clark was hostile towards her when they filmed their first scenes on 31 January. To him, like many others still reeling from Kirtley Baskette's 'Hollywood's Unmarried Husbands And Wives' exposé, she was little more than a common tart. Over the last few weeks, much had been made in the press over his involvement with Carole, yet here was a woman virtually no one in Hollywood had heard of until now – a *married* woman with a child, back in England, cohabiting with a married actor under everybody's noses!

On top of this, he was fighting Selznick over his differences with George Cukor. His accusing the director of favouritism before the first frame had been canned was but the first in a long list of complaints. Back in the December he had had a bust-up with Selznick over Cukor's decision that *everyone* should speak with a Deep South accent – after all, this was where the action was taking place. Cukor denounced Clark's Ohio-Cumberland twang in *Mutiny On The Bounty* as ludicrous, and did not want Rhett Butler lampooned by the critics as just another Gable extension. Clark flatly refused to pronounce his lines in any accent but his own – even if it meant walking off the picture, which he said he had never really been bothered about doing in the first place.

Next he grumbled about the script – or lack of it, for all he had to work on were 92 pages of instructions, delivered to his home by motorcycle courier the day before shooting began, detailing how Selznick wanted Rhett to be played. For once, the producer declared, Clark would portray a character exactly as written. Gable turned up for work in a foul mood, intent on having it out with Selznick. Aware of this, Carole tried to cheer him up by having a parcel delivered to his dressing room. Inside was a hand-knitted 'cock-sock' and a card which read, 'Don't let it get cold. Bring it home hot for me'. Clark calmed down for the moment, but caught up with Selznick later, and this time there was a blazing row over his costumes. Selznick had handed over a cool $150,000 to *Gone With The Wind*'s costumes department, ordering them to spare no attention to detail – even the extras' shoes, socks and petticoats had to be authentic because, he believed, they would give better performances *knowing* they were wearing them. Clark complained that the tight collars he had been given made his neck appear too bull-like, and that his too-short jacket sleeves over-exaggerated his wrists and hands. He also hated wearing tight trousers because they drew attention to his crotch and, he claimed, made him look 'faggy'.

He was further aggrieved that Selznick spent his every waking hour on the set, breathing down everyone's necks – and that the producer opted to shoot almost everything out of sequence, beginning with the burning of Atlanta, to get the most arduous scenes out of the way. He was additionally against Selznick's insistence that all the actors be costumed and on set from the start of the day's shooting, whether they were required or not. This was a dodge subsequently adopted by *Giant* director George Stevens, who Clark later admitted he would not have worked alongside for all the money in the world. Years later, while working with Montgomery Clift in *The Misfits*, he howled with laughter upon hearing how Monty, while shooting Selznick's *Indiscretions Of An American Housewife* (1954), had publicly addressed the finicky producer as 'Interfering Fuck Face'.

Clark could do nothing about Selznick – it was simply a case of grin and bear it – but he was determined Cukor would have to go, unless Selznick wanted to find himself a new Rhett Butler. This, of course, was something the public would never have accepted after all the hype surrounding the current one. His initial excuse for not wishing to work with Cukor was that he regarded him as a 'woman's director', and therefore sure to show favouritism towards Vivien Leigh. To a certain extent, this was true. Cukor had a solid track record for taming temperamental actresses: his success stories in this respect included Harlow, Crawford, Judy Garland and Ingrid Bergman, but most especially Katharine Hepburn, with whom he made nine films.

Clark could have handled the situation more sensibly and diplomatically when petitioning for Cukor's dismissal. Instead, he marched into Selznick's office, guns blazing, and bawled, 'I will *not* be directed by that fairy, Cukor!' Until now Selznick had been unaware of Cukor's sexuality, and had Cukor not been so gentlemanly he might have enlightened Selznick of how, not so very long before, his accuser had been an active participant during his trips to Pershing Square with William Haines, Joan Crawford, et al. Haines had recently decorated Cukor's house – Clark and Carole attended the completion party – and visited him several times during the first week of shooting *Gone With The Wind*. This made Clark edgy because he had seen Haines and Cukor chatting and laughing, and suddenly become paranoid that one of them might let something slip.

The crunch came one morning when Clark cornered Cukor on the set and growled, '*I* only like working with *real* men!' – bringing the tarty response, 'So do I, my dear!' This resulted in Cukor sending Gable the aforementioned birthday gift of soap and Listerine. Eleven days later, on 12 February, production was suspended when Selznick fired Cukor, and for the time being Clark's secret stayed safe. But, as Kenneth Anger aptly observed in *Hollywood Babylon*, 'One of the great directorial shifts in film history took place in 1939 because of a few blow-jobs given by Bill Haines.' Unperturbed, Cukor began shooting *The Women* sooner than scheduled – over the moon, he declared, to be working 'amongst his own'. And to make up for her disappointment over losing out on Scarlett O'Hara, Paulette Goddard was added to its distinguished cast.

To replace Cukor – again on Gable's insistence – Selznick brought in Victor Fleming, whom Clark maintained had remained his favourite director since working with him on *Red Dust*. Fleming had been directing Judy Garland in *The Wizard Of Oz*, and his departure from this picture inadvertently resulted in its becoming more popular than it might have done, had he stayed. Fleming had been against a sequence containing what would become Judy's signature song, 'Over The Rainbow', which was subsequently filmed by King Vidor.

Victor Fleming (1883–1949) was a gifted director, but when in

Gable's company was a deeply unpleasant individual – as indeed was Clark whenever they were together. Inasmuch as both were 'gay-friendly' in the company of homosexual colleagues but viciously homophobic behind their backs, so too were they virulently anti-Semitic, a trait wholly unacceptable and deplored in an environment where the studio hierarchies were predominately Jewish. Having denounced Sidney Howard's script (according to film buff Gavin Lambert) as 'no fucking good', forcing Selznick to commission a new one from Ben Hecht to the tune of $15,000, Fleming next attacked the man behind the camera. Lee Garmes (1898–1978) had been Marlene Dietrich's favourite photographer – his innovative use of light and shade in von Sternberg's *Morocco* and *Shanghai Express* were truly inspired, and fortunately around one third of *Gone With The Wind* bears his unmistakable stamp. Shooting was held up for a week while Fleming secured the services of Ernest Haller (1896–1970), another Expressionist genius nevertheless who had recently filmed *Jezebel* with Bette Davis. Some years later, Haller would capture the anguished glory of James Dean in *Rebel Without A Cause*.

Fleming's tenure at the helm of *Gone With The Wind* would be brief. Vivien Leigh and Olivia de Havilland, having been spoiled by George Cukor, resented working with him and consulted with Cukor behind his back. Leslie Howard persistently argued with him and Selznick's round-the-clock presence on the set ground him down. Two months into the production he had an almighty bust-up with Vivien Leigh who, when riled, could be extremely unladylike and turn out as many expletives as him. When Fleming tried to bully her into making her character more bitchy than she believed Scarlett could have sensibly got away with, he flung the script at her and yelled, 'Miss Leigh, you can stick this up your royal British arse!'

The press were told that Fleming had temporarily left the production to recover from exhaustion. Actually, he suffered a nervous breakdown. Shooting was held up for two weeks, and when he returned to the set Selznick brought in Sam Wood (who had directed two Marx Brothers' films and recently completed *Goodbye Mr Chips* with Robert Donat) to share the workload. The film would be completed with Wood and Fleming shooting different scenes at different times of the day – with Clark still insisting he be directed only by Fleming, and with his leading lady and Olivia de Havilland still taking advice from George Cukor.

A gorgeous score composed by the master of the genre complements the scenario. Viennese-born Max Steiner (1888–1971) was a former child prodigy who studied under Mahler, composed his first operetta at 14 and evaded Nazi persecution by fleeing to New York, where he composed for Florenz Ziegfeld before hitting Hollywood with the advent of sound. In a career spanning 40 years and over 200 film scores, Steiner received a staggering 26 Academy Award nominations though *why* he did not win an Oscar for *Gone With The Wind* may only be adjudged a crime against art.

As Scarlett O'Hara, Vivien Leigh is no different on the screen to how she was in her private life: selfish, spoilt, mentally unstable, flighty and capricious where men are concerned – what would today might be called a 'prick-tease'. Only one person can tame Scarlett and the O'Haras' other two 'white trash' daughters – Mammy (Hatty McDaniel), their firm but loveable housekeeper who is treated more like a member of the family than a slave. David Selznick's first choice for the part had been Louise Beavers, younger than McDaniel but already a veteran of 100 such roles. Clark and McDaniel had been close friends since *Saratoga*, and would remain so until her death, 13 years later from breast cancer. He insisted upon her playing Mammy – delaying the production slightly because, as a native of Colorado, she had to be coached how to speak like a Southern slave. As such she effortlessly steals every scene in which she appears, even from Clark and Vivien Leigh.

Against Selznick's wishes, Rhett Butler is but an extension of Clark Gable: coarse, egotistical, arrogant, tough in the sense that he persistently has to be seen to be proving himself, caddish and smug, impervious to women, admired by their menfolk, who regard him as a redoubtable role model. The film opens with Scarlett, flirting with a couple of obligatory beaux, who are discussing the fast-approaching Civil War, a subject she finds boring. All she is interested in is the barbecue about to be held at Twelve Oaks, the Wilkes' mansion, where Ashley (Leslie Howard) will celebrate his birthday and announce his betrothal to his cousin, Melanie Hamilton (Olivia de Havilland). For generations the Wilkes have been in-breeding to keep their bloodline pure, and Scarlett has decided that she will hate Melanie for no other reason than *she* wants Ashley for herself. This despite her father (Thomas Mitchell) assuring her that as heiress to Tara, the O'Haras' plantation, she can have her pick of all the young bucks in the county.

Scarlett flings herself at every eligible bachelor who attends the party, but is initially standoffish towards Rhett, a visitor from Charleston, whom few appear to like. 'He looks as if he knows what I look like under my shimmy,' Scarlett observes. Rhett *does* have a bad reputation. He was expelled from West Point, though we are not told why, none of his family have anything to do with him – and he once 'ruined' a girl by taking her out, without a chaperone, then refusing to marry her! The first of his and Scarlett's many heated exchanges occurs when, hiding in the library at Twelve Oaks, he overhears her trying to seduce Ashley – who rejects her because he is so devoted to Melanie. Rhett further ruffles a few feathers when, after pacifist Ashley protests that war only brings misery, Rhett declares that, being too ill equipped, the South will not win the War in any case. 'All we've got is cotton and slaves and arrogance!' he growls. And when Scarlett *wants* to give Melanie a piece of her mind for 'stealing' Ashley, she finds this impossible because the girl is so utterly nice and never sees the bad in anyone.

Unable to have Ashley, Scarlett accepts a proposal from the first man who asks her – Melanie's brother, Charles (Rand Brooks). They wed the day after Ashley and Melanie, on the eve of his departure for his regiment. He proves an early casualty in the conflict, succumbing to pneumonia, but hailed a hero just the same. Feeling nothing for her loss, Scarlett rejects widowhood and stays with Melanie in Atlanta, where she will be close at hand when Ashley comes home on leave. [Melanie's mother is played by Laura Hope Crews, whose nephew and Clark's former lover Earl Larimore was barred from visiting the *Gone With The Wind* set – following his problems with Cukor, Clark clearly wanted no more reminders of his salad days.]

In Atlanta, news comes of General Lee's latest victory, and Rhett shows up as a blockade runner – popular with wealthy locals now that he can keep them supplied with essential luxuries. At a party, he charms well-heeled war-widows into donating unwanted jewellery to help the war effort – but while Melanie sacrifices her wedding ring, saying this is what Ashley would want, Scarlett gives hers away because she never wanted it in the first place. For now, Rhett's actions appear just as selfish. He *claims* to be obsessed with feathering his own nest and caring little for the cause, but not unlike Gable himself, a few years from now, within the brawny cynical frame there lurks a profound conscience.

That Rhett regards all women as traditionally the sport of the warrior – drawing more comparisons with Clark – is proven when the action jumps to his return from a trip to Europe. He has bought a hat for Scarlett, and (in the very first scene he filmed with Vivien Leigh), shows her how to put it on *and* audaciously tells her she should not be wearing pantalettes. Of the gift he growls, 'I never give anything without expecting something in return, and I *always* get paid.' Then, to reassure her that his intentions are *not* honourable, he adds, 'Don't flatter yourself. I'm not a marrying man!'

The scenario moves to July 1863, and the aftermath of Gettysberg, which marked the turning point in the war. Ashley comes home, embracing his wife while Scarlett scowls with envy. He is morose, believing the end may be near, so Scarlett promises to look after Melanie, pregnant and in frail health, should the worst happen. She does this because caring for Melanie will always remind her of her unrequited love for him. Then fighting erupts closer to home as enemy troops sweep through Georgia towards the sea, taking Atlanta and almost razing it to the ground. Despite her condition, Melanie becomes a nurse – helping wounded soldiers just in case the next one could be Ashley. Scarlett pretends to care for their welfare, but as usual is begrudging. 'Melanie, I hate you,' she says to herself, 'I hate you, I hate your baby! If only I hadn't promised Ashley!' Inadvertently she is caught up in the siege of Atlanta, and is rescued by Rhett, who drives her back to Melanie's house. However, the baby is due so she returns to the scene of the carnage to fetch the only doctor in the city.

As she wanders through the streets, the picture pans out until she is lost in a sea of corpses, a disturbing scene for European audiences who got to watch this only months after the outbreak of World War II. The doctor, of course, needs her to help *him*, though for once she has an excuse for being selfish, and she returns to Melanie, whose health suffers a setback after the baby's birth.

Rhett takes the women back to Tara, where they will hopefully be safer. In a truly tremendous scene they drive through the burning city, narrowly escaping death when the Confederates blow up their ammunition supplies to prevent them from falling into enemy hands. When Scarlett has a fit of hysterics, Rhett comforts her, though from now on she will have to fend for herself. No longer wishing to stay home while the others are off fighting, Rhett decides to enlist, though he *does* act irresponsibly, leaving his charges in the middle of nowhere to fend for themselves. Scarlett begs him not to go, now that the War is almost over and she needs him. 'Selfish to the end, aren't you?' he chides, 'Thinking only of your own precious hide, but never a thought for the noble cause.'

Rhett's mood changes when he explains *why* he is leaving: 'Maybe it's because I've always had a weakness for lost causes, once they're *really* lost – but maybe it's because I'm ashamed of myself.' If this is the case, she responds, then he should die of shame for leaving her alone and helpless. Here, Rhett and Gable become one – the man who is never happier than when curt and aggressive towards his women, though Scarlett does exact a confession that he loves her more than he has loved any other – and that he has waited far too long before getting physical with her. 'We're alike,' he drawls. 'Bad lots both of us, selfish and shrew, but able to look things in the eyes and call them with the right names.' Scarlett fights off his advances, though she really doesn't want him to stop: he kisses her, she slaps and insults him.

Following this Scarlett drives the trap containing Melanie, her baby and her loopy maid (the magnificent Butterfly McQueen) – not to Tara, but through storms and the corpse-strewn terrain to Twelve Oaks. Again, she thinks only of being reunited with Ashley. The Yankees have been here, and the place is deserted save for a solitary cow, which they hitch to the trap and head for Tara. Here, Scarlett's mother has succumbed to typhoid and her father has lost his mind: the enemy have used the house for their headquarters, stripping it bare and absconding with all the food.

In one of the film's most moving scenes, beautifully captured by Lee Garmes prior to his dismissal, Scarlett stumbles out into the barren field, pulls up an inedible root, sobs, then suddenly becomes filled with hope. This is Vivien Leigh's most glorious moment, the one that reputedly clinched her Oscar for Best Actress – the lonely figure silhouetted against the wasteland backdrop, who defiantly proclaims, 'As God is my witness, they're not going to lick me! I'm going to live through this, and when it's all over I'll never be hungry again . . . If I have to lie, cheadle, cheat or kill, as God is my witness I'll never be hungry again!' It is a classic image much referred to, in Europe especially, as the horrors of World War II unfolded and rationing beckoned.

The credits for the next sequence tells us how Tara has survived to face the hell and famine of defeat yet this is but the beginning of adversity as Scarlett drives everyone – her sisters and the slaves – remorselessly to get the plantation back on its feet. 'I don't like the way you're treating them,' her father admonishes. 'You must be firm with inferiors, but you must be gentle with them, especially darkies.' But Scarlett shows no mercy (in a scene directed by George Cukor *after* being replaced by Victor Fleming) when an army deserter shows up, bent on plunder. When he menaces her, she plugs him between the eyes, relieves him of his money, and she and Melanie bury him. Then, as the War ends and the survivors come home – Ashley among them – Georgia faces another enemy in the form of carpetbaggers, opportunists who have augmented the Yankee cause. One such is the O'Haras' former overseer, Jonas Wilkerson (Victor Jory), who as Tara's new landlord demands money which Scarlett has no hope of raising. She solicits Ashley, who the conflict has made cynical and bitter: having been involved with the carnage, he now sees himself in a world worse than death, a place in which he no longer feels he belongs. Scarlett wants him to run away to Mexico with her and start over – with Melanie too weak to have any more children, she says, there is nothing to keep him here. 'Nothing,' he responds. 'Nothing except honour!' Yet for a moment he is tempted: he kisses her passionately before reality strikes home and he reminds her that, just as he would never desert his wife and child, so she will always put Tara before any man.

Scarlett is still worrying about Wilkerson's demands when he turns up and offers to *buy* the plantation. Her father chases him off the land, falls from his horse and dies. As a last resort she goes to see Rhett, now languishing in a Yankee prison. Within minutes they are engaged in a slanging match – and in any case he cannot help her because the Yankees have confiscated his money. Thus the man who not so long ago sent her senses reeling is dismissed as a skunk. Again, Scarlett marries a man she does not love: Frank Kennedy (Carroll Nye), a once-poor soldier who was sweet on her sister before the War but now has the wherewithal to support her. Scarlett lies, saying her sister, tired of waiting, is engaged to somebody else. And *still* she has designs on Ashley, getting so upset when he announces that he and his family are relocating to New York, so much so that Melanie rebukes *him* for being selfish towards Scarlett, who has done so much for them! He therefore elects to stay in Georgia, knowing he will never be safe from her clutches.

Using her new husband's money to employ convict as opposed to slave labour, Scarlett starts up a lumber business, beating the Yankees at their own game by doing business with them and fleecing them, becoming the scourge of polite society. She is still sluttish towards Rhett when he recovers his finances and buys himself out of jail – yet he springs to her defence when she is almost murdered by Yankee robbers while driving home through the woods. He, Ashley and Frank retaliate by routing the area. Ashley is wounded, but Scarlett is more concerned for him than she is for her husband, who is shot dead – she cannot even bear to look at Frank's photograph. Rhett calls on her, to be informed by Mammy that she is 'prostrate with grief': she sheds a few crocodile tears, pretending to feel guilty for stealing Frank from her sister. What follows may well be the most camp, most sarcastic marriage proposal in movie history, one which required a dozen takes before Gable got it right without cracking up:

Forgive me for startling you with the impetuosity of my sentiments, my dear Scarlett – I mean, my dear Mrs Kennedy – but it cannot have escaped your notice that for some time past, the friendship I had felt for you has ripened into a deeper feeling – a feeling more beautiful, more pure, more sacred. Dare I name it? Can it be *love*?

Rhett adds he cannot spend the rest of his life catching her between husbands. She has had a boy, then an old man, so now it is time for the real thing – someone who kisses her with such passion that her legs buckle beneath her (an experience later repeated with Doris Day in *Teacher's Pet*). It matters little that they do not really love each other: they simply have enough bad qualities in common! So they marry and honeymoon in New Orleans, though she cannot wait to get back to Tara once he tells her she can spend as much money as she wants restoring the plantation to its former glory. They have a child, Bonnie (Cammie King), but Scarlett still keeps a picture of Ashley close at hand, and makes it clear that she wants no more children unless fathered by him. Rhett seeks solace in his ex-mistress, Belle Watling (Ona Munson), a whorehouse madam, who gave more to the war-effort than most, and who now reminds him that his daughter is worth ten of her mother.

Now realising the error of her ways, Scarlett goes to see Ashley, but all they do is reminisce over what might have been – and when their friendly embrace is witnessed by his sister, the rumour spreads that they are having an affair. For once Scarlett is innocent, yet Rhett insists on her wearing a scarlet – in other words, a *whore's* – dress when they attend a party at Twelve Oaks. 'Nothing modest will do for this occasion,' he snarls. 'And put on plenty of rouge. I want you to look your part tonight!' Never has Scarlett/Vivien Leigh looked lovelier, but his ruse backfires when Melanie welcomes her with open arms – aware that much as he might want to, Ashley would never cheat on her.

Back home, Rhett gets drunk and there is a repetition of Clark's scene with Norma Shearer in *A Free Soul* – save that this time he pushes her back into her chair *twice*. 'Observe my hands, my dear,' he purrs, wrapping his massive paws around her neck, then her head. 'I could tear you to pieces with them, and I'd do it if it'd take Ashley out of your mind forever. But it wouldn't. I'll remove him from your mind forever *this* way – one on each side of your head, and I'll smash your skull like a walnut. *That'll* block him out!' Like the majority of Clark's female fans, Scarlett only finds such threats acting like an aphrodisiac. She retorts that he will never frighten *her*, and her fearlessness makes him horny. For a while he has been barred from her bed while she has been thinking only of Ashley, but as he sweeps her up into his arms at the foot of the staircase he announces that tonight he will take her by force!

The next morning Scarlett awakens, obviously having enjoyed the rough sex which has taken place (a trait for which Vivien Leigh was legendary – in her last years going out into the night and picking up nameless men in the park near her London home). But it is not long before they are back to bickering. 'I've always thought a good lashing with a buggy-whip would benefit you immensely,' he growls, after calling her an unfit mother and demanding a divorce. They survive a little longer, but only on account of Bonnie – and the fact that Scarlett is pregnant again with the child she tells him to his face she wishes could be anybody's but his. 'Cheer up,' he quips. 'Maybe you'll have an accident!' He speaks too soon, for she slaps him, falls down the stairs and suffers a miscarriage.

For the first time ever on the screen (it had *almost* happened in *Hold Your Man*) we witness the ultra-macho Gable in tears, a scene which took weeks of persuading him to even consider shooting. Real men did not cry, he yelled at Selznick and Victor Fleming, whatever the circumstances. Contemporary reports suggest the tantrums he threw on the set – threatening to walk off the picture and declaring that this time he meant it – gave many cause to believe he was little different from the 'prima donna fags' he was forever deriding, until Olivia de Havilland effected a solution. The scene was shot twice, in single takes – one *with* the tears, the other without so that Clark could watch the rushes and decide for himself. He plumped for the former, comforted in the scene by Melanie, who adds to his emotion, confessing she is risking her own life by having another child.

When Bonnie dies in a riding accident identical to the one that killed her grandfather, and when Melanie also dies, we instinctively know the end of the Butlers' marriage is imminent. 'I've loved something that really doesn't exist,' says Scarlett of Ashley, while Rhett laments of Melanie, 'She was the only completely kind person I ever knew – a great lady.' He also realises the path is clear for Scarlett and Ashley to be together, if this is what they want, and therefore decides to return to Charleston to start a new life. Then comes the sequence where she begs him to take her with him, culminating with the infamous line which, in 2005, would be voted the most popular movie quote of all time by viewers of a Channel 4 television poll:

> RHETT: I'm through with everything here. I want peace. I want to see if somewhere there isn't something left of life with charm and grace.
> SCARLETT: I only know that I love you!
> RHETT: That's your misfortune . . .
> SCARLETT: Rhett – if you go, where shall I go? What shall I do?
> RHETT: Frankly, my dear, I don't give a damn!

David Selznick anticipated a tremendous struggle getting the word 'damn' past the Hays Office censor so as a safety precaution he filmed an alternative take, where Rhett tells Scarlett, 'Frankly, my dear, I don't care!' This of course would have robbed the scene of its essential clout – by this stage in their relationship Rhett has had enough of the fickle woman. The Hays Office permitted the original epithet but only after Selznick handed over a $5,000 'fine'. And if seats were vacated 'in disgust' when the film went out on general release, with this 'filthy talk' coming right at the end, Selznick was convinced it would not spoil the rest of the audience's enjoyment.

As for Scarlett, as always she has the last word and must be commended for her belief in the precognitive dream – the fact that all will turn out well in the end, so long as this is what one wishes. Sobbing on the stairs, which in the past have seen such passion between her and Rhett, she hears voices from the past – Ashley, her father, Rhett – then she looks up, her face lighting up with hope for the future as she defiantly pronounces, 'I *will* have him back. After all, tomorrow is another day!' Then we see her for the last time, silhouetted against the still desolate landscape – interpreted by millions around the world as the symbol of the woman waiting for the soldier to come home from the War – as the credits roll.

Magnificence does not begin to describe what can be witnessed over three-and-three-quarter hours, $4 million well spent on arguably one of the greatest films ever made, and a box-office phenomenon. *Gone With The Wind* would gross four times this amount during its first year and figures released at the end of 2006 declared it had made over $500 million.

## Chapter Seven

# LOVE CONQUERS ALL

On 8 March 1939, while shooting *Gone With The Wind*, Ria Gable was granted a Las Vegas divorce on grounds of desertion. Ben Maddox must have been tickled to report the statement issued by her lawyer, part of which read, 'Marriage between a society woman and a movie star has a far better chance of surviving than one between two movie stars'. 'Well, this one didn't,' Maddox concluded in *Screenland*, though one wonders what his readers would have had to say, had they known that *he* and not Carole Lombard had been party to much Gable pillow-talk while Clark was deciding whether or not to end his marriage. Or that one of the grounds for desertion cited in Ria's petition referred to Clark's many lovers, including the handsome young reporter.

Carole was bombarded with questions concerning the divorce. Would they marry now that Clark was free? She refused to commit herself either way. The divorce had come smack in the middle of negotiations for a new contract that saw her signing a three-picture deal with RKO for a staggering $450,000 – far more than Clark ever dreamed of earning. Her first film was to be *In Name Only*, monopolising on the Gable situation. In this drama, starring another of her lavender friends, Cary Grant, she played the mistress of a married man whose wife, Kay Francis, refuses to grant him a divorce. Carole joked with reporters in what would be her only reference to recent events, 'If I'd been the casting director, I'd have given Ria Kay's part because the old bag's got a monopoly on hearts of stone!'

On 28 March, before shooting got underway on the new Lombard picture, the major studios closed for several days so that the executives and stars were free to attend the San Francisco première of Fox's *Alexander Graham Bell*. Accompanying them on the trip were just about every reporter in Hollywood. Clark and Carole took advantage of the situation by eloping, undetected. Clark's press officer, 34-year-old Otto Winkler, had married the previous week in Kingman, Arizona, so he and Carole decided to do the same. Accompanied by Winkler, they set off on the 350-mile trip early the next morning, wearing old clothes and with Carole's hair in pigtails so that they hopefully would not be recognised en route. They arrived during the early afternoon, were married at once by a Methodist-Episcopalian minister, and by three the next morning, 30 March, were back in Hollywood at Carole's house.

On the way home Winkler called Howard Strickling to break the news. Strickling arranged a hasty press conference, for which Carole was instructed not to curse or discuss her husband's alleged short-comings in the bedroom or his false teeth. This was about to begin when an angry call was put through from Louella Parsons, demanding to know why *she* had not been given an exclusive. Carole told her to jump into her car, that she would hold off the press conference until she arrived and would answer Louella's questions first. Parsons' response was that such gatherings were beneath her – unless Carole sent everyone home and afforded her a one-to-one she was not interested. For a while, Carole would find herself snubbed by the snooty hack. Following this, it was back to work for the newlyweds.

In September 1939, war erupted in Europe, though for the time being few in the film capital showed interest in a 'far away feud' which might never concern them. Marlene Dietrich, who like Carole would do more than her fair share for the war effort, labelled these people 'Lazy Sunbathers' because, even when the situation in Europe worsened, they still did not wish to be involved. Between now and the various *Gone With The Wind* premières in December, Clark and Carole had contractual obligations. She was about to begin her second RKO picture, *Vigil In The Night*, but on the eve of shooting was rushed to the Cedars of Lebanon Hospital with severe abdominal pains. This time it was Otto Winkler's turn to hoodwink the press into believing she was suffering from the usual appendicitis. Carole had in fact suffered a miscarriage.

Clark, meanwhile, made what would be his last film with Joan Crawford – *Strange Cargo*, based on Richard Sale's allegorical novel, *Not Too Narrow, Not Too Deep*, and directed by Frank Borzage – but only after Spencer Tracy had turned it down. Tracy had read critic W.H. Mooring's comment in *Film Weekly*, 'The title has a ring of a spade against earth, hasn't it? And Hollywood loves to dig graves.' Supporting was Ian Hunter and two fine Hungarian actors mostly typecast as villains at around this time: Paul Lukas and Peter Lorre. The film was shot on location at Pismo Beach and the neo-tropical Pico National Park – a first for Joan, who had not worked outside a studio since her silents days. It was also her least taxing on MGM's costumes department: the trio of 'bargain basement' dresses she wears cost less than $100.

*Strange Cargo* is second only to *Possessed* in the eight Crawford-Gable vehicles, but even they are not as impressive here as Ian Hunter (1900–75), whose character, Cambreau, is a thinly disguised Jesus Christ. Surprisingly, this caused no problems with the Hays Office anti-blasphemy brigade, or with any other religious groups. The characterisation, the finest of Hunter's distinguished career, is honest, intensely moving, and never over the top. As Cambreau/Christ, Hunter *looks* just as holy as Robert Powell in the later *Jesus of Nazareth*. No, what saw *Strange Cargo* part-banned in some American states was the implication of some of the dialogue. Coming hot on the heels of Clark complaining over George Cukor calling him 'dear', here we have Gable, the tough he-man convict, addressing his cohorts as 'sweetheart'. Also, for the undisputed homophobe who was absolutely paranoid about anyone thinking him less than 100 per cent *übermensch*, there is a homoerotic scene where he almost kisses Hunter on the mouth, albeit reverently.

The action takes place in an uncivilised penal colony 'off the coast of one of the Guianas', a hell hole where past, present and future are one. The toughest prisoner here is Verne (Gable), a thief who now believes the only thing worth stealing is his freedom. He has bungled so many escapes that the Governor has put him to work outside the prison walls – this way he will see that the jungle beyond is impenetrable. On the wharf he watches hard-bitten *chanteuse* Julie (Joan) – when she tosses away a half-smoked cigarette he retrieves it, sniffs and licks it, then finishes smoking it. Julie is currently being lusted over by obnoxious stool-pigeon Monsieur Pig (Lorre), who is not put off when she snarls, 'Men die all the time and pigs live on and on – and you'd think that their own smell would kill them!'

Neither is Julie any more sympathetic towards Verne, engaging him in bitchy banter that only makes him more intent on having her. It matters little to him that he will end up in solitary confinement for failing to return to the prison with the rest of the work-party: one night with this fire-brand will make the suffering worthwhile. What he does not know is that Cambreau has latched on to the work-party to make up the numbers – emerging from nowhere, and knowing everything about the disciples he will soon gather about him. They, however, know nothing about him save that his teachings make sense and his prophesies always come true.

Verne sneaks into Julie's room and after more sniping she changes her mind about giving him a good time – he reminds her too much of her former lover, so she shops him to the authorities, a ruse which backfires when both are arrested. Fraternisation with convicts is against colonial law and Julie is given mere hours to vacate the island. Cut to the prison, where Cambreau addresses his flock, which includes top-dog Moll (Albert Dekker), who makes little secret of the fact that his love for pretty blond youngster Dufond (John Arledge), is more than brotherly – mirroring the pair's relationship away from the screen. (Clark hated working with both actors, no doubt terrified of his own 'secret' emerging. In 1968, cross-dresser Dekker, after being outed by the tabloids, was found hanging from his shower-rail, wearing women's lingerie.) Verne grabs the Bible, and drawls a quote, 'So, God created Man in his own image. How d'you like that? Take a look at me. Do *I* look like a god to you?'

When Cambreau learns that Moll and Dufond are planning an escape and that several others are contributing towards the cost of the boat waiting beyond the jungle, he pays for Verne and himself to accompany them. Moll, however, does not want him along and bashes him (Dekker later claimed he would have loved to have done this to the homophobic Gable for real), and leaves him for dead. The prisoners make a break for it, but Cambreau has effected a miracle: Verne recovers from his life-threatening injuries, finds the map that Cambreau has drawn in the back of his Bible, and he too escapes. Before catching up with the others, he must find Julie. She is desperately trying to raise funds to leave the island and Pig offers to help in exchange for her favours. '*You're* the one man in the world I'd never get low enough to touch,' she tells him, settling for assistance from the only slightly less odious official, Marfeu (Bernard Nedell) – long enough to attempt to kill him and abscond with his cash. Something that is prevented by Cambreau's disembodied voice, 'Not *that* way, Julie!'

Verne rescues Julie, but still treats her like dirt, comparing her with the cheap food she feeds him: 'Garbage, but good enough for a man when he's starving. You'll do, baby. This is no time to be particular!' This of course was the Gable philosophy – treat 'em mean, keep 'em keen. A woman did not have to be attractive to end up in his clutches, which from the point of view of overzealous female fans meant that, given the circumstances, Gable was not out of their reach, either!

Still thinking him a louse, Julie leaves with Verne and they catch up with Cambreau and the others at the shore, their numbers reduced, just as Cambreau predicted, by a series of incidents in the jungle. A chance remark that Julie is here solely for the crew's gratification sees Verne and Moll scrapping for supremacy. Verne wins, naturally, and assumes the role of captain while Julie stands, like Garbo in the closing scene from *Queen Christina*, spread-eagled before the mainsail as they embark. When she brazenly kisses Verne, one of the men gruffs, 'What good can ever come from a man like that, a *woman* like that?' Cambreau is non-judgemental: he sees her as Mary Magdalene, maybe even the Holy Virgin, and philosophically replies, 'I've heard of it happening before. Why can't it happen again?'

Cambreau's philosophy – that others will die during the struggle for survival – comes true. In a fit of pique, one man throws the water barrel into the sea, then gets eaten by a shark while retrieving it. Dufond goes insane and Moll slaps him, accidentally killing him. With nothing left to live for, he tests the barrel's contents to see if it contains salt water. It does, and he chokes to death on his swollen tongue.

The survivors reach the mainland to find Pig and the Colony Governor are there first not having had to risk the jungle. Verne pays a fisherman to take them to Cuba, but Julie changes her mind about going with him – she blames herself for his being on the run and considers herself unworthy of the risks he is taking. Verne, Cambreau and the fisherman set sail as a storm is brewing. Cambreau knows his mission is nearing completion, that it is time for him to move on and help others. As the rain lashes the deck he engages in a battle of words with Verne, the Doubting Thomas – *begging* him to kill him, knowing of course that he is immortal.

Verne knocks him overboard, where he floats, cruciform, before being rescued – and Verne, now aware Cambreau/Christ has died for *him*, bursts into tears and *wants* to kiss him, but instead clutches him to his breast. Clark had little difficulty crying for this scene. Firstly it was raining heavily and therefore his tears could not actually be seen and secondly, he believed any man would have been overcome with emotion upon meeting Jesus Christ. The actual kiss was filmed, but the footage destroyed on the orders of the Hays Office.

The film ends as Verne and Julie are reunited, and with him giving himself up. At last he has found honour and will serve the remainder of his sentence because he knows the woman he loves will be waiting for him on the outside. And as Cambreau exits the scenario just as mysteriously as he arrived, the fisherman makes the sign of the Cross.

A massive row erupted between Joan Crawford and Louis B. Mayer when, at the film's preview in April 1940, she was 'mortified' to see that he had contravened the terms of her contract by placing Gable's name above hers in the credits. Clark had demanded this as part of *his* contract. By the time of the première, two weeks later, Mayer had effected a compromise: their names were printed side by side, but in alphabetical order, which effectively meant that Joan had won!

Prior to this, another battle of egos raged between Mayer and David Selznick over Clark's billing for *Gone With The Wind*. Selnick had promised him that his name would appear above the film's title, but now insisted on this being replaced by his own. Clark had no objection to this, so long as his name appeared above Vivien Leigh's. Initially, he wanted nothing to do with the Atlanta première scheduled for 15 December, even when told that his not being there would affect the box-office. His beef was that while the city dignitaries and every *white* person involved with the film had been invited to the event, to be preceded by a parade through the streets, Hattie McDaniel and the black cast had not. Owing to Georgia's absurd segregation laws, they would be compelled to stay in blacks-only hotels, and barred from the theatre.

Clark and Carole, like Tallulah Bankhead, had already caused controversy by hiring black staff to run their homes, and McDaniel was of course a dear friend. He was eventually persuaded to attend by Carole, but by now his already low esteem of Selznick and Mayer had plummeted. He refused to travel to Atlanta with the Selznick party, instead chartering a plane for himself and Carole, Otto Winkler and Howard Strickling. Then there was a last-minute hitch when he threatened to pull out of the première because Victor Fleming's name had been omitted from the programme, allegedly on Selznick's orders on account of Fleming's anti-Semitic ravings – though in this respect Clark had been no less culpable.

As the Governor of Georgia had declared the weekend of the première a state holiday, with an estimated 500,000 visitors flocking to the city to see the stars – and with Clark as their clear favourite – he had no option but to capitulate, though even then it was a forced effort. Earlier in the day he had paid tribute to the original scriptwriter, Sidney Howard, who had died in an accident in the August. Now, a sound system was set up outside the theatre so that his speech – all 30 seconds of it – could be relayed to the vast crowd. He was here, he said, as just another spectator, and wished to be treated accordingly. This night, he concluded, belonged not to him but to Margaret Mitchell and the people of Atlanta. Neither did he sit through the whole 222-minute film. He was introduced to Mitchell

just before curtain-up, and the two of them retired to the ladies room
– locking the door behind them – until the interval. What happened
there has never been made public.

At the Hollywood première, Clark was slightly more relaxed but
still refused to be seen with Selznick. He and Carole, wearing a gold
lamé Travis Banton gown, arrived with Marion Davies and Raoul
Walsh. Carole had wanted her father-in-law to share their limousine
but William Gable insisted on making his own way to the theatre and
flatly refused to wear a tuxedo. None of the Gables attended the New
York première, though Clark and Carole did show up at the Oscars
ceremony in February 1940.

*Gone With The Wind* won an unprecedented 10 Academy Awards.
Selznick won Best Producer, Vivien Leigh Best Actress, Victor
Fleming Best Director, Ernest Haller Best Cinematography, William
Cameron Best Production Designer, Hal Kern and James Newcome
jointly Best Editors, Lyle Wheeler Best Art Director. Best Supporting
Actress went to Hattie McDaniel, the first ever black recipient.
Astonishingly, Max Steiner did not win an Oscar for one of the most
superlative scores in movie history. Though nominated for Best
Actor, Clark was prevented from winning in yet another act of
extreme spite from Louis B. Mayer. He pulled the necessary strings
to ensure that Robert Donat won for *Goodbye Mr Chips*. This had not
been doing too well at the box-office and with *Gone With The Wind*
breaking all records for takings, Mayer must have felt that his other
baby needed the boost in publicity.

No sooner had Clark recovered from doing the rounds with the
Selznick film than he was assigned to *Boom Town* with Spencer
Tracy, while Carole completed her third RKO production, *They
Knew What They Wanted*. She is thought to have been suffering from
depression – the traditional curse of the comedienne – a
combination of not seeing as much of Clark as she would have liked
over the last few hectic months and also longing for a child – thought
to have been exacerbated by watching the bonding scenes between
Rhett Butler and his daughter. Also, despite his fondness for Carole,
Clark had never stopped playing away from home. While making
*Gone With The Wind* there had been a fling with Ona Munson, who

would never really get over him, as well as the experience of playing a key role in one of the most prestigious movies of all time. With his usual flair for helping friends in their hour of need, Clark would try but fail to get Munson parts in several of his future films – for some reason, MGM were never interested. Her only decent-sized role would be as another whorehouse madam, two years later, in Josef von Sternberg's *The Shanghai Gesture*. In February 1955, shortly after calling Clark to wish him a belated happy birthday, she would bring down the curtain with an overdose of pills.

In *Boom Town*, scripted by John Lee Mahin and directed by Jack Conway, Clark and Spencer Tracy were wildcatters working in the oilfields, a role which must have resurrected horrific memories of Gable's youth. He played 'Big John' McMasters, while Tracy was 'Square John' Land. Their first encounter takes place in the street, when they square up to each other over who has the right of way across the wooden planks preventing pedestrians from wading ankle-deep in mud. Both are equally aggressive, their stubbornness zigzagging between friendship and rivalry as they make and lose respective fortunes. This more or less sums up the film, confusing the viewer en route. Square John dreams of settling down with Betsy (Claudette Colbert), the girl he left at home. When she unexpectedly arrives in town, Big John welcomes her and they spend the night together – it is only afterwards that we learn they have married by special licence. Big John accepts the union and only snaps when his prospecting partner cheats on her with his secretary (Hedy Lamarr). All ends well, of course. Big John sees the error of his ways and, happy to be poor again now that he and Square John have been declared bankrupt, they walk off arm-in-arm, with Betsy between them, across the undrilled field that they have every confidence will make them rich again.

There was considerable off-screen rivalry between Gable and Tracy, who later said that he hated making the film because Clark had been given the juiciest part. Clark also insisted on doing his own stunts, refusing the stand-in provided for the punch-up scene with Tracy, which is as hammy as it gets. Tracy's stand-in smacked him in the mouth (allegedly on purpose, having been told by Tracy to teach him a lesson for trying to act too tough), cutting his lip and chipping his dentures. Shooting was held up for a week while the injury healed and his dentures were repaired – with Louis B. Mayer docking Clark's pay because he had 'risked life and limb' by not using the stand-in. And Tracy swore never to work with him again, though they would soon make up and remain friends for the rest of Gable's life.

Hedy Lamarr (Hedwig Kiesler, 1913–96) was an exquisitely beautiful Austrian import, who shot to fame in 1932 with a 10-minute full-frontal nude scene in the Czech film, *Extase*, regarded as pornographic by non-European audiences. Though six-times married and divorced, she never concealed the fact that sexually she preferred women to men. It must have come as a blow to Clark's macho pride that, despite being on much friendlier terms with Claudette Colbert than the first time around, his female co-stars in *Boom Town* were more interested in each other than in him. Not that he went without his obligatory fun while shooting *Boom Town*. It later emerged that among the several movie magazine reporters allowed on to the set were freelancers May Mann and the ubiquitous Ben Maddox. Both spent at least an hour with Clark in his dressing room, with strict instructions that they were not to be disturbed. Mann arrived wearing a cocktail dress, Maddox in his usual grey suit and trilby. Whereas all the usual conclusions were drawn over what Clark might have been getting up to with an attractive woman, in an unenlightened world it was assumed he and Maddox could only have whiled away their time drinking and engaging in buddy talk.

In January 1940 Clark and Carole travelled to Mexico in their new station wagon for what was described in the press as a belated honeymoon. In fact, the trip was part-financed by *Photoplay* in a deal with MGM to promote the Gables as Hollywood's No. 1 couple in the wake of the Kirtley Baskette fiasco. It was agreed they should be allowed a week on their own 'to make a baby'. They would then be joined at the La Grulla Hunting Club in Baja California, some 60 miles south of the border, by Otto Winkler and a *Photoplay* photographer – along with Baskette or Ben Maddox. The baby that Carole wanted so badly, but Clark was apparently indifferent towards, would never happen. The following year both would undergo fertility tests at the Johns Hopkins Medical Center in Baltimore, and be told that there was nothing physically wrong with either of them. The story fed to the press at the time, in an age when male movie stars simply could not be considered incapable of fathering children unless they were gay, was that Clark had been having treatment for a slipped disc following a fall from a horse . . . eight years earlier.

One may be assured that neither Clark nor Carole wanted anything to do with Kirtley Baskette – similarly, that Clark would not have wanted Ben Maddox around during his 'honeymoon'. He therefore removed himself from temptation – of punching the former's lights out and succumbing to the latter's charms – by setting off with Carole for Encenada, on the Pacific Coast. Unfortunately, they forgot to inform Otto Winkler of their revised itinerary and when they drove into a storm and opted to rough it in the back of the station wagon, this sparked off an international alert. Ben Maddox, still in Hollywood, drew the conclusion that the Gables had been kidnapped my Mexican terrorists, which brought a complaint from the Mexican government, who were appalled by Maddox and his colleagues' published opinion that the country had returned to the lawlessness of the previous century. Louis B. Mayer ordered Winkler to charter a plane and organise a search party – which subsequently found Clarke and Carole shooting duck on the outskirts of Encenada, wondering what all the fuss was about.

For the umpteenth time, Clark avoided suspension by the skin of his teeth – saved this time by the phenomenal box-office success of *Boom Town*. Because of this, Mayer once more cast him opposite Hedy Lamarr in *Comrade X*. Directed by King Vidor, this was promoted as a spin-off from Ernst Lubitsch's sparkling comedy, *Ninotchka*. A massive hit the year before, it had been promoted with the slogan, 'GARBO LAUGHS!' The film saw Clark as an American reporter visiting Russia, who falls for a trolley-bus conductress suspected of being a Communist. It had its moments, but another *Ninotchka* it was not.

Carole, meanwhile, had just completed what would be hailed the best of her screwball comedies: *Mr And Mrs Smith*, co-starring Robert Montgomery and directed by Alfred Hitchcock. By all accounts, despite the on-screen clowning around, she was still feeling pretty low. Once shooting wrapped, however, she was apparently back to her old self, playing pranks, going on hunting trips with Clark and his pals – and according to Louella Parsons, 'Still cussing like it was going out of fashion.'

In February 1941, soon after celebrating his fortieth birthday, Gable began shooting *They Met In Bombay* with Rosalind Russell, with whom he had made *China Seas*. Directed by Clarence Brown, this saw them playing rival jewel thieves, who trail an English duchess to the Far East, attempting to outwit each other while trying to steal her diamonds. Eventually they become partners, and naturally they fall in love. Then the story becomes ludicrous with the over-application of the essential Gable gung-ho element. While masquerading as an army officer he is assigned to an offensive against the Japanese, for which he is awarded the Victoria Cross – and a lighter jail sentence when finally apprehended for his crime on account of his heroics.

Carole visited the set each day. She was temporarily out of work because her RKO contract had expired and David Selznick was no longer interested in signing her to a new deal because of Clark's antagonism towards him during the *Gone With The Wind* premières. Carole blamed her inactivity on Myron Selznick – out of fear of upsetting his brother, she said, he was 'sitting on his fat ass, watching the world go by'. Because she had signed a contract with him that would not expire until late 1943, she was unable to look for another agent, therefore she handed the matter over to arbitration. Her victory would be Pyrrhic. Though the court found in her favour and permitted her to drop Myron Selznick, she was forced to pay him $27,000 – the estimated amount the judge worked out she would have had to pay in commission, *had* Selznick found her work between now and the end of their contract! Several of Selznick's other clients would leave him out of sympathy for Carole. He was to hit the bottle and would die an embittered alcoholic three years later.

Carole's new agent was Nat Wolff, one of Clark's hunting buddies. Within weeks of taking her under his wing he signed her to two comedy dramas – *They All Kissed The Bride*, to be shot in the spring of 1942, and for now, *To Be Or Not To Be*, with Jack Benny. One of her finest films, it was directed by Ernst Lubitsch and tells the story of a theatrical group, living in Nazi-occupied Warsaw, who attempt to stage a production of *Hamlet* while being harassed by the Gestapo. Clark, meanwhile, moved on to *Honky Tonk*, his first cowboy picture since *The Painted Desert*, co-starring Lana Turner and Claire Trevor. He played trickster Candy Johnson, who rides into a corrupt backwater town and chisels his way into running the place. He falls for a saloon girl (Trevor), only to drop her when the virginal Lucy Cotton (Lana, very much against type!) enters the scenario. They marry, and she attempts to turn him into the good guy – in the process suffering a miscarriage and a near-death experience. Carole visited the set each day, though for different reasons than last time. From the first day of shooting there were rumours that Clark and Lana were having an affair – said to have been Lana's revenge on Carole for getting her fired from *Idiot's Delight*.

Lana certainly was a very busy lady. Recently she had been seen about town with celebrity lawyer Greg Bautzer, almost Ben Maddox's legal alter ego in that in return for an almost 100 per cent success rate in the courtroom, he was famed for bedding just about every one of his A-list female clients. Bautzer (1911–87) was currently involved with Joan Crawford – indeed, Maddox predicted he would be her next husband. The two had dated before, and Lana had broken up with Bautzer after Joan had asked her around for tea – and warned her to back off, or else! On the rebound, Lana married bandleader Artie Shaw, a serial cheat who had recently made Betty Grable pregnant while two-timing *her* with Judy Garland. Like Lana, Shaw would make eight trips down the aisle – and Lana had cheated on him with fellow bandleader Tommy Dorsey, drummer Buddy Rich, singer Tony Martin and muscle-bound actor Victor Mature!

News of Turner's wayward character reached Louis B. Mayer and he threatened her with suspension unless she curbed her ways. Lana compromised by dropping her beaux, divorcing her husband and returning to Greg Bautzer – only to begin an affair with James Stewart, her co-star in *Ziegfeld Girl*. Needless to say, Carole had grave concern now that Hollywood's most illustrious tramp had been teamed up with a man who, in her words, 'didn't know how to keep it in his pants'. The visit to the set of *Idiot's Delight*, she said, had been but a polite warning – this time she intended catching them at it and 'kicking some ass'.

Louis B. Mayer stepped in and informed security that Carole should not be allowed within 100 yards of her husband when he was working. Her rage only intensified when Clark and Lana were photographed for the cover of *Life* magazine. The headline read, 'Today's Hot New Team!'. Her hackles were further raised by *Variety*, which reported, 'Lana Turner clicks with Gable in this lusty Western and makes you wish you were there!' When she confronted her husband at home, however, he reassured her in his own particular way that if these one-night stands and little love-trysts meant absolutely nothing to *him*, likewise they should not be taken too seriously by her!

Because of its stars' reputations, *Honky Tonk* was completed quickly so that they could be rushed into other projects. Lana was assigned to *Johnny Eager* with Robert Taylor – enabling Taylor to evade the gay tag once more by boasting that Lana was *so* hot, any red-blooded male would be willing to risk five years in jail for raping her! The story was fed to the press that, after spending just one night with Lana Turner, Robert Taylor asked Barbara Stanwyck for a divorce. It was all hogwash, but good for the Taylor image. Not so long before, while shooting *A Yank At Oxford*, a London journalist had marched up to him in a Piccadilly pub and asked, 'Mr Taylor, are you queer?' Taylor had unbuttoned his shirt, displayed his hairy chest and responded, 'Does that look like a queer to you?' Now, Louis B. Mayer was faced with a dilemma: who to team Lana with next, Taylor or Gable? The superlative reviews for *Honky Tonk*, with critics begging for more of the torrid Gable-Turner chemistry, decided the toss. Their schedules were cleared and they were immediately put into *Somewhere I'll Find You* – which ironically would be directed by Wesley Ruggles, who directed Clark and Carole in *No Man Of Her Own*.

In the meantime, more and more Hollywood characters began taking an interest in the War. Until now, this had been regarded by many as someone else's conflict and perhaps not serious enough to lose much sleep over. Pearl Harbor changed this. The unprovoked Japanese attack on the US Pacific naval base in Hawaii on 7 December 1941 – while Japanese envoys were holding so-called peace talks in Washington – brought America into World War II on account of Japan's AXIS pact with Italy and Germany. Over 2,000 US servicemen were killed and a large section of the Pacific Fleet destroyed. President Roosevelt, anticipating more Japanese attacks, announced on the radio, 'Yesterday was a date which will live on in infamy: the American people in their righteous might will win through absolute victory'. Speaking to reporters, Carole was more to the point: 'If it was left to me, I'd go to the pacific and kill those fucking Japs with my bare hands!'

To a certain extent such comments, though interpreted as racist today, in 1941 led to a purge of Japanese workers. At the studios gardeners, seamstresses, technicians and labourers, many of whom had lived in the country for decades, were now branded 'enemy aliens'. They were laid off until the Government informed the moguls what to do with them. Germans in Hollywood, on the other hand, were not suspect. Marlene Dietrich had long since publicly denounced Hitler and became an American citizen. Most of those who worked during the Weimar Republic had followed suit. Ernst Lubitsch, the director of Carole's final film *To Be Or Not To Be* was absolutely beyond reproach – though Carole suspected his German majordom was not all that it seemed. The FBI was brought in to investigate: he was found to be involved with a Nazi espionage ring, arrested and interned.

As had been happening for some time across the Atlantic, major cities in America adopted blackouts and air-raid drills. The stars, too, began offering their services. James Stewart had recently won an Oscar for *The Philadelphia Story*, but despite his success and the lucrative offers which had come winging his way, he joined the US Navy. Henry Fonda, Tyrone Power and Mickey Rooney had enlisted, prompting Walter Winchell – a Lieutenant-Commander with the Naval Reserve – to observe in the October 1941 issue of *Photoplay*, 'How about awarding Oscars, or at least some sort of recognition to other movie men who have traded their make-up kits and megaphones for duffle-bags?' Robert Montgomery was also with the Naval Reserve. Robert Taylor had joined up, proving to detractors that he was as much a man, if not more so than those who had been excused from military duty citing paltry excuses, chief of which, according to top war-bond saleswomen Carole Lombard and Tallulah Bankhead, was cowardice. Figuring among these 'lazy sunbathers' were future president Ronald Reagan, Humphrey Bogart and even the mighty John Wayne.

Clark and Carole were included in the guests in the White House Oval Room on 30 December 1940 when President Roosevelt delivered one of his Fireside Chat speeches on national radio. These were so popular that in most cinemas the features were arranged around them so that they could be broadcast during the intermission. 'Never before has our American civilisation been in such danger as now,' Roosevelt began, accusing Nazi Germany of enslaving Europe. Then he urged America to support Britain in preventing Hitler from dominating the rest of the civilised world. 'If Britain goes down,' he concluded, 'all of us in the Americas would be living at the point of a gun.'

Though under current draft regulations Clark, at 40, was too old to be called up, there was nothing to prevent him from volunteering. He wrote to Roosevelt, begging him to find him *something* to do. Despite his busy schedule, the President afforded him a reply wherein he advised the Gables to stick to what they were best at – making movies and maintaining public morale. Carole was having none of this. It was all very well for 'FDR sitting in his wheelchair and spouting crap', she declared, but brave men were dying out there – men who did not need movie glamour, but medical assistance and muscle. She was scheduled to begin shooting *They All Kissed The Bride* for Columbia early in the New Year, but announced that *she* was putting this on hold so that she could join the Red Cross. She would return to making movies only when the War was over, and dared the studio to even *think* of suing her for breach of contract.

As for Clark, Carole declared, he would be enlisting to fight, whether Louis B. Mayer approved or not. He was interviewed by the film industry's war-time liaison officer Lewell Mellett, who told him what he already knew: he was too old. Mellett then gave a statement to Walter Winchell, who syndicated this across the country: 'Gable is one of the American people's daily habits and we don't want to rob them of their steady habits all at once. That's the one thing we have copied from the Goebbels' propaganda machine.'

Some recompense came when Clark was asked to chair the Actors' Division of the Hollywood Victory Committee, the body formed to organise and recruit movie talent for hospital and camp tours, fund-raisers and war-bonds rallies. His first job was to draw up a 15-strong committee, which met on 22 December 1941 at the Beverly Wilshire Hotel: Bette Davis, Rosalind Russell, Ginger Rogers, Charles Boyer, Myrna Loy, Bob Hope, Claudette Colbert, Irene Dunne, Jack Benny, Ronald Colman, Cary Grant, Gary Cooper, Tyrone Power and John Garfield.

On 24 December, shooting wrapped on *To Be Or Not To Be*, and Carole and Clark celebrated what would be their last Christmas together, beginning with a party that same evening for soldiers at MGM. Clark helped man the buses ferrying the men to the bash, while Carole greeted each one at the door with a kiss. Judy Garland and Eleanor Powell headed a hastily put together revue and Wallace Beery, one of the most miserable actors in Hollywood who hated Christmas *and* children, dressed up as Santa Claus!

Usually a shopaholic when it came to Christmas presents, Carole mailed her hundreds of friends and colleagues cards, announcing she had donated cash in their names to the Red Cross. Many doubled the donation. Her last gift to Clark was a gold cigarette case inscribed, 'To Pa. I Love You. Ma'. He gave her diamond and ruby clip-on earrings to match her wedding ring and the heart pendant he had given her the previous Christmas. The festive season itself was a muted affair in Hollywood: with no one sure what was lurking around the corner, few felt like celebrating.

Three days after Christmas, Clark was made aware of the new draft bill, approved by Congress. Effectively, all males between the ages of 18 and 64 would be able to register for active service, but with priority going to those between 20 and 44. Louis B. Mayer intervened, as he had with Robert Taylor and Mickey Rooney, claiming the studios needed these men more than the military, to boost public morale. Mayer was, of course, thinking only of himself and when Clark refused to listen, he called Lowell Mellett and ordered him to find Gable a position as a commissioned officer – in other words, a desk job in Washington so he could be called upon to work. Before Clark was given the opportunity to speak for himself, Carole called Ben Maddox. Her husband was not interested in Mayer's 'phoney bullshit commission' – he wanted to set an example for the rest of the country by starting military life as an ordinary private. His enlistment would take place, she added, as soon as he had finished *Somewhere I'll Find You.*

Carole's war-bonds promotion came about by way of Howard Dietz and Clark himself. Dietz had been shanghaied into the project by Secretary of the Treasury, Henry Morgenthau – and as the drive was to be launched in Indiana, Dietz plumped for the state's best-known Hoosier, Carole Lombard. To acquire her services, however, Dietz had to petition the head of the Actors Victory Committee – Clark, who would regret his decision to let her go for the rest of his life. The drive was scheduled to peak in Indianapolis on 15 January, with Carole taking the long route via train, as opposed to flying, so that she could stop off at Salt Lake City, Chicago and Ogden (Utah), and at Albuquerque and Kansas City on the way home. It was her intention to make the Hollywood première of *To Be Or Not To Be* on 18 January. Clark should have accompanied her, but Louis B. Mayer would not release him from his contract, which meant that for the first time since their marriage began they would be apart for more than a week. His place was taken by Otto Winkler and when best friend Fieldsie dropped out owing to illness, Carole's mother Bessie Peters was invited to tag along.

Neither did Clark see the group off from Union Station – according to the statement given by Howard Strickling because he was scheduled that day to begin working on *Somewhere I'll Find You.* And in any case, Strickling added, he would not have wished to rob his wife of her moment of glory. The real reason for him not being there appears to have been because that morning the couple had had an almighty bust-up over Clark's tomcat ways – one of those arguments that sees both parties flinging insults they do not really mean, which in this case would haunt him for ever.

This was an age when film stars turned out *looking* the part, so Carole's wardrobe had been carefully selected for the trip – the proven theory being that the better she presented herself, the more money she would raise for her cause. Irene Sharaff provided her with several black creations to match the sombre political climate. For her main speeches she would wear an ankle-length gown adorned with huge white roses representing the quest for peace – over which she wore the sable coat Clark had given her to protect against the frequently sub-zero temperatures. The diamond and ruby clip-on earrings he had bought her that Christmas were attached to either side of the plunging neckline so they could be close to her heart, which suggests she had not taken their argument too seriously.

Before leaving Hollywood Carole gave her secretary, Jean Garceau, a bundle of *billets-doux* to be passed on to Clark at the rate of one a day while she was away. Though this has never been disputed, Garceau later added to the mystery that there had been just five of these, and not six or seven, which would have covered the period between her leaving and the première of *To Be Or Not To Be*. In other words, it was suggested Carole had *planned* defying Howard Dietz's strict no-flying policy. As all the protagonists are now dead, we shall never know whether Garceau made up the number to add to the drama, or simply made a mistake on account of her own distress. Neither does the suggestion hold good that Carole departed Hollywood in a miserable mood, as if forewarned of impending doom. With her usual zaniness she left a gift in Clark's bed – a large-breasted love-doll wearing a Lana Turner wig – along with a note that read, 'So you won't be lonely'. She knew *exactly* what Clark might have been getting up to during her absence and this was undoubtedly her offbeat way of reminding him that she was on to him, and that there would be merry hell to pay when she returned home. The fact that Clark *knew* she was on to him was apparent from his reaction: he had a couple of friends 'customise' a male dummy with a 12-inch erect penis, so that he could place it – forming a tent – in Carole's bed to surprise her. This related to a private joke between them that she had made public. Clark, boasting that he was known as 'King of Hollywood' because he had a penis which measured a 'regal' 12 inches, had been put in his place by his wife, who retorted, 'One inch less and you'd be the *Queen* of Hollywood!'

The rally in Indianapolis concluded with Carole tearfully leading the crowd at the Cadle Tabernacle into 'The Star-Spangled Banner', then encouraging them to give Churchill V-sign salutes and cheer 'loud enough to be heard in Tokyo and Berlin'. When this happened, rarely for her, she burst into tears – and did so again upon learning that her efforts that day had raised a staggering $2 million. Each bond had been dispensed with a receipt carrying a personally signed photograph and the printed logo, 'Thank you for joining me in this vital campaign to make America strong'. Sitting hunched over a table for six hours, Carole signed thousands of these and never once complained. Unlikely support for her truly inspired campaigning came from clean-up merchant Will Hays, a fellow Hoosier (Sullivan, Indiana), who not so long ago had denounced her as immoral. Though Carole was still describing him – more than once to his face – as 'that vomitable old fuck', this did not prevent Hays from dispatching a telegram to Clark, via Louis B. Mayer: 'Carole was perfect, really she was MAGNIFICENT! Sold in this one day $2,017,513 worth of bonds. Everyone deeply GRATEFUL!'

Carole had not spoken to Clark since leaving Hollywood, but she wired him at least once and Jean Garceau passed on her notes. One of these is said to have read, 'Hey, Pa. You'd better get into this man's army!' – ribbing him to the very end over his frequent lack of confidence in his machismo. This was hardly helped by his father's persistent reminders that 'real men' were going off to fight and die while he was wasting time play-acting. *Why* Carole changed her mind about taking the train and opted to fly back to Los Angeles has been much discussed over the years, giving way to the pure speculation that inevitably arises in the wake of a tragedy when the victim is young and beautiful. The demises of Valentino, James Dean, Elvis Presley and Princess Diana have all loaned themselves to some of the wildest and highly improbable conspiracy theories.

It is highly unlikely that Carole would have wanted to hurry home just to catch Clark with Lana Turner. As already explained, she would not have put anything past him where an attractive woman was concerned and she knew that even if she *did* end his antics with this one, he would have another waiting in the wings. Cheating had always been part of Clark's nature, and had he not already convinced her that his sleeping around did not mean he had become any less enamoured of her? Equally far-fetched seems to be the story put about that Carole's mother had been warned not to fly by her astrologer and that she had declared 3 and 16 to be her 'unlucky' numbers: the plane was a TWA DC-3, Carole was 33 and the date was the sixteenth. Had this been so, Bessie Peters would have been suspicious of the fact that the train journey also took three days, and that there were three in the Lombard party.

The real reason for Carole's change of plan almost certainly pertained to her being a practical woman. Barring the visits to Albuquerque and Kansas City, which she promised to make after the *To Be Or Not To Be* première, the war-bond tour was over. It had been more successful than anyone could have imagined, but quite simply she wanted to get back to her regular life as expediently as possible. This was a fact reiterated by a reporter from *Life* magazine who spoke to her on the Saturday evening after the Cadle Tabernacle rally. Observing how exhausted she looked, he expressed his surprise that she was not planning an early night so that she might be properly refreshed before taking the train the next morning. Her response had been that if she caught the 4am so-called 'milk-train' flight from Indianapolis – an unusually long 17-hour flight – she would be home for dinner with Clark, and then be able to sleep in her own bed. 'And in any case,' she added, 'I don't like choo-choos!'

Howard Dietz had imposed a no-flying ban on his stars for good reason: on account of the blackouts, fewer beacons were kept lit for private flights. Carole, however, was permitted to ignore this ruling because this was not a private flight but a military one chartered to convey up to 20 Army personnel. The fact that she was doing war work automatically entitled her to a seat: her mother, Otto Winkler and several other civilians were allowed on board only because there was room. Clark was wired with news that the plane was scheduled to touch down in Burbank at around 9pm and as he was still at the studio, he arranged for MGM publicist Larry Barbier to meet the plane. A few times along its route it was delayed. In Albuquerque, several civilian passengers were ordered off and left to make their own way to Los Angeles when their seats were required for men from the Flying Command. Because the plane was overloaded and owing to the night-landing restrictions, the next stop on the route (Boulder, Colorado) was cancelled and the flight diverted to Las Vegas for refuelling – otherwise it would have flown straight to its destination. Instead, at 7.20pm on 16 January, 15 minutes after take-off and some 30 miles south west of Las Vegas, Carole's plane crashed into a ball of flames 70 feet from the summit of Mount Potosi (aka Table Rock Mountain). All 22 on board died instantly.

Larry Barbier was first to hear the news and notified Howard Strickling, who chartered a plane to transport Clark, MGM's second-in-command Eddie Mannix, Stuart Peters (Carole's brother, whom Clark could not stand) and Jill Winkler to las Vegas. By the time they arrived here, the first search party consisting of Army personnel was about to set off to clear the snow-blocked passes to enable the medical team to get through. There was no road up the 8,500-foot mountain, and the only way to bring any survivors or bodies back down would be via stretcher or mule-train. Clark wanted to accompany the medics, but was persuaded not to and sequestered a bungalow at the El Rancho Las Vegas hotel. One report stated he had to be physically restrained from heading off up the mountain – Louis B. Mayer did not want one of his biggest investments to come a cropper less than a week into his new film, so Eddie Mannix went in his place. It was he who wired Clark from a mountain way station with the news that Carole was dead.

The recovery of the bodies took three days on account of the snow and harsh terrain. One part of the mountain was so treacherous that a mule transporting a bodybag slipped on the ice and plummeted over a rock-face. Clark was permitted to watch from a safe distance, and through his binoculars had a clear picture of the mangled, still-smoking wreckage. All the victims were burned beyond recognition

– there was no question of identification, even by checking dental records. Most, including 'a young female', almost certainly Carole, had been decapitated on impact. Found close to the wreckage was one diamond and ruby ear-clip that Clark had given her: he would have it set in a locket and wear it for years until he eventually lost it. The matching heart péndant was never found. One fanciful journalist wrote that it had been embedded within Carole's own heart. Scattered across the snow were charred pages from *They All Kissed The Bride*. None of the relatives of the dead were permitted to see what was left of them. And all that Clark could mutter to a friend was, 'Ma's gone.'

Among the thousands of letters of condolence was a telegram from Buckingham Palace and there was a personal eulogy from President and Mrs Roosevelt, who would later posthumously present Carole with a medal bearing the citation, 'The first US woman killed in action in the defence of her country against the AXIS powers'.

The Roosevelts observed,

Carole was our friend, our guest in happier days. She brought great joy to all who knew her not only as a great artist. She gave unselfishly of her time and talent to serve her government in peace and in war. She loved her country. She is and always will be a star, one we shall never forget nor cease to be grateful to.

On 19 January, Clark helped load the wooden crates inscribed with the names of his wife, mother-in-law and best friend onto the train bound for Los Angeles. Identifying the charred remains, in pre-DNA days, had been mostly guesswork. The grisly truth is that each bodybag contained a head, four limbs if possible, but not guaranteed to have come from the same person. Clumps of blonde hair found at the crash site were assumed to have been Carole's, but really they could have been anybody's and it is very likely that the crates in Clark's charge contained the remains of servicemen, as well as those of his loved ones.

To avoid the media circus expected in Los Angeles, Clark and his grisly cargo disembarked at Colton, the next but last stop before

Union Station. Here, the crates were loaded onto the back of a truck that conveyed them to a funeral parlour. Carole had died serving her country, and as such was entitled to a funeral with full military honours. Clark would not hear of this nor of the Government erecting a monument in her memory. Cynics suggested he did not wish for her to be more fêted than he was. Attention was also drawn to the fact that in August 1939, five months after their marriage, Carole had drafted another will. This was common practice among the Hollywood fraternity, as was the clause within which Carole stipulated that no one but her immediate family should see her body after death. Garbo, Dietrich and Hepburn made similar requests, expecting to live until they were old and no longer possessed of the great beauty that had contributed to their fame.

Fashionable to the last, Carole had asked to be laid out in a white gown designed by Irene Sharaff, though this of course was her being her usual wacky self – there is no way she had expected to die at just 33. Even so, the dress was commissioned and added to the steel casket that would be sealed without Clark looking inside. Carole wanted to be buried in a 'modestly priced' crypt at Forest Lawn. Clark bought three: one for Carole, one for Bessie Peters and the third for himself. No matter *who* he married in the future, he declared, when his time came he would lie next to Lombard because he had loved her more than he could possibly love anyone else.

Carole and her mother were buried on 22 January, with the Methodist service conducted by a Reverend Chapman at the Church of the Recessional. To Clark's grief-stricken way of thinking, no God could have robbed him of his anchor, so there were neither prayers nor hymns. He did consent to the reading of Psalm 23, a short poem that Carole had loved and a quotation from the self-proclaimed Persian prophet and leader of the Baha'i faith, Baha-Allah: 'I have made death even as glad tidings unto thee. Why dost thou mourn at its approach?' Just 46 mourners were invited to the ceremony, including Carole's brothers, who Clark refused to acknowledge – he had always dismissed them as scroungers. The only stars present were William Powell, Myrna Loy, Fred MacMurray, Dorothy Lamour, Spencer Tracy and Jack Benny. With the exception of friends Adela

Rogers St Johns and Ben Maddox, along with 'acquaintances' Lloyd Pantages and Louella Parsons, the press were excluded.

Throughout the proceedings Clark sat motionless – between his father and stepmother – and revealed no outward emotion. Even in the wake of such a colossal tragedy the macho man within prevented him from shedding tears. The storm would break later when Carole's secretary, Jean Garceau, handed him the last of her *billets-doux*, the contents of which were never revealed. 'That was just too much,' Garceau told Gable's biographer Lyn Tornabene. 'He'd borne up so well to that point, but when he read Carole's last note he just went to pieces and broke down. And that's pretty hard to watch in a big man.' Otto Winkler was buried the next day, with Clark personally escorting his widow, Jill, to the ceremony.

Carole Lombard's death was a national tragedy – not as all consuming and hysterically received as Valentino's, 16 years earlier, but almost on the same scale as that of Marilyn Monroe, 20 years hence. As had happened with Jean Harlow, the studios held two-minute silences and closed down for the day. Louis B. Mayer had not been one of Carole's favourite people: when asked by a foreign reporter if she knew what the 'B' in his name stood for, she had retorted, 'Bastard!' She therefore would not have appreciated his hypocrisy – placing a black-edged advertisement in several Hollywood trade papers depicting a still from her last film – below which was a cartoon of the MGM lion, black-clad and holding a wreath.

More reverent, but bizarre, was the magazine, *Carole Lombard's Life Story*, which appeared unexpectedly, bearing neither the name of its publisher nor any of the contributors. We now know it was financed by William Randolph Hearst and those paying tribute included Marion Davies, Adela Rogers St Johns and Ben Maddox, who had not wanted the world to accuse them of making a fast buck. In fact, the proceeds were donated to the Red Cross. The publication contained over a dozen stunning photographs, and to reassure his readers that the Gables' marriage had been the strongest and happiest in Hollywood, Hearst made up the story of how Clark had seen Carole for the last time when kissing her goodbye at Union Station. Ernst Lubitsch, who burst into tears upon hearing of Carole's death, recalled the 'tastelessness' of rush releasing Jean Harlow's last film, and persuaded United Artists to postpone the première of *To Be Or Not To Be* by a month. One of its lines was cut – in the scene where the actors are plotting their escape from Poland and Carole asks Jack Benny, 'What can *happen* in a plane?'

Not everyone was pleased with the massive attention paid to Carole's death, though. A powerful detractor was CBS Radio's Elmer Davis, who became embroiled in a syndicated column row with Walter Winchell over whose deaths had been the more tragic – Carole, her mother and Otto Winkler, or the 15 military personnel and 4 crew members who died with them.

From the American nation's point of view, *everyone* had known Carole Lombard, while comparatively few had heard of the others apart from friends, families and colleagues – an undisputed fact, but no less distressing for the ones they had left behind. 'There is plenty of evidence that newspaper headlines misrepresent the feelings of the public,' Davis argued. 'It is a very sad reflection of our times that the death of an artist however distinguished and popular could be regarded as more important to the future of a nation than the loss of a group of trained men upon whom the country had depended for its victory.' Winchell's response was a curt, insensitive but truthful, 'We can train 15 more pilots, dreadful as their loss was. But could *you* dredge Hollywood from one end to the other and find another girl who could get out there and sell *so* many war-bonds?'

The inquest into the crash, conducted by the Civil Aeronautics Board, was primarily concerned with determining what had happened to its own, and if Carole's actions had had any part in this. They had been tipped off that the plane might have been sabotaged by the Japanese, following comments made by Carole over what she would do to them, in the wake of Pearl Harbor. One eyewitness claimed to have seen the plane exploding into flames *before* hitting the mountain, but a Western Airlines pilot, deemed more reliable, swore under oath that he had seen it hit the rock face. He was supported by Dan Yanish, a watchman at a diamond mine near Las Vegas, who told the inquest, 'The plane cracked in two like a piece of kindling wood.'

The findings laid the blame on the pilot, Wayne Williams, citing his 'inability to make proper use of his navigational facilities'. Williams diverted the plane a second time after leaving Las Vegas to make up for the time he had already lost and had been flying too low. Had he survived, he would almost certainly have been charged with reckless piloting, if not actual manslaughter. It subsequently emerged that he had been disciplined several times in recent months for failing to observe flight instructions.

Chapter Eight

# Death Wish In The Clouds

For Clark, Carole's death was the beginning of the end – a protracted, agonising 18-year decline. He would laugh again, love again but he would never really be happy bereft of his beloved 'Ma'. Also, he was consumed with guilt (as indeed was Howard Dietz, who blamed himself for setting up the war-bonds tour in the first place) for assigning his wife to her fateful mission. And if the decision to eschew the train for the plane had been Carole's alone, he could not alter the fact that her eagerness to get back to *him*, for whatever reason, had cost her her life.

This does not mean to say that, had she lived, the Gables' already-shaky marriage would have survived. One instinctively recalls the 'great loves' of French chanteuse Edith Piaf (boxing champion Marcel Cerdan) and Elizabeth Taylor (showman Mike Todd), which would not have remained so, had they not perished in similar air disasters to the one which claimed Carole. The fact that these tremendously passionate but stormy affairs ended so tragically while at their zenith *made* them greater than they would have been. Given the track records of all the participants, they would almost certainly have petered out, like every one of their predecessors and those following in their wake.

Clark Gable was a serial adulterer. For him it was almost a mental condition that Carole may or may not have tolerated indefinitely. He was not an especially attractive man in his post-Lombard years, and neither was he overtly charismatic – many have called him surly at times, even boring. His impatience and halitosis are reputed to have got worse. But he *was* Clark Gable, a magnet for women of all shapes, ages and sizes. Absolutely no one would have refused his advances: all he had to do was snap his fingers and the most faithful or prudish female would have offered herself to him on a plate.

The Gables' referring to each other as 'Ma' and 'Pa' had been sincere, offering proof of a couple contented with their lot. Similarly, from the cynic's point of view, the appellations might just have easily have been contrived to give an *impression* of contentment. This is something we shall never know. Though Carole tended to be open with her feelings, often towards the point of humiliating her husband, Clark kept his well under wraps – his father's bullying had seen to that – so whatever he and Carole were really like as a couple is anybody's guess.

His friends and supporters all agreed that the best way of getting him to even try to come to terms with his loss would be to help him get his life back on track by going back to work. Louis B. Mayer may have appeared outwardly sympathetic, but Mrs Gable had not been on his payroll and now his prime concern was less for Clark's welfare and fragile state of mind, but that *Somewhere I'll Find You* should not run overbudget. Not wishing to feel beholden to Mayer, Clark had refused his paychecks for the five weeks the film had been held up. Naturally, Mayer had not put up a fight.

In the film, Gable and newcomer Robert Sterling played war correspondent brothers who fall for the same girl – cub reporter Lana Turner who, after being promoted to the Foreign Desk, is dispatched to Indo-China, where she disappears. The brothers go off in search of her and find her working in Bataan as a nurse with the Red Cross on the eve of the Japanese invasion. It being unthinkable that Clark Gable should not get the girl in the last reel, the scriptwriter assigned to Sterling a hero's death. The title of the film alone, coming so soon after Carole's death and the fact that this was supposed to be a semi-comedy, could not have helped Clark's neurasthenia. MGM pretended to help by changing the title to *Red Light*, but as soon as shooting was over it was switched back again. It was, however, a huge success.

With his customary lack of tact, Louis B. Mayer contacted Joan Crawford *before* Carole's funeral and ordered her to stay away from

Clark – while Lana Turner, whom Joan and a good many more held indirectly responsible for the tragedy, was encouraged to offer him a friendly shoulder to cry on. It was Joan, however, who did all the comforting: in her memoirs she claims Gable dropped in for dinner most evenings after leaving the set of *Somewhere I'll Find You*, and there seems no reason not to believe her. Joan had adored Carole and was deeply hurt that she and William Haines were not invited to her funeral. Of course Mayer had exercised complete control over the invitations and in his eyes Crawford and Haines were social pariahs.

Snubbed by Mayer for what would be the last time now that her MGM contract was coming to a close, Joan decided the best tribute she could pay to her late friend would be to play tough-talking businesswoman Margaret Drew in *They All Kissed The Bride*, whether or not Mayer approved of her loan-out to Columbia. He certainly voiced his disapproval when producer Edward Kaufman informed Joan that the part was hers – but stepped down from his podium when she told the press that she would be donating her entire $125,000 fee to Carole's charity, the Red Cross. Later, when she learned that her agent, Mike Levell, had deducted his usual 10 per cent, she fired him!

While Joan might have wanted Clark as her co-star once more, to cast him opposite the stand-in for his deceased wife would have been unthinkable. Therefore the part of her love interest in the film went to Melvyn Douglas. At the time fans and the general public must have found it inconceivable to even imagine melodrama queen Joan Crawford attempting screwball comedy, yet she handles herself admirably, dropping her voice half a tone in the way Carole did, but never emulating her. Carole could not have wished for a finer tribute.

Joan had recently adopted a child – Christina, who immediately after her death would attempt but fail to trash her name by penning *Mommie Dearest* – and was in the process of adopting another with the help of lawyer lover Greg Bautzer, still two-timing her with Lana Turner. In the meantime, she was so eager to introduce a father figure into her children's lives that she began *auditioning* candidates for the role. There were just two stipulations: the man had to be handsome and lusty, but also exempted from military service because she did not wish to be widowed unnecessarily and end up raising her brood herself. Clark headed her list, and of course passed the test – a few hours playing with Christina, and a night in the sack with her mother – but turned her down, claiming he had no intention of ever marrying again. Among the other contenders were Glenn Ford, John Wayne and Gable lookalike James Craig, who recently failed to woo Marlene Dietrich while shooting *Seven Sinners*. Eventually, Joan plumped for 33-year-old Philip Terry, a little-known actor she claimed was Clark's exact size in every anatomical detail and who, like him, had acquired his beefcake physique working alongside his father in the oilfields. The pair were married in July 1942.

After completing *Somewhere I'll Find You*, for a while Clark lost himself at his ranch, spending much of his time tending his horses or wandering about the fields and orchards, as he had with Carole. Shortly before her death they had been thinking of selling the place (of late they had been pestered by intrusive fans and press). Now he had no intention of moving: as long as he lived in Encino, he said, Carole's spirit would stay with him. Whenever he spoke of her to friends, it was always as 'Ma', always in the present tense. He bought a huge motorcycle and roared around the surrounding neighbourhood, earning himself a roasting from Louis B. Mayer who, though he disliked the man, did not wish to see one of his biggest investments 'wrapping himself round a tree and breaking his stupid neck'.

Carole had left around $600,000 in her estate aside from modest trust funds to her brothers, the bulk going to Clark. The ranch, it emerged, she had bought in his name. There was also her collection of furs, valued at $25,000, and around $30,000 worth of jewellery, riding and sports equipment, and guns. Clark would eventually give most of these items to friends for keepsakes. Until then, for several months the house became a mausoleum: everything stayed exactly as Carole had left it, even down to the powder spilt on her dressing-table and the ashtrays containing cigarette stubs with traces of her lipstick.

It is now known that on 23 January, just seven days after Carole's death when Clark had been feeling truly suicidal, his scriptwriter friend Sy Bartlett, now a captain in the US Army, cabled him at

MGM regarding a position he had found for him in the Air Corps. The cable had bypassed Louis B. Mayer, but ended up in the hands of Howard Strickling. Rather than get in touch with Clark, Strickling conspired with Mayer to get him into another picture as quickly as possible. From the studio's point of view, Bartlett was informed, Clark was doing more for the war effort as a movie star than he ever could as a soldier. For 10 years he had figured in the Box-Office Top Ten, therefore it was essential he should remain in Hollywood to entertain his own 'troops' – in other words, cinema-goers ploughing money into the MGM coffers, a mercenary attitude destined for failure when the stooge was Clark Gable.

Strickling announced that Clark *would* be joining the Air Corps – fictitiously, on the set of *Shadow Of The Wing*, to be directed by Victor Fleming. Clark himself counteracted this by telling Mayer to his face that he would be making no more films at all until after the War. Initially, Mayer threatened him with suspension, though he soon capitulated: to take such action at a time when other stars were enlisting would have earned him few plaudits with the patriotic press. Mayer then decided to go along with 'Gable's foible', as he called it. He would allow him to enlist, but work behind the scenes to zip him through the ranks as quickly as possible, then recall him once he had got the urge to fight out of his system.

On 11 August 1942, leaving the ranch in the capable hands of Jean Garceau, Clark joined the queue at an Air Corps recruiting office in downtown Los Angeles. Normally, so as not to cause a media frenzy, movie stars were given private appointments, but this had been orchestrated as a publicity stunt by Howard Strickling. He was sworn in as Private Gable, Serial No. 191-257-41 and left that same day for the Officers Candidate School in Miami, Florida. His training schedule lasted 13 weeks and proved an ordeal, bearing in mind that he was a good 20 years older than most of the other recruits. Miami Beach had been seconded to the forces and transformed into a base, its plush hotels now doubling as barracks. Much of the time the temperature was over 100 degrees, and no leeway was initially given towards him for being a celebrity – quite the reverse, for as the other men rightly guessed his presence was just for show, he was resented. What made matters worse was that despite only being a private, he had been assigned his own batman – cameraman Andrew McIntyre, whose first task was filming him having his moustache shaved off. Neither did he gain many friends when, in a short space of time, he was rapidly promoted through the ranks – Sy Bartlett's theory being that the public would never accept Clark Gable as a 'low-ranker'.

Attitudes changed somewhat when he knuckled down to training. Inasmuch as he preferred the company of technicians and the like in Hollywood, so he professed to enjoy the 'anonymity' of Air Force life. He struggled with the physical aspects of the training, but coped well with the written work – years of working with scripts had given him a photographic memory, and in his final exams he was reported to have finished 'a third-way down the line of about 3,000'.

However, Clark did suffer from periods of black depression, brought about by the other men's persistent chattering about their wives, mothers and girlfriends, when he had no one but Jean Garceau to write home to. Lyn Tornabene quotes one soldier, Philadelphia radio executive Raymond Green, as saying, 'Sometimes I wondered if he had a death wish. He never talked at all about what he would do when the War was over. He had a cut-off point in his mind.' Green recalled how, with Miami Beach constantly under threat of attack from German submarines, he and Clark formed part of the nightly patrol and that on one occasion a lifeguard station within yards of them had been struck by lightning. 'I told him I was going to get him relieved from guard duty,' Green added. 'He wouldn't let me. I said, "You're carrying a rifle, you could get killed." He said, "So?". He had no fear of death, and he didn't seem to care. If he died, he died.'

On 27 October, Clark left the OCS as Second Lieutenant Gable and delivered his graduation speech – very definitely a scripted publicity exercise that was filmed by Andrew McIntyre and shown in newsreels across the country in the hope of boosting morale. It could just as easily have been a scene from one of his movies:

I've worked with you, scrubbed with you, marched with you, worried with you whether this day would ever come. The important thing, the *proud* thing I've learned is that we are *men*. Soon we will wear the uniforms of officers. How we *look* in them is not important. How we *wear* them is a lot more important. The job is to stay on the beam until in victory we get the command! *Fall out!*

A few days later, he received a personal command from H.H. Arnold, Lieutenant General Chief of the Army Air Forces. As part of a location unit he would be shooting and narrating a propaganda training film about aerial gunners, which the services were having difficulty in recruiting owing to the high mortality rate. On 8 November he and Andrew McIntyre were dispatched to the Tyndall Field Gunnery School, Florida, then on to Fort Wright, Solkane, for training in war photography. On 7 January 1943, feeling morose because it was coming up to the first anniversary of Carole's death, Clark was cheered somewhat by being awarded his aerial gunner wings – again, the ceremony was captured on celluloid for the newsreels. His smile, however, was forced. He had just declared in a letter to Jean Garceau, 'I have everyone anyone could want, except one thing. And all I really want is Ma.'

By 28 January, Clark was seconded to the 508th Squadron of the 351st Heavy Bombardment Group, First Air Division, 8th Air Force. As part of the same exercise – ensuring his exploits were comprehensively recorded and relayed to his *real* base, MGM – Andrew McIntyre went with him. The pair were relocated to Pueblo, Colorado, to prepare for action in Europe under the command of Colonel William Hatcher: the 351st HBG was nicknamed 'Hatcher's Chickens', which in modern day Hollywood parlance would have a totally different meaning directly in contrast with Clark's all-important macho image! Clark and McIntyre's mission would be to chronicle the day-to-day activities of the group and release this as a training film also to be shown between cinema features.

Effectively, he was given carte blanche with the project, which suggests his rapid promotion through the Air Force ranks had been but honorary. He took liberties assembling his team, which he audaciously named 'The Little Hollywood Group'. To head his production team he demanded John Lee Mahin, currently assigned to aircraft identification duties with Combat Intelligence, in Mexico. Mahin was one of many who were intent on cracking the Nazi Enigma Code and he was against giving up what he saw as vital work to make what looked like being just another documentary. Hatcher pulled the strings, however, and Mahin was told to fly with Clark to London. Accompanying them, also apparently against their will, were sound technician Howard Voss and cameramen Mario Toti and Robert Boles.

If Clark was expecting a regal welcome in England, he would be disappointed. As had happened with the OCS, he was initially despised and mistrusted by everyone he came into contact with. London had suffered terribly during the Blitz and thousands of young men were dying at the Front, so the last thing wanted on this side of the Atlantic, where the anti-American motto was, 'Over-sexed, over-paid and over here!' was some swaggering Hollywood movie star. Clark may never have stopped reminding everyone that he considered himself no one special, just one of the guys who enjoyed roughing it with the rest of them but each time he did not get his own way, he would become moody and pull celebrity rank. He would always get away with it. It was only when he began putting on displays of bravado and taking risks, as had happened in Miami Beach, that he was shown any respect – though as will be seen, this would be short-lived.

At the end of April, he was transferred to Polebrook, 80 miles north of London, between Huntingdon and Peterborough, where the 351st HBG would be flying B-17s. Clark got his men on side by offering to 'design' the group's logos for the planes' fuselages. Actually, he wired MGM's Cedric Gibbons to send him several designs to choose from, which he passed off as his own work. He also used his celebrity clout to have contraband goods smuggled into the camp – fruit, chocolate and toiletries. Having learned his lesson in London, he asked to be billeted *away* from the top brass and stayed in the officers' quarters with John Lee Mahin. Then he spoiled it all by refusing to wear the uniform supplied to him – the one he had stressed during his OCS graduation speech did not matter *how* it looked – having several made to measure by one of the most expensive tailors in Bond Street.

Clark's first aerial mission – supervised by Colonel Hatcher, who went up with him – was almost his last. It took place on 14 May during an attack on Courtrai airfield, in Belgium – against Hatcher's better judgement, Clark's way of proving he really was making an effort to fit in. Until now, as had happened back in America, everyone regarded his presence as a publicity stunt. Maybe Clark *did* have the death wish referred to by Raymond Green. The mission resulted in him being hailed a hero by the British and European press when a German shell pierced the fuselage of the plane, took off the heel of his boot, then ricocheted within an inch of his head.

From this point on, he really was one of the boys, and for a man reputed to have been tight with his money, did little to stop his colleagues sponging off him. Also, with so many women literally throwing themselves at him, he would pass the 'spares' on to his buddies. Formerly ignored, he was invited to join in the fun on leave, accompanying them on charabanc trips to Brighton, Southend and even Blackpool. On one occasion he and a pal rode all the way to the resort on a motorcycle he had bought especially for the occasion. On other leave weekends, Clark hung out with David Niven and his wife, Primula, at their cottage near Windsor. 'He was caught between two extremes,' Niven observed, 'Those who fawned upon him and those who automatically thought he ought to be chopped down.' Niven also recalled how he was still distraught over losing Carole, how Primula had found him in their garden, hunched over a wheelbarrow, weeping uncontrollably.

The news of his near-death experience was wired back to Louis B. Mayer, in whose eyes Clark was anything but a hero. As strings had been pulled to get him to Europe, so Mayer would bring him home – dead movie stars, he declared, were no use to anyone. Clark's response to Howard Strickling – 'I'm staying put. Tell Mayer to go fuck himself!' – never reached the mogul, and when he was designated more missions, the Germans put a price on his head. A propagandist tabloid had 'researched' the family trees of several major Hollywood stars and determined that 'Gable' was a derivation of 'Goebbels', a theory which did not sit well with the Nazi

Propaganda Minister. When a substantial reward was offered for his capture, Clark confided in David Niven that though his flying missions over Northern Europe terrified him, if push came to shove he would never bale out on account of what Hitler might do to him, should he be captured. 'That sonofabitch'll put me in a cage and charge 10 marks a look all over Germany!' he told Niven. Actually, Hitler is said to have wanted Clark's ears and overworked genitals in a glass case at the Reichstag!

The bounty tag proved too much for Clark's peers – both in the military and back home at MGM. The risks he was persistently taking were too great, not just for him, but for those accompanying him on his flying missions. The fact that in a very short time he had been awarded an Air Medal, a European Campaign Medal and an American Campaign Medal did not impress them. In their eyes he had confused heroism with stupidity: the obsession yet again with asserting his manhood, which had never been questioned in the first place. Clark may have had little or nothing to live for, but his comrades had, and at the end of October, having shot around 50,000 feet of film, the United States War Department summoned him, Mahin and McIntyre to return to Washington, where the farce continued. H.H. Arnold, the man who dispatched Clark to Europe, could not remember *why* he had done so – and in any case, he responded when Clark enlightened him that the film was no longer required! One of the country's top directors, William Wyler, had been given a similar commission and had come up with *The Memphis Belle*, a much more polished production, which had subsequently gone on general release. Therefore, with nothing better for Clark to do, Arnold informed him that he would have to wait until January 1944 before being transferred to the Air Force photography unit at Fort Roach, Culver City, where he and his team would be able to edit the footage which, ostensibly, nobody wanted.

Few 'soldiers' had been awarded quite so many privileges – and promotions – as those heaped upon Clark Gable in a little over a year's military service. He got away with refusing to work at Culver City, petitioning the man he hated more than any other – Louis B. Mayer, who halved his pay to $3,750 a week from the day he enlisted

– to allow him to work on his project at MGM on *full* salary. He commuted daily, not from a designated base but from his ranch instead. Mayer renegotiated the contract early in December. The terms were the same: $7,500 a week for 40 weeks of each of the next seven years but a new clause was added to the effect that if Clark so required, he could also be hired to produce or direct his movies. For the aerial film project, Mayer loaned him Blanche Sewell, one of MGM's most accomplished editors, and John Lee Mahin was retained to write the script. *Combat America* was panned by the few critics who watched the 60-minute production. It was screened in some cinemas between Gable features, and at the odd war-bonds rally, though within a few months it would be assigned to oblivion whereas William Wyler's *The Memphis Belle* still crops up in retrospectives, 60 years on.

On 15 January 1945 Clark was guest of honour at the launching of the 10,500-ton rescue ship, *Carole Lombard*, though Louis B. Mayer presided over the ceremony to mark the start of another Hollywood war-bonds campaign. Mayer effected the supreme insult by asking Irene Dunne to perform the christening, and not Clark. Unexpectedly for him, he burst into tears and this public expression of his bottled-up grief gained him considerable respect from some detractors, who were finally seeing him as a flesh-and-blood human being.

There were now two women in Gable's life: Virginia Grey, whose relationship with him is still said to have been platonic, and Kay Williams, an MGM contract player 16 years his junior, who he said reminded him of Carole. The characteristics were certainly similar: blonde, petite, witty and suitably filthy-mouthed – like Carole, Kay 'cursed with class' and was immediately accepted into her 'I can say shit because I'm a lady!' circle by his other lively friend, Tallulah Bankhead. Clark and Kay met the first Christmas after Carole's death when mutual friends tried but failed to push them together. According to the much-repeated story, Kay passed the Lombard test during their first date when Clark asked her to go upstairs and undress – bringing the tarty response, 'Why don't you go shit in your hat?' Their affair would not amount to much then. Over the next two years she was but one of a half-dozen Gable regulars – but in years to come, she would prove the most important woman in his life after Lombard and Crawford.

The film project completed and with time on his hands, Clark's name augmented the rota of the controversial MPA (the more familiar name for the long-winded Motion Picture Alliance for the Preservation of Ideals Against Fascism and Communism). By the spring of 1944 this was a forerunner for the next decade's McCarthy witch-hunts, which caused more than its share of unnecessary strife for Hollywood during the last years of the War. The MPA's dictum was, 'We refuse to permit the effort of Communist, Fascist and all Totalitarian groups to pervert this powerful medium [the movie industry] into an instrument for the dissemination of un-American ideals'. What it did *not* promote was any kind of antidote against racism and anti-Semitism by taking on board the likes of Clark, John Wayne and Victor Fleming. Within a month of its formation the MPA was besieged by angry protests from members of the Jewish community – by no means a minority in Hollywood, so much so that the matter was addressed by the *Los Angeles Times*. MPA chairman James McGuinness counteracted the accusations with a statement far more comprehensible than his organisation's logo: 'We are not anti-Semitic in a community where the most active opponents of Communism *are* the Jewish race.' Few believed him though his defence was countersigned by Robert Taylor, Ward Bond and Hedda Hopper.

In May 1944, having done absolutely nothing to earn this, Clark was promoted to Major Gable. In Hollywood, of course, then as now frequently out of touch with the real world, he was fêted for his phoney heroics. However it was a self-hyped bravado brought about by sorrow and self-pity, for with Carole gone and with her the reason for living to his way of thinking during all those aerial missions, death would have come as a merciful release. His rapid scaling of the military ladder proved an acute embarrassment a few weeks later, in the wake of D-Day, when thousands of men gave their lives doing considerably more than filming documentary footage that no one wanted. On 12 June, six days after D-Day, the press were informed in a statement not issued by the War Department, but by MGM, 'Clark Gable has been relieved from active duty by his own request'. This was pure fabrication. If he had enlisted with the Air Force, according to the original statement, 'For the duration of the war, plus six months', then he would not have been permitted to request discharge now unless for health reasons. A more likely theory is that Louis B. Mayer had worked behind the scenes to *get* him discharged – worried about his investment. Having been rushed through 45 films in 11 years, Clark had not faced a movie camera in the last two, and there was the possibility that his popularity might have been on the wane, threatened by any number of new kids on the block.

MGM, not wishing such information to be divulged to the press, organised a number of 'welcome home' parties – the most important being in Washington, where Clark presented his edited aerial training film to the Pentagon. This was also broadcast to a largely uninterested audience at New York's famous Stork Club, where the man of the moment, having been introduced to wealthy socialite Dolly O'Brien, eschewed the showing to whisk her back to his hotel suite!

At 50, Countess (through another marriage) Dolly Hyman Hemingway Fleischmann O'Brien Dorellis was six years Clark's senior and their affair was almost a repetition of what happened after Ria. His self-confidence had taken a battering in the wake of Carole's death and the European farce, so he needed a more forceful woman to get him back on track. Dolly was, like Carole and Kay Williams, blonde and witty – though in photographs taken at the time, she wears so much make-up that at times she resembles a drag queen. The daughter of a Philadelphia insurance man, her claim to fame had been her divorce from yeast tycoon Julius Fleischmann. This brought a $5 million settlement, though had she waited a little longer she would have received $66 million following his fatal fall from a polo pony.

Neither was Dolly particularly interested in Gable, the man. She had always been heavily into toy-boys, but liked to add big-name notches to her bedpost to increase her social standing. Clark *believed* she was sufficiently smitten to think of their setting up home together, but the nearest they got to this was when he spent two weeks at her

Palm Beach villa that December. He returned to Elcino for the festive season to divide his time between Kay Williams and Virginia Grey.

It was then back to work. In the United States, as in Britain, the War effected drastic changes within the movie industry. Former top-liners Garbo, Shearer, Flynn, Crawford, Dietrich, MacDonald and Eddy – and on the other side of the Atlantic, Gracie Fields and George Formby – had seen a slump in their careers, though most would soon return to fight for their crowns. The public were currently clamouring for the 'stars of tomorrow', some of whom were already established: Elizabeth Taylor, David Niven, James Mason, Judy Garland, Katharine Hepburn, Stewart Granger, Van Johnson, Greer Garson, and the ubiquitous Lana Turner. Louis B. Mayer, for all his efforts to get Clark out of the military and back onto the lot, did not know what to do with him now. At 44 he was considered too old for a credible romantic lead and not yet suitable for the fatherly and avuncular roles in which the likes of Lionel Barrymore excelled.

Since that fateful night in January 1942, Clark had substantially increased his liquor consumption. He was also addicted to Dexedrine, a weight-loss drug he had begun taking since returning from England, where he had piled on the pounds on account of the stodgy Air Force diet. This reacted badly with the alcohol, causing him to have the shakes and making close-ups frequently impossible. Neither was he happy with the series of radio dramas lined up by his agent, Phil Berg – at $7,500 a shot, the idea being that being heard but not seen might help him with his nerves. He taped just one before throwing in the towel, playing a submarine commander in *Take Her Down*.

Meanwhile, there *was* a world outside of his movie career. Like Errol Flynn, who had founded the FFF (Flynn's Flying Fuckers) – an adventure group comprising male friends who shared his passion for sex, sailing and drinking – Clark and his director buddy Howard Hawks formed the Morago Spit & Polish Club. This was mostly a middle-aged, racist, anti-Semitic motorcycle gang which convened most weekends at Hawks' house on Morago Drive, and who would drive out to the Mojave Desert in search of their lost youth, eager to prove themselves as adept on two wheels as the speed-freak younger generation. The gang members included actors Andy Devine, Ward Bond and Keenan Wynn, besides Victor Fleming and several hunting friends.

For the second time, Louis B. Mayer issued Clark with a warning to stay off motorcycles, but it was his Duesenberg that got him in trouble. On 24 March 1945, on his way home from a party celebrating the US capture of Iwo Jima – drunk and quite possibly driving on the wrong side of the road – Clark crashed into a tree in the middle of a traffic roundabout on Sunset Boulevard and Bristol Avenue. Luckily for him it was around four in the morning and there were no witnesses, so how he arrived at the Cedars of Lebanon Hospital remains a mystery.

The hospital had its own network of well-paid spies lurking to report back to the press on the latest celebrity indiscretion, so MGM chief of police Whitey Hendry stepped in to prevent the inevitable headlines. The story was put out that Clark, who had not touched so much as a drop of liquor all evening, had been driving on *his* side of the road when he swerved to avoid a drunk-driver speeding towards him on the same side. How Hendry came to the conclusion that the other driver had been drunk, when he had not stopped was of course immaterial. And was it not a coincidence that Clark had crashed not into the roundabout, in Hendry's version of events, but into the front garden of talent scout Harry Friedman?

Clark was forcibly subjected to a brief drying-out period before beginning work on *Adventure*, originally commissioned for former child star Freddie Bartholomew, now 21 and just returned from serving with the Air Force as a real fighter pilot. Bartholomew was to have played the son of the lead characters (Clark and Greer Garson), but dropped out of the production, disapproving of Clark's ersatz heroics overseas. Though Clark got along famously with his other co-star, 36-year-old Joan Blondell, he took an instant dislike to Greer Garson, accusing her of being sour-faced and devoid of a sense of humour. The cause for this dissension was due to Garson's lack of amorous interest in him – and Clark's aversion to Louis B. Mayer's slogan for the film: 'Gable's Back And Garson's Got Him!'

Additionally, Garson (1903–96) was a favourite of William Wyler, who had directed her in *Mrs Miniver*, one of the most successful films of the war years – and Wyler had of course gazumped him with the aerial gunner documentary. She had also appeared in *Goodbye Mr Chips* with Ronald Colman, who had walked off with the Oscar Clark believed *he* should have received for *Gone With The Wind*.

In the film, Clark played a womanising merchant sailor whose ship is torpedoed by the Japanese. He and his men are rescued when an Irish tar prays for a miracle – which comes in the form of stuffy librarian Garson, for whom he falls while having a doxy (Blondell) on the side for the sex he may not be getting from Garson. They wed, and when the marriage fails, he goes back to sea. He then sees the error of his ways just as Garson is about to have the baby she never told him about. The child is stillborn, so this time *he* prays for a miracle, and the child comes back to life! The film was absolute nonsense, attracting more bad reviews than good. The *New York Times'* Bosley Crowther, the most influential critic of his day, bemoaned the lack of nuclear fusion expected from two stars as potent as Gable and Garson, concluding, 'What should have been a bombshell is about as explosive as a slightly ancient egg'. Even the usually Gable-friendly *Photoplay* was puzzled by it all, observing, 'What we can't understand is the vociferous and he-mannish Mr Gable consenting to mouth the innocuous, and at times whimsical dialogue that means just nothing'.

Despite such panning, *Adventure* did well at the box-office, though largely because fans flocked to the cinemas to see if it really was as bad as the critics were making out. MGM released the film two weeks before Christmas, in time to catch the end-of-year Oscar nominations. It was completely overlooked, though Greer Garson was put forward for Best Actress for her other film of that year, *The Valley Of Decision*. Clark publicly gunned for one of the other contenders, Joan Crawford, and must have been thrilled when she won for *Mildred Pierce*. Best Actor went to Ray Milland for his portrayal of an alcoholic in *The Lost Weekend* – playing his brother was Joan's new husband, Phillip Terry.

Because of the success of the film, Louis B. Mayer considered a Gable-Garson re-match which neither wanted. He was therefore offered *The Hucksters* with Deborah Kerr and Ava Gardner. Initially he refused the part of brash advertising executive Victor Norman, declaring he had left his years as Crawford and Shearer's hardbitten foils behind him – that from now on he wanted only intelligent and sophisticated roles similar to the ones the studios were offering Gary Cooper and Spencer Tracy. Mayer's response was that he was *still* a contract player, obliged to obey orders. Temporarily, the great Gable was losing his swaying power, though he brazenly demanded a screen test with 'unknown quantity' Deborah Kerr before agreeing to work with her. The Scots-born actress, then 24, had started out with the Sadlers Wells Ballet Company before turning to acting. Her film debut, *Contraband*, had been with Conrad Veidt in 1940, though her scenes have been deleted from the final print. The following year she triumphed in *Major Barbara*, released shortly before she was informed that she would be working with Clark. Mayer went along with the screen test, but it was only to humour him.

Ava Gardner (1922–90), one of the last of the screen's truly great love goddesses, had just scored her first success with *The Killers*. By pitching her opposite Gable, Mayer was hoping to spawn a partnership as hot as the ones with Harlow, Crawford and Shearer. Like the former two, Ava had had lovers galore before marrying Mickey Rooney in 1942, then divorcing him the following year. Her marriage to Lana Turner 'reject' Artie Shaw had been similarly short-lived: they filed for divorce within weeks of her landing the part in *The Hucksters*. Yet even with the presence of these distinguished leading ladies and the gargantuan Sydney Greenstreet, the film was no great shakes. Even so, fans flocked to see it to find out, as promised, if the Gable-Gardner pairing matched up to the others, and its success returned Clark to the Box-Office Top Ten.

At this time, Clark was seeing a lot of David and Primula Niven and their two small children at their rented home in Beverly Hills. He had not had much to do with Niven while married to Carole, who for some reason had disliked him. Niven recalled in his memoirs how she had called him 'a pain in the ass', but only, he believed, because she had been unable to stand anyone who could shoot and fish more efficiently than herself. Clark and the Nivens went on hunting trips, played golf and partied, a brief but idyllic period which ended in tragedy on 20 May 1946 when the trio were invited to a pool party chez Tyrone Power. While playing hide-and-seek, 28-year-old Primula climbed into what she believed was a closet – and fell headlong down a steep flight of stone steps leading to the basement and fracturing her skull. She never regained consciousness and died the next day.

Primula's body was flown back to England and interred in the churchyard at Huish in Wiltshire, where she and Niven had been married. Clark wanted to accompany his friend, but Louis B. Mayer prevented this – worried he might not come back. Even so, when Niven returned to Hollywood, for two weeks Clark never left his side. Niven recalled, 'During that long period of utter despair, Clark was endlessly thoughtful and helpful, and he checked constantly to see if I was all right. Without me realising it he was drawing on his own awful experience to steer me through mine.'

Gable next swallowed a huge chunk of humble pie in an attempt to heal the rift *he* had opened between himself and David Selznick, apparently fulfilling a promise (quoted by his biographer Lyn Tornabene) made to a colleague while on one of his flying missions: 'What did the guy ever do to me except force me to be in the most important film I ever made? If I get out of here alive, I'm going to apologise!' And he had much to apologise for – his snubbing of Selznick during the *Gone With The Wind* premières, his personal and prejudiced remarks. But there was a sound reason for his grovelling: Selznick was about to re-release the film, which had been removed from theatre bills in the wake of Pearl Harbor, on account of its distressing aftermath-of-war scenes being considered 'inappropriate' for those millions across the world touched by the real war.

Naturally, the re-release would catapult Clark back into the limelight, but also alert everyone to the fact that the roles he was currently being offered paled to almost nothing compared with that of Rhett Butler. This he did not mind, for Selznick (who had sold his share of the original production for $500,000 to help keep his company afloat) now had high hopes of there being a sequel. It is said that Margaret Mitchell was asked to begin working on this, but as it had taken her 10 years to complete the first book, few were surprised when the project fizzled out. Nor was Selznick in a forgiving mood so far as Clark was concerned, though there was an unexpected bonus when, after gatecrashing one of the mogul's parties, he was introduced to 30-year-old Anita Colby, the former actress-model now employed as a $100,000 a year consultant for Selznick Productions.

Clark was still seeing a non-sexual partner (Virginia Grey), an older woman (Dolly O'Brien) and numerous others. Now, in a throwback to his pre-fame days he latched onto the sexually ambiguous Colby (Anita Counihan, 1914–92) ostensibly in the hope that her influence on Selznick might rectify the slump in his career. The producer was still not buying, so Clark ditched Colby to concentrate on Kay Williams – too late, it turned out, for she was about to become the fifth wife of millionaire Alfred Spreckles. On the rebound, Clark took up with thrice-married Standard Oil heiress Millicent Rogers, a woman possessed of characteristics that define her as being at least partially insane.

Around Clark's age, Rogers, a champion of Red Indian rights, would turn up for their dates wearing authentic costume – on one occasion as a squaw, on another as the Madame de Pompadour. When Gable tried to end their relationship after one red face too many, she began stalking him, tipping waiters so that she could sit at an adjacent table when he was entertaining other lady friends. Having finally driven home the message that it really was over between them, Rogers wrote him a farewell letter – forwarding a copy to Hedda Hopper, which of course ended up in her column:

> You're a perfectionist, as am I. I followed you last night as you took your young friend home. I'm glad that you kissed and that I *saw* you kiss, because now I know that you have someone close to you and that you'll have enough warmth beside you. God bless you, my most darling darling! Be gentle with yourself! Allow yourself happiness!

On account of Millicent Rogers' hounding, and to offer himself breathing space from the press, Clark secretly rented a suite at the Bel Air Hotel – with its own driveway and entrance down a side-street, so that he could come and go, hopefully without being seen. His neighbour was fellow serial cheat Greg Bautzer, who had been living there at his refuge for dodging spurned lovers and their angry partners, off and on for the past decade. Surprisingly the two became friends – for years they had been rivals over Joan Crawford and Lana Turner. Occasionally they would go for long drives into the desert and swap anecdotes in Clark's latest 'baby' – an expensive Jaguar XK-120, top speed 130 mph.

In the midst of this bed-hopping confusion, Clark made *Homecoming* with Lana Turner, Anne Baxter and John Hodiak – a potential recipe for disaster if ever there was. Since last working with Gable, Lana had wed and divorced actor Stephen Crane, an unsavoury character with mobster connections – they had had a daughter, Cheryl. Hodiak (1914–55) was a volatile individual who had recently emerged emotionally scarred from a torrid affair with Tallulah Bankhead on the set of Hitchcock's *Lifeboat* – to take up with Lana while shooting the ironically mistitled *Marriage Is A Private Affair*, and all while married to Anne Baxter. On the rebound, Lana ended up in the arms of Tyrone Power, separated from his French actress wife, Anabella – and also involved with Cesar Romero, who had recently ended a relationship with John Hodiak! Salvation of sorts had kept the outing brigade from Power's door when Lana had fallen pregnant – though she had subsequently had an abortion, by no means her first – and to 'prove' he was not gay, Power had moved on to 16-year-old starlet Linda Christian.

Directed by Mervyn LeRoy, the publicity slogan for this one was, 'THE TEAM THAT GENERATES STEAM!'. Clark played Ulysses Johnson, a Park Avenue doctor serving with the medical corps in North Africa during World War II, who has an adulterous affair with an army nurse, played by Lana; 25-year-old Anne Baxter played his long-suffering wife, a union criticised by moralists because of the great age difference at a time when such things were unacceptable. Morality also wins the day when Ulysses returns to her, heartbroken, after Lana dies of injuries sustained during the 'Battle of the Bulge'. Generally, the film was a lacklustre affair with rival stud John Hodiak running rings around Clark in every scene they shared.

'Battle of the Bulge' was a term used by several critics to describe Gable's rounded appearance and he was further ridiculed when the press were given 'privileged' information that he had begun applying haemorrhoid ointment to reduce the bags under his eyes. He went into a sulk, and disappeared for three weeks on a fishing expedition.

Only slightly better was *Command Decision*, directed by Sam Wood, an all-male production which had no love interest other than the not inadvertent admiring stares exchanged between John Hodiak and Van Johnson. Many Gable detractors thought he had a nerve playing a US Air Force commander who sent his men on suicide missions, flying B-17s over Germany to bomb munitions factories. In real life, he had zipped through the ranks basically for being Clark Gable – and now here he had been promoted to Brigadier General.

On 4 August 1948, William Gable, who had never really got over the death of his wife, Edna, the previous year, died of a heart attack. The press stated his age to be 78, but this was merely guesswork. Clark was holidaying in Europe with Dolly O'Brien at the time, having sailed to Le Havre on the *Queen Mary* on 12 July. After spending a few days in Deauville with the Duke and Duchess of Windsor, he and Dolly drove to Paris to attend one of Elsa Maxwell's 'multicultural' society parties. They then went on to Dolly's villa in Cannes, and finally back to Paris where Howard Strickling's wire had caught up with him. Clark pretended to be devastated for the sake of the press, but in truth he was relieved. The pair had never really got along and despite the money and attention he had lavished on the old man, his taunts over Clark's supposed lack of manliness had made his younger life a misery.

Clark made no effort to hurry home. After leaving the Air Force he had sworn never to take another plane, a vow he would keep until 1952. He wired Strickling with the instruction to have his father placed in cold storage and boarded the next available liner for New York. Publicly, he had displayed very little grief over the death of his wife so it was hardly likely that he would be caught weeping for a father he secretly despised. For this reason, MGM played down William's demise, releasing only the basic facts to the press. It was essential for the world to be informed though, according to the brief obituary notice in the *Los Angeles Times*, paid for by the studio, that Clark was deeply distressed after losing the father he had worshipped. After the funeral he set about removing every trace of his father from his life. He threw away William's clothes, gave away his possessions and sold the bunglow he had bought for him and Edna at a loss.

On 6 January 1949, Victor Fleming died suddenly of a heart attack, aged 65. This time Clark was genuinely devastated. Fleming had hunted, fished and roughed it with him in the most adverse conditions and had been regarded as invincible. The fact that he had not been ill – or if he had, no one had known – not only made his death harder to bear, but it forced Clark, in light of his own excesses, to become terrifyingly aware of his own mortality.

Chapter Nine

# STRANGE INTERLUDE

In the aftermath of World War II, MGM, like all the major studios, started to feel the pinch. One report revealed the studio to be over $6 million in the red. Hoping to combat the dilemma, Louis B. Mayer brought in 43-year-old Dore Schary, with whom he had always had a shaky relationship. Born in New Jersey, Schary worked as a stock actor, then as a scriptwriter for Columbia, joining MGM in 1937 to work on Spencer Tracy's *Boys Town* and *Edison The Man*. Six years later he had fallen foul of Mayer's unpredictable temper, and left to produce for Vanguard and RKO.

Politically opinionated and a close friend of David Selznick, Mayer figured Dore Schary would never get along with Clark Gable, who loathed him from the start and never shied away from telling him to his face. Sparks started flying when Schary – well aware of Clark's paranoia over his machismo – suggested him for the role of centurion Marcus Vinicius in the Roman epic, *Quo Vadis?*, the script of which had been gathering dust in MGM's archives for some time. Clark roared that he 'would not be seen dead in a fucking skirt!' – and that was that. Nor was he happy when Schary commissioned *Any Number Can Play* especially for him: he wanted to do *Nothing Wrong*, scripted by Preston Sturgess. Schary informed him, as Mayer had done innumerable times, that as a contract player he would stick to the rules.

Clark dismissed the film, a throwback from his formative years directed by Mervyn LeRoy, as 'second-rate crap'. He played alcoholic, chain-smoking casino owner Charley King, whose marriage is on the rocks, and whose teenage son (Darryl Hickman) hates him. To cap it all, Charley has a heart-condition and eventually loses his business in a card game.

No sooner had he recovered from this dreary fare than Schary put him into Robert Riley Crutcher's romantic comedy, *Key To The City*, of which the less said the better. This saw him working with Loretta Young again, and proved a less pleasurable experience than their first outing, 15 years before. Since then, Loretta had borne Tom Lewis two children in the space of two years, and was pregnant again. Judy still did not know her real father's identity, but her husband is thought to have suspected something.

In the new film, Clark and Loretta played rival contenders in a small town mayoral election campaign. He is a hard-bitten, chauvinistic ex-stevedore, she a frigid spinster that he, of course, thaws out, and to tie in with Clark's machismo and celebrity, *he* is the one who gets to be mayor, while she gives up her career to become his wife and skivvy for him. The by-now obligatory slogan for this one – dreamed up by Dore Schary, who was aware of past history – was, 'THEY CLICK LIKE A KEY IN A LOCK!' Some of the components of this particular lock, however, were decidedly rusty! In some scenes, despite just a 12-year age gap, Clark looks old enough to be Loretta's father.

The production was blighted by a series of problems. John Wayne regularly visited the set in his official capacity as an MPA agent tracking down a Communist said to have infiltrated Schary's staff. The subsequent investigation – silly but upsetting for the man in question – proved clean. Halfway through shooting, Loretta Young collapsed and was rushed to hospital, where she suffered a miscarriage. Then, in the September, a few days after the film wrapped and two hours after playing golf with Clark, 59-year-old Frank Morgan – his friend who plays the fire chief in the film – succumbed to a fatal heart attack. Clark was a pallbearer at his funeral.

So far as is known, Clark had first met 'Lady' Sylvia Ashley in December 1939, shortly after the death of her third husband, Douglas Fairbanks. He and Carole had taken time out from their hectic *Gone With The Wind* promotional drive to console the widow at her Santa Monica mansion, though why they had done this when they hardly knew Fairbanks, or her, is baffling. The two met again in April 1949 at New York's Park Sheraton Hotel, at a fundraiser ball organised by Elsa Maxwell, introduced by Lady Cavendish – aka Adele Astaire, Fred's sister whose husband had died during the War, leaving her extremely wealthy. A few weeks later Clark showed up at Sylvia's home and the press, with Maxwell leading the charge, soon reported them as going steady.

His new amour – one of a half-dozen he squired around town at the time – was no longer a bona fide member of the British aristocracy. Born Edith Louisa Hawkes in Paddington, London, in 1904, this stable-hand's daughter and decidedly rough diamond's first attempt at bettering herself had involved taking elocution lessons to rid herself of her harsh Cockney accent. After World War I she modelled lingerie and posed for French postcards, and appeared as a chorine in a number of Soho revues. Little more than a prostitute, she encouraged a succession of wealthy admirers to vie for her affections, pampering her with furs and jewels. In 1927 she married Lord Anthony Ashley, heir to the 9th Earl of Shaftsbury.

Marriage and an elevated position had not prevented Sylvia from scandalising London society by engaging in any number of very public affairs – the best known with ageing swashbuckler Douglas Fairbanks, whose supposed fairytale marriage to 'America's Sweetheart' Mary Pickford had been on the rocks. She divorced Fairbanks in 1936, around the same time as Ashley divorced Sylvia, citing Fairbanks as co-respondent. Sylvia and Fairbanks had married at once. No longer Lady Ashley, but purloining the title to maintain her position in a society, many of whose members were little less corrupt and immoral than she was, Sylvia persuaded Fairbanks to buy a house in London's Park Lane. She also coerced him into changing his will, well aware that he was ill. Upon his death, in 1939, she had inherited his London and Santa Monica homes, a citrus farm and the Rancho Zorro in California, a small fleet of Rolls-Royces, and around $4 million in cash. Fairbanks' son, Douglas Jr, had been bequeathed little in comparison.

In 1944, the money-grabbing widow remarried into the British aristocracy: Lord Edward Stanley, 6th Baron Sheffield and Alderly.

They had met in New York, where as a conscientious objector he had lived for the duration of the War. Sylvia knew all along that her (albeit subsequently four-times wed) husband was gay, and used this as an excuse to shame and divorce him four years later, whence she had reverted to calling herself Lady Sylvia Ashley, which legally she was not entitled to do. In 1948 she relocated to the Fairbanks' mansion in Santa Monica, until then occupied by 'caretaker' tenants – her sister Vera and brother-in-law: British film producer Basil Bleck. When Sylvia took up residence, the Blecks stayed put.

How Sylvia managed to ensnare a man as stubborn as Clark Gable into marrying her mystified his friends. During most of 1949 he was rarely seen twice in the same week with the same woman, so when he and Sylvia married that year, on 20 December 1949, in Solvang, a Scandinavian community in Santa Barbara County, even the sharpest tacks among the press were caught by surprise. In 1941, he promised Otto Winkler that if he ever married again – suggesting that despite their closeness, he had not regarded his union with Carole as potentially long-term – that Winkler would be best man. With Winkler gone, Howard Strickling, alerted to the wedding plans three days earlier, was asked to take his place. Clark and his bride dressed unconventionally in blue serge, just in case they were spotted heading for the Danish Lutheran Church. Suspicious reporters, he hoped, would assume they were attending someone else's wedding and not their own. Jean Garceau was a witness and Sylvia given away by Basil Bleck.

Clark had insisted on strict secrecy but Strickling, in the position as Louis B. Mayer's official mouthpiece, brought along a photographer to record the happy event. Not for the first time, the register was falsified: Sylvia lied that she was 39 – she was six years older. The gossip-columnists had a field day unearthing all the juicy details of her past, though most of these were too lurid for public consumption. The honeymoon took place in Hawaii, by which time the press were hot on the Gables' heels. While Clark and Sylvia travelled the leisurely way to Honolulu on the SS *Lurline*, Strickling and his wife flew on ahead to brief reporters and ensure they refrained from asking too many impertinent questions.

Louella Parsons had not forgiven Clark for snubbing her the last time around. Staying put in Hollywood, she sniped in her column, 'I doubt if any characters in history – Antony and Cleopatra, Helen of Troy and all the rest – can equal the careers of these two.' It did not take a genius to work out that she was referring to their respective 'careers' in the bedroom department! Ben Maddox, now out of Clark's life for good, followed up on this by suggesting his new bride had 'more in common with the Queen of the Nile than most would imagine'. Any serious historians among Clark's fan-base were left with little doubt that Maddox was referring to the chronicled event when Cleopatra fellated 100 Roman soldiers in a single night! Quite clearly, the *faux* Lady Ashley commanded little respect other than from those within her inner sanctum.

When Sylvia began styling herself Carole Lombard's replacement within days of moving into the Encino ranch, it was a foregone conclusion that the marriage would not survive. She brought her personal maid and white cook – Jesse, Clark's black cook, was shown the door. Next, Sylvia complained the house was too small: she liked to paint, therefore she needed a studio, and it was also essential her staff have their own space for receiving guests so that these might not be seen by *her* high-ranking friends. Her greatest folly, however, was bringing in decorators to refurbish Carole's room, the former shrine to her memory that was now turned into an English bedsit, cluttered with antiques from her former homes – souvenirs, she said, of *her* marriages. Clark refused to enter the room once she had its walls painted shocking pink. Sylvia next took a leaf out of her predecessor's book and began 'scorning' her husband's machismo – not by making wisecracks, as Carole had got away with so well, but by getting him to carry her tiny pooch with its painted claws and diamond collar. Not so long before Clark had taken Joan Crawford's husband, Phillip Terry, to one side and told him how 'faggy' he looked carrying hers.

Sylvia discouraged his hunting, fishing and motorcycle fans from visiting the ranch, fearing that 'outdoors' language and behaviour might shock her friends. In London she had frequented Mayfair circles: likewise in Paris her 'local' had been the Hotel Continental, off the Place de l'Opéra. Attempting to re-create these soirées, she invited only English and French showbusiness people to the ranch: Clifton Webb, Brian Aherne, Merle Oberon, Robert Douglas, Joan Fontaine, Charles Boyer, Louis Jourdan and Noel Coward – mostly people Clark could not stomach. A permanent resident during the early months of their marriage was Timothy Bleck, Sylvia's teenage nephew, who appears to have developed a crush on him.

Though wealthy in her own right, Sylvia's improvements to her new domain – including transporting hundreds of antiques from England – had been effected by Clark dipping into his wallet, something he had rarely done for his other wives, who always insisted on paying their way. Most of her money, she claimed, was tied up in property and business deals across the Atlantic. The press picked up on this. They had never stopped making comparisons with this snooty Englishwoman, who looked down her nose at anyone non-European – and Carole Lombard, adored by all and accessible to all but a few, and above all sincere. Their conclusion was that 'Lady Ashtray', as Joan Crawford called her, was the same with Clark as she had been with the other men in her life – a kept woman.

Sylvia's assets and holdings were made public. They were two beach houses, the mansion in Santa Monica and the 3,000-acre Rancho Zorro worth in excess of $6 million, the $50,000 profits invested from the movies Douglas Fairbanks bequeathed her and around $750,000 in jewels and bonds lodged in a London bank vault. When journalists commented on how well she looked decked out in all her finery – but that Clark was starting to look jaded and henpecked – he ordered her aboard the next ship to England, not to come home until she had released the revenue from some of these assets. She was also told to take Timothy Bleck with her. The youth and his friends, Clark declared, were eating him out of house and home, and always pestering him for money. Sylvia was also told to put her beach properties on the market and evict her sponging relatives – something she refused to even consider.

Initially, she stayed put, claiming she had arranged for her London lawyers to transfer funds to a Los Angeles bank. She also promised to curb her spending and was almost good to her word while Clark was shooting To Please A Lady, which saw him returning to the caveman

Gable of old. His co-star was Barbara Stanwyck, whom he had memorably socked in the jaw 20 years earlier in *Night Nurse*. Director Clarence Brown was therefore asked to guarantee cinema-goers a repeat performance and Clark did not disappoint as ruthless racing driver Mike Brannon, whose uncompromising way of competing on the track has seen several rivals killed or seriously hurt. Eventually he has to give up the sport because the crowds hate him so much, and he ends up as a stunt driver with a travelling sideshow. Enter all-powerful journalist Regina Ford (Stanwyck), who has built up a smear campaign against him to ban him from driving, period.

Needless to say, love enters the equation though Mike still treats Regina shabbily, as he does everyone else. One of their set-tos ends with him warning her, 'You'd better listen to what I'm saying, or I'll *knock* that smile off your face!' 'Knock it off,' she responds – and he does, before kissing her hungrily then marching off in a strop. Twenty years ago, or even ten, this scenario would have worked – now, however, at 49 and 43 respectively, Gable and Stanwyck were too old to be playing supposedly young romantic leads.

The locations were shot over a three-week period at the Indianapolis 500 and included footage of the actual race – initially depressing for Clark, for this was the city from which Carole had embarked on her fatal flight. He was faced with an additional dilemma when Timothy Bleck showed up with a group of friends, taking over several rooms at the Marriot Hotel where the Gables were staying – and charging the bill to their account. When Sylvia received a wire from her London lawyers informing her that they had finally sorted out her complicated business interests, she decided to travel to England herself – with Clark ordering her to take Bleck with her and make sure he stayed there.

She was away for just three weeks, and when she returned to Hollywood all she had with her was $100,000 of jewellery, which she planned putting up for auction. Unfortunately, she let slip to columnist Sheilah Graham that she had smuggled this into the country: Graham included the snippet in her syndicated column, Sylvia was arrested by the FBI and fined $5,000 for contravening customs regulations. As if she had not humiliated him enough, Sylvia was an even bigger nuisance when, in July 1950, she accompanied Clark to Durango, Mexico, for the locations of *Across The Wide Missouri*. The great female icons – Garbo, Dietrich, Crawford and Marion Davies at the height of their popularity had got away with demanding palatial dressing-rooms on the studio backlots, but never in the history of the studio system had a star's *wife* made such demands as Sylvia.

Budgeted at $5 million, Clark's first Technicolor film since *Gone With The Wind* was directed by William Wellman, who after their set-tos on the set of *Call Of The Wild* had vowed never to work with him again. Time had cooled their tempers: now it was *Mrs* Gable who gave Wellman an almighty headache, transforming her husband's 'man's man' dressing-room cabin into a mock English country cottage. Not only did she commission a wicker fence and have the exterior landscaped with turf, rose bushes and even trees in gigantic sunken tubs so that she could relax in a 'homely' environment and paint – she hung pink lace curtains up at the windows! To Clark's way of thinking, this was Sylvia's way of launching yet another attack on his manliness. Most of the time, when not working, he went off hunting and slept rough under the stars with his buddies.

*Across The Wide Missouri* was promoted as an exercise in racial tolerance and harmony between the French and Scottish fur-trappers and the Blackfoot Indians upon whose territory they encroach. Clark played Flint Mitchell, whose peaceful expedition to found a settlement among the Blackfoot sees him falling for the chieftain's daughter (Maria Elena Marques). They marry and have a child. Needless to say MGM's unspoken anti-interacial policy ensured the marriage was short-lived and she is killed when Mitchell's men cause the Blackfoot to go on the warpath.

Clark's acceptance of the role led to his first major row with Sylvia. A champion for their cause, she resented the Indians in the film being played by made-up American actors delivering their lines in Blackfoot dialogue, with translators incorporated into the scenario so that each line was pronounced twice. She approached William Wellman and asked him why real Indians could not be used and subtitles added to the bottom of the screen. But he refused to listen.

The finished film bored preview audiences senseless and the director was forced to cut all of this out, reducing the production from 135 to 78 minutes, leaving over $2 million of Technicolor footage on the cutting-room floor. Wellman then completed the farce by hiring musicals star Howard Keel to narrate the story, in flashback, to fill in the missing chunks. Few were surprised when the film bombed.

The Gables' marriage limped along until the end of the year, by which time Clark had begun working on another Western, *Lone Star*, directed by Vincent Sherman. Co-starring were Ava Gardner and Broderick Crawford. Still reeling from the losses incurred by its predecessor, MGM commissioned this one to be shot in monochrome – an exercise which would not only cost less, but eliminate by way of its more subtle lighting techniques the ravages of premature ageing starting to show in Clark's face. According to Sylvia, she was relaxing in the tub when Clark barged into the bathroom, announced that he had had enough and that he was filing for divorce. The next day she sailed for the Bahamas, ostensibly to give him breathing space in the hope that he might change his mind. He did not, and when she returned to Elcino at the end of May, Clark had 'done a Joan Crawford' by having the locks changed.

Sylvia was the first to instigate divorce proceedings. She hired Jerry Giesler, long renowned as the best – and most expensive – celebrity lawyer in California. Giesler (1886–1962) had successfully defended mobster Bugsy Siegel when accused of killing Harry Greenberg; he had got Busby Berkeley off the hook from a triple-fatality drink-driving rap; and cleared Errol Flynn of statutory rape. Naturally, when Giesler filed a petition on Sylvia's behalf in Santa Monica on 31 May, Clark grew worried. He was convinced Giesler would encourage Sylvia to take him for every penny he had, as had happened with most of his other divorce cases.

To cope with the stress, and several years ahead of James Dean, Clark turned rebel at 49. He, Vincent Sherman, producer Wayne Griffin and the equally hard-drinking and bombastic Broderick Crawford hit the town every night, 'chasing skirt', as they called it, and there were reports of brawls and other booze-fuelled incidents. On one occasion the four ran amok at celebrity eaterie Chasen's, smashing tables and chairs, slinging food at the walls and the other diners. Clark paid for the damage, but was asked not to darken the establishment's doorway again. Another prank backfired when he paid a studio technician to rig Griffin's car: this exploded, very nearly writing off the vehicle and setting the producer alight. This time he was summoned to Louis B. Mayer's office and given a dressing down. Clark blamed it all on his failed marriage, and told Mayer to mind his own business.

In fact, Mayer had more than his share of problems to deal with as the dissension between him and Dore Schary escalated. Personality clashes notwithstanding, this was a repeat of what happened between Mayer and Thalberg: Schary had triumphed with a number of film projects that Mayer had wanted to reject, deeming them uncommercial. Mayer further accused his rival of courting publicity by using such films to exploit political propaganda, which of course was true. The matter was decided during the early summer of 1951 by MGM president Nicholas Schenck, who also took into consideration Mayer's failing health (he would die of leukaemia in 1957), and the fact that Schary was 20 years his junior.

Schenck, who would take a tumble himself a few years later and be demoted to company chairman, had until now played little active part in the creative side of filmmaking, leaving this to Mayer and Thalberg. Now he was called upon to exercise the upper hand over which of these war-mongering moguls would go: each had his own band of sycophants, and should both be permitted to stay, Schenk feared the studio would split into two factions and ultimately sink. Naturally the deciding factor was money. Schary's recent films had taken more at the box-office than Mayer's, and had attracted more Oscar nominations. According to Mayer's biographer, Scott Eyman, the choice of Schenk was an obvious one, simplified by Mayer having told one of MGM's directors, Bob Rubin, over the telephone, 'You can tell Mr Nicholas Schenck and Dore Schary that they can take the studio and choke on it!'

The next day, 31 May, *Variety* reported that Mayer would be tendering his resignation within the week, to take effect on 31 August. His golden handshake would be a cool $3 million, upon which by special arrangement he would have to pay only 25 per cent tax. Schenck, two-faced as they come, lied to the press that Mayer was retiring 'by mutual agreement', adding, 'Mr Mayer has given our industry leadership and inspiration, and now, in parting, his associates at [parent company] Loews's wish him success and happiness in his future activities.'

With Mayer gone, Clark and a few other 'shit-stirrers' were individually summoned to Schary's office: if the mighty Mayer could be toppled they were told, then absolutely no one in Hollywood was indispensable. Besides a new boss, Clark had to contend with a new agent. Phil Berg retired, prompting a pouting Gable to swear never to speak to him again. He signed with George Chasin of MCA, an organisation then in favour of liberating their clients from the restricted confines of the studio system so they could branch out and experience independence. Even so, despite his hatred of Schary, Clark would have to suffer working for him for another three years until his MGM contract expired.

In the meantime, there was his divorce. After lodging her petition, Sylvia had left for Honolulu again, hoping he might change his mind about reconciliation. Instead she was contacted by an intermediary and asked to remove her effects from the ranch. When she failed to do this – and Clark was informed by the Blecks that she had every intention of taking him to the cleaners – he decided to act first by applying for a Nevada divorce. This meant taking up a minimum six weeks' residency within the state, with the law declaring that should he leave the state boundary for more than 23 hours during this period, his application would be null and void.

Closing his California bank accounts so that these could not be seized (one newspaper reported he had stuffed his cash into suitcases and thrown these into the back of his car!) he drove to Nevada. Never one to do things by halves he had rented a ranch in Carson City. Here, with typical aplomb, he fell for young socialite Natalie Thompson, who far from the prying eyes of the press went hunting with him by day and kept his bed warm at night.

Because he was not permitted to leave Nevada, MGM sent work out to him: the terms of his contract offered him script, director, cinematographer and co-star approval and he was visited by producer Arthur Hornblow Jr to discuss his next project, *Sometimes I Love You*. Clark informed Hornblow that he would do the film with Ava Gardner – then just as quickly changed his mind, declaring he did not want to do it at all because the script was 'absolute shit'. When Dore Schary threatened him with suspension, his response was that he did not care. George Chasin was negotiating a deal that, if successful, would allow him to work for 18 months in Europe – still under contract to MGM, but tax-free. In fact, this was the studio again being parsimonious because rather than paying Clark from their US assets, his salary would come from MGM's European holdings, the funds from which could not be transferred back to America due to European currency laws introduced during the War. Similarly, European studio overheads were considerably cheaper than their Hollywood counterparts.

Taking Natalie Thompson with him – the press were fed the line that she was visiting her mother, who lived nearby – Clark returned to Encino for Christmas. The pair stayed together until the New Year but parted amicably. Clark then received word that Sylvia had obtained an injunction on his Nevada divorce – ostensibly because she had filed first – but that Jerry Giesler had drawn up the papers ready for him to sign. The parting of the ways took place on 3 February 1953 – the day after Clark's fifty-first birthday – in a New York hospital to which Sylvia had been admitted after breaking her leg in a fall. That same evening Clark showed up at Madison Square Garden, where he participated in a Republican rally organised to urge Eisenhower to stand for president in the November elections.

Clark returned to Hollywood – Dore Schary's executives had persuaded him not to suspend him. There he was presented with the script of *Mogambo*, a re-hash by John Lee Mahin (with more than a dash of Hemingway!) of his earlier *Red Dust*. In the wake of the hugely successful Stewart Granger-Deborah Kerr adventure film, *King Solomon's Mines*, Granger wanted to make another film with an Africa-based theme, but Schary had other ideas: the new *Red Dust* could *only* have Gable as its central figure. His character would be yet another extension of himself – the brash, but impervious to women white hunter let loose in a picturesque Kenya-Uganda setting. He asked for Ava Gardner as his leading lady, and his wish was granted.

Dore Schary tried to persuade Clark to waive the tax-free clause in his contract, which neither Clark nor George Chasin would agree to. Schary backed down, but a codicil was added. Unless given express permission to do so by Schary himself, Clark would be allowed to work in England only Monday through to Friday – his weekends would have to be spent on the Continent on account of the tax laws affecting MGM's United Kingdom holdings.

Within days of his agreeing to the new deal, Clark received a wire informing him that Sylvia had obtained a provisional divorce, citing the irreconcilable breakdown of their marriage owing to his mood-swings. And, contrary to what he had expected, the settlement drawn up by Jerry Giesler and the court was a reasonable one: Sylvia would receive 10 per cent of Clark's earnings during the coming year and 7 per cent for each of the next four – a predicted total of around $150,000. This was a mere drop in the ocean for a very wealthy woman who, soon afterwards, would marry the Prince Dimitri Djordjadze and dispense with Douglas Fairbanks' Rancho Zorro for a staggering $7.5 million.

On 6 May 1952, Clark sailed for France on the *Liberté*, waved off by 2,000 fans told they would not be seeing him again until the end of the following year. The previous day, he visited Loretta Young and 16-year-old Judy Lewis – the first and last time Judy would meet her father, though she would not find out for some time who he really was.

Judy had every reason to feel bitter. However, when speaking on *Living Famously* in her autobiography, *Uncommon Knowledge*, she is surprisingly calm – maybe the years in between had tempered her anger. In the documentary, she explains how she had come home from school and found Clark Gable standing in the living room. Taken aback, she assumed him to be there to see her mother on movie business and had excused herself. Loretta begged her to stay: she and Clark had sat on the couch and talked for over an hour. 'I was terrified,' she recalled, adding how warm he had been while questioning her about her life. 'Then he said it was time to go, and I got up and walked him to the front door. He bent down and kissed me on my forehead – and walked out the front door and out of my life.'

From Le Havre, Clark headed for Paris, where he spent a month in the company of a leggy 27-year-old Frenchwoman named Suzanne Dadolle, a mannequin with Elsa Schiaparelli, and needless to say another Lombard lookalike. How, where and when they met is not on record, but their affair was serious enough for their photograph to appear on the front page of *France-Soir*, with Dadolle flashing the topaz 'engagement' ring Clark had given her. They were also filmed by Paris-Pathé for the French newsreels, dancing in the Place de la Republique on Bastille Day.

Contractually, he was still tied to *Sometimes I Love You*, but while the script for *Mogambo* was being polished he made *Never Let Me Go*, with Gene Tierney and Kenneth More. In this lukewarm anti-Communist drama, something of a poor man's *Ninotchka*, he plays a hard-boiled reporter for the umpteenth time, this time falling for a Soviet ballerina. The reviews were appalling. The *New Yorker's* John McCarten drew his readers' attention to Clark's dimples, which he said now resembled craters on the moon – and concluded by way of a back-handed compliment, 'Mr Gable, at this point in his career, is grizzled, not withered'. Bosley Crowther of the *New York Times*, comparing this with Clark's last Russian excursion, observed, 'This is the same Gable as *Comrade X* – but a little older, a little fatter, a little shrewder and more cynical.' For Clark, it would prove his third turkey in a row.

He hated making the film, but said he had loved working with Gene Tierney. His preoccupation at this time, however, had not been attempting to seduce his co-star or wondering what his French girlfriend might be getting up to across the Channel – but with the customised Jaguar he had ordered upon his arrival in London. It was said to be the only one of its kind. The vehicle was delivered to him in Mullion Cove, Cornwall, where the locations were filmed – a region notorious for its narrow roads and sharp, dangerous bends. It was certainly ill suited for driving a monstrosity with a top speed of 100 mph, which Clark at once insisted on taking for a spin.

*Never Let Me Go* wrapped in the September, and Clark and his Jaguar boarded the boat train for Paris. A few days later he and Suzanne Dadolle set off on what should have been a slow drive to Rome, then Naples. By the time they reached Lake Como, Clark argued that he had driven far enough, and for three weeks they stayed at the Villa d'Este, where he spent virtually every waking moment on the resort's famous golf course. Dadolle was left to make her own way back to Paris when Clark received the call-to-arms from producer Sam Zimbalist, waiting for him in Rome. Zimbalist, the man responsible for *King Solomon's Mines*, was currently a white-hot property: his *Quo Vadis?* had just been announced as the highest grossing film since *Gone With The Wind*.

The locations for *Mogambo* (the Swahili word for passion) were to be filmed in Kenya, whose political climate was unstable, to say the least. The Mau Mau, the country's secret militant Kikuyu guerilla movement, had been operating for several months. Its aim was to end colonial rule – a goal achieved 10 years hence with the granting of independence and the election of Jomo Kenyatta. Before this happened, however, colonial government forces would set up a despicable exercise in ethnic cleansing, killing over 10,000 Kikuyu (Kenya's largest ethnic group), causing the Mau Mau to retaliate with unprecedented brutality. Sam Zimbalist and director John Ford were warned that nowhere in Kenya was guaranteed to be safe and that for everyone's sake it would be a case of getting in and out of the country as quickly as possible.

Faced with such a tense situation, MGM should of course never have been making the film in the first place. Zimbalist elected to fly everyone into Kenya, as opposed to travelling by the (then) more practical sea-route. This brought fierce protests from Clark, who had sworn never to fly again. For several days he ranted and raved, but on 2 November he, too, boarded the plane for Nairobi. This flew into a hailstorm over North Africa and had to make an emergency landing: several small planes were sent out to rescue the stranded passengers, and Clark is reported to have arrived at his destination looking more than a little green. Three days later he, Ford and the crew flew the 50 miles to the game reserve on the banks of the Kagera River, near Mount Kenya, which would serve as the film's backdrop. This was a journey which, on account of the Mau Mau's presence, they would make twice a day rather than staying put. Even so, the stars were afforded every conceivable luxury while shooting: 20 fully upholstered marquees which served as dining and dressing rooms, a movie theatre and fully equipped hospital, and a sports-entertainment centre, all with hot and cold running water in an area where this was in very short supply.

Evenings were spent propping up the bar at Nairobi's New Stanley Hotel. Clark and John Ford, both heavy drinkers, were matched glass for glass by Ava Gardner and her husband Frank Sinatra – officially accompanying her at her expense to celebrate their first wedding anniversary on 7 November, and her 30th birthday on Christmas Eve. And unofficially there because he wanted to keep an eye on her while she was around Clark for five months. It was here, during a meeting with the British Governor and his wife, that one of Ava's one-liners, secondary in their vulgarity only to Tallulah Bankhead's, entered Hollywood folklore. John Ford loathed Sinatra, and asked Ava in front of their distinguished guests what she saw in this '120-pound runt' – bringing the response, 'Oh, there's only 10 pounds of Frank, but 110 pounds of cock!'

Sinatra's sojourn in Africa was brief. Only days after Ava's outburst he was wired by his agent: Columbia Pictures wanted him to test for Fred Zinnemann's *From Here To Eternity*, which he hoped would put his flagging career back on track. He flew back to Hollywood, flunked the test (though the studio would subsequently change their mind and give him the part), and a few weeks later returned to Nairobi. Any hopes of Clark having a fling with Ava during his absence had been scuppered, however, when she was taken ill on the set. As per usual, a malady (amoebic dysentery) was invented for the benefit of the press, and by the time she was reunited with Sinatra, another troublesome pregnancy had been dealt with courtesy of a lightning trip to London's Chelsea Hospital.

John Ford was never an easy director to work with at the best of times. He had not wanted Clark for the film, and because he could not stand Ava Gardner either, he had pleaded with Sam Zimbalist to get him Maureen O'Hara for the part of Eloise Kelly. Zimbalist overruled him, explaining that of all the actresses he had considered for the part, only Ava was as 'sympathetically sluttish' as Jean Harlow had been. Ford, one of the rudest directors of his generation, would wind everyone up by addressing them by their surnames and made an example of Ava by frequently bawling her out in front of the entire unit, deriving sardonic pleasure from the stream of invectives which followed. On one occasion when he was *almost* kind to her, just to get his back up and feel comfortable with the Ford she had come to hate, Ava ripped off her clothes and ran around the set in the nude! Eventually, when he realised that he would never be able to outcurse her, Ford relaxed his hostile attitude towards her and they became friends.

The film's third lead, playing anthropologist's wife Linda Nordley, should have been English rose actress Virginia McKenna, but when she dropped out Zimbalist brought in 24-year-old Grace Kelly, the blonde, Philadelphia-born ice-maiden who had recently starred opposite Gary Cooper in *High Noon*. After *Mogambo* she would make just eight more films – most notably Hitchcock's *To Catch A Thief* (1955), before marrying Prince Rainier of Monaco and retiring from the movies.

*Mogambo*'s singular advantage over *Red Dust* is the colour photography and an authentic exotic location, as opposed to leftover sets from an old *Tarzan* film. Otherwise it lacks the raw sensuality of the original, made at a time when attitudes towards sex were less liberal, resulting in such productions being regarded as revolutionary in their approach to the very subject the Hays Office had been founded to condemn. Ava Gardner's brassy showgirl is at the same time warm and vibrant, the perfect homage to Harlow's Vantine. Grace Kelly, on the other hand, undeniably exquisitely beautiful, lacks the innocence of Mary Astor's earlier characterisation and is so *dull*, one wonders what white hunter Victor Marswell (Clark) sees in her, though he too looks weather-beaten throughout most of the film.

His saving grace is his tough-guy mien and a charisma which all but leaps from the screen.

Victor, who supplies animals for the world's zoos, arrives home from a hunting trip to find he has an unwelcome visitor – Eloise 'Honey Bear' Kelly, who has come here from New York to meet up with a maharajah, only to have missed him. 'A little trinket that's dropped from the maaharajah's turban,' someone says of her. And now she must stay put until the next boat arrives, the one which will be bringing anthropologist Donald Nordley (Donald Sinden) and his wife, Linda. Victor is tense because he has not seen a white woman in over a year. Even so he is apprehensive about the inarticulate showgirl who mistakes a rhinoceros for a kangaroo. 'I've seen 'em in London, Paris, Rome,' Victor growls. 'They start life in a New York nightclub and end up covering the world like a paint advertisement. Not an honest feeling from her kneecap to her neck!'

What Victor does not know is that just weeks after their wedding during the War, Kelly's fighter-pilot husband was killed in action and that she only turned to the high life in an attempt to blot out the tragedy. He changes his attitude towards her when she ends up in his arms after being frightened by his pet snake – they kiss passionately, and in the next scene she is at his piano crooning 'Coming Through The Rye'. Despite this heated moment, both feign indifference when the time comes to say goodbye. Victor gives her money to help with the journey ahead, adding that he will brain her if she does not accept it, and that in any case the money is only 'a 99-year loan'. 'This is one loan I'll pay back if I have to live 99 years to pay it back,' she retorts.

The Nordleys arrive. He is a stuffed shirt, while she is giddy, strait-laced, but devilishly pretty, and Victor loses no time in flirting with her once Kelly is out of the picture. Their relationship speeds up when Donald develops a tropical fever and she lashes out at Victor for the inadequate medical treatment she feels he is getting. 'What do you expect me to do,' he asks, 'Crawl into bed with him and hold his hand?' His reward is a slap across the face, followed by a show of hysterics. Then Linda decides to go walkabout in the jungle: Victor follows, rescues her from a marauding panther and they get caught in a storm that brings her suppressed feelings to the fore. This is a repeat of the scene in *Red Dust*, for by now Kelly has returned unexpectedly to the camp after her boat was marooned on a mud-bank.

At first, the two women in Victor's life are civil towards each other, a situation that disintegrates when all the protagonists dress formally for dinner, and Kelly quaffs too much wine. Henceforth, the scenario mirrors the earlier film. The men go off on a safari, where Victor intends coming clean about his feelings for Linda – until Donald reveals he dotes on her and that they will be starting a family once they get back to England. As before, the angry Linda pulls a gun and wings him when he confesses he has only been stringing her along, and once more Victor ends up with the strumpet – save that this time he intends making an honest woman out of her.

If Clark was hoping to get fresh with Grace Kelly, once the production moved to its secondary location in Uganda – by arranging a weekend trip to the beach resort of Malindi in the Indian Ocean – he would be disappointed. Aware of his intentions, Grace invited the Sinatras along for company. Then the unit moved to London, to finish off the sound-stage work.

For several weeks Clark stayed at the Connaught Hotel, drinking heavily most of the time and attending parties hosted by other 'exiled' Americans who, like himself, were taking advantage of the tax-free situation to work overseas. He forgot about pursuing Grace Kelly once he learned that old flame Lana Turner was in town, minus her husband of several months – Tarzan hunk, Lex Barker. Two years later, America's most controversial trash-mag ever, *Confidential*, would report (as was its wont, with little proof) that for a brief period in London, Ava and Lana were an item.

The *Mogambo* company split in April 1954. Clark travelled to Paris to meet up with Suzanne Dadolle. They drove to Rome, where the press reported their engagement, then just as quickly printed a retraction when Clark told reporters, 'I am – and so far as I can see – will remain a single guy until the right woman comes along. Unfortunately, she hasn't come along yet.' He returned to Paris, holed himself up at the Hotel Raphael for a few weeks and, in the September, completed his 'tax-exile trilogy' by travelling to the

Netherlands to make *Betrayed*. This would be his last film with Lana Turner and his last for MGM.

His agent, George Chasin, had flown to London at the studio's expense to personally hand him the script for the new film – and to inform him that, because of recent low box-office receipts, MGM were no longer interested in negotiating the new long-term contract they had discussed with him back in the States. As a compromise, Chasin added, the studio *were* willing to extend his current contract by two years. Clark refused to discuss the matter, and his stubbornness was interpreted – and welcomed – by Dore Schary as tantamount to him handing in his notice.

The locations for *Betrayed* were filmed in Amsterdam and Arnhem, and much was made of the fact that this was the first ever all-American production to be made in the country – though most of the supports were British. Directed by Gottfried Reinhardt, it was photographed by Freddie Young, who used the new Eastmancolor process to emulate the dark hues favoured by the Dutch masters. As such, it is a grim, pretty depressing affair. Set during the Nazi occupation, Clark played a Dutch intelligence officer and Lana dyed her hair dark to appear more convincing – according to the publicity – as a spy. *Newsweek* summed it up perfectly as 'a clumsy, overslow piece of melodrama'.

In the December, Clark returned to Hollywood, $500,000 richer, but unsure of his future, regretting his attitude towards MGM over his contract, but too proud to meet up with Dore Schary with a view to resolving the matter. He had 'compared notes' with old (and still occasionally burning) flame Joan Crawford, whose massively successful 16-year partnership with MGM had ended acrimoniously with her marching into Louis B. Mayer's office in June 1943 and announcing that she had had enough. Privately, she had hoped that Mayer might plead with her to stay and offer her a better deal with the studio than the one she already had, but he had called her bluff *and* demanded $50,000 to release her from her contract! Clark therefore knew that he would only be wasting his time talking to Schary, who was far more pig-headed than Mayer had ever been. Like Joan he left quietly, collecting his belongings from his dressing room, shaking a few hands and driving literally into the sunset to demolish a bottle of Scotch.

Reading some of the grossly exaggerated reports of his exit from MGM, one visualises the penultimate scene in *Queen Christina*. Following her abdication (a few years before Garbo's own departure), the much-loved Swedish monarch weaves her way through her tearful courtiers, who plead with her to stay and touch her gown as if it is some holy relic. There were no tears when Gable walked out of MGM for the last time, simply because no one *knew* he was leaving until he had passed through the front gates. Neither were the press entirely sympathetic. Louella Parsons and Hedda Hopper would never forgive Clark for not giving them an indication – not to mention an exclusive – of his plans. Ben Maddox was no longer interested in speaking to him because at a press gathering Clark cracked one 'fag' joke too many. Indeed, Maddox had been approached with a view to writing a piece for *Confidential*, who offered him a huge fee in exchange for a story that might have involved any one of the scores of actors and actresses he had serviced 'in the line of duty'. He had chivalrously declined the offer and it was therefore left to arch-enemy Dorothy Manners, who had had an axe to grind since Clark had threatened to punch her, to let the world know that he had been fired. This was not because his last few films had bombed but simply because he had gotten too big for his boots. According to Dore Schary, he was unworthy of the $500,000-plus MGM had been paying him, too.

Howard Strickilng, who would remain a close friend until the end, defended Clark vociferously: Gable was the most popular star MGM had ever had on their roster and everyone had adored him, from the executives down. This was what Strickling *believed* – but he had left out the most powerful executive of them all, Dore Schary. Ironically, had Schary waited a little longer – until after *Mogambo*'s release – things might have been different. The film opened to rave reviews and was a huge hit around the world. Offers of work flooded in from every major studio now that Clark was freelancing, offering massive fees, but he rejected them all. He needed to relax, he said, with the new woman in his life – or rather an old flame with whom he had recently become reacquainted, Betty Chisolm. A widow, another Lombard lookalike, and the extremely wealthy heiress to the Jones Meat-packing Company, she first met Clark in 1947 when he had been 'juggle-dating' with Anita Colby, Virginia Grey, Kay Williams and a few others.

There also appears to have been a fling with Grace Kelly, who had rejected Clark's advances before. They met again at the 1954 Oscars ceremony, where Grace had been nominated Best Supporting Actress for *Mogambo* – she lost to Donna Reed for *From Here To Eternity* (one of the film's eight awards), for which Frank Sinatra won Best Supporting Actor for his comeback role. Ava Gardner, nominated for Best Actress for *Mogambo*, lost out to Audrey Hepburn, who won for *Roman Holiday*.

A few days after the ceremony, Grace turned up at the Elcino ranch and presented Clark with a burro (a tiny Mexican packhorse) and it was his trysts with her that encouraged him in his latest eccentricity – emulating his white hunter character in their film. He bought a jeep, which he customised with zebra-skin seats and big-game hunting stickers. For weeks he drove around in full safari-suit and pith helmet, rifle across the dashboard, until reporters began hinting he may have been slightly mad. He even wore the get-up when summoned to script meetings, the first of which was with MGM editor Sam Marx – sent by Dore Schary to woo him back to the studio, only weeks after giving him his marching orders. Clark pretended to be interested in a project yet to be revealed, getting Schary to keep upping his fee – then telling him to shove his offer 'up his ass'.

It was Twentieth Century-Fox's Darryl F. Zannuck who eventually coaxed Clark out of 'retirement', assigning him to two films: *Soldier Of Fortune* and *The Tall Men*. The money was more than he had ever dreamed of earning with MGM – $400,000 per film, plus 10 per cent of the gross. For the first time in his career, he would be a millionaire. In the meantime, he decided to sort out his complicated love life. Betty Chisolm and Dolly O'Brien were, he declared, good pals who kept him company on outdoor jaunts, and fine for the odd tumble in the sack. What he really needed, he said, was the kind of stability he had had with Carole. Many of his friends were taking bets that the next Mrs Gable would be Grace Kelly, with Betty Chisolm sitting on the reserve bench. But Clark surprised everyone by announcing that his next wife would be another blast from the past.

Like himself Kay Williams was no shrinking violet. Born in Erie, Pennsylvania, in August 1916, she had married a local college student and the pair had relocated to New York, where she had worked for a while as a photographic model. Courtesy of a magazine photospread, she had met the Argentinian playboy millionaire, Martin de Alzaga Unzue, more familiarly known as Macoco. Kay divorced her husband, wed Macoco and the marriage had lasted all of 10 days. Next, she latched on to sugar tycoon Adolph Spreckels – often referred to as Adolph Hitler on account of his Nazi tendencies and psychotic streak.

Kay had married Spreckels in 1945, despite being warned by friends that he was a thoroughly bad lot. His first four wives all divorced him because he had bashed them senseless. A dancer with whom he had had a fling sued him for maiming her during a drunken rage, then trying to set her alight! His sixth wife (the one after Kay) would put up with him for a month, then have him arrested for breaking both her arms. Even after their divorce, Kay would not be safe from this obnoxious beast: during an argument over custody of their children, he kicked her unconscious and for his pains received a 30-day prison sentence. Few would be surprised when he came to a sticky end, in 1961, of a brain haemorrhage sustained by an unexplained blow to the head.

Already wealthy following the Unzue settlement, divorcing Spreckels in 1953 had left Kay $700,000 richer, with properties in San Francisco and Los Angeles. Her children with Spreckels – 3-year-old Joan and 5-year-old Adolph Jr, nicknamed Bunker after the location of Hitler's suicide – had each been set up with a $1 million trust fund by Spreckels' mother to make up for the harm her son had inflicted on Kay. At their divorce hearing, Kay testified that she had hardly ever seen her husband sober during the first three years of their marriage – that he frequently punished her by beating her with his shoe and once had come at her with an axe.

This second time around, to make her more his own, Clark addressed her only as Kathleen. The couple were inseparable until November 1954, when he flew to the Far East to make *Soldier Of Fortune*, a film almost doomed by way of the very manner in which it was assembled. Clark played Mike Lee, an exiled American trickster who smuggles counterfeit goods out of China into British-ruled Hong Kong. His co-star was Susan Hayward, recently divorced and the mother of 9-year-old twin boys she wanted to take with her on location. Fearing he might never see his sons again, her ex-husband obtained a court order preventing this, so Hayward felt she had no choice but to stay in Hollywood. Therefore all of her Hong Kong scenes were shot with a double, and the critics, weary of trying to work out who was who in the rear/disguise shots, gave the production a thumbs-down.

*The Tall Men*, with Jane Russell, fared little better. Directed by Raoul Walsh, this told of the rivalry between two cowpokes, Clark and Robert Ryan, on the Texas-Montana cattle drive (but filmed in Mexico). Naturally, Russell is the trophy they fight over, and there were no prizes for guessing whom she ended up with.

No sooner had Clark and Kay announced their marriage plans than, courtesy of an 'exclusive' in *Confidential* magazine, Josephine Dillon re-entered the Gable arena. The most feared scandal-rag of its day – selling upwards of 4 million copies per issue and with its motto, 'Tells The Truth And Names The Names' on the cover beneath the title, it had been launched by Robert Harrison in 1952. Its purpose, according to him, was to explore the nucleus of America's so-called den of iniquity – Hollywood – and flush out its corruption, though few were more corrupt than Harrison himself.

The gullible American public lapped up every word. While the more orthodox tittle-tattlers Hopper, Parsons and Maxwell checked the authenticity of their stories before publishing Harrison and his team employed devious methods to obtain their 'exclusives'. Whores of both sexes were paid to coerce stars into compromising positions, while a tiny machine, concealed in the bedroom, whirred away recording the evidence. For 'special' cases such as Elvis Presley and Rock Hudson (homosexuality), Lana Turner (sharing lovers) and

Errol Flynn (two-way mirrors) Harrison supplied his 'detectives' with tiny, sophisticated infra-red cameras. 'We all read it,' Marlene Dietrich told me. 'Not because it was any good – it was rubbish, worse even than some of the garbage you get on newsstands nowadays – but to find out if we were in it. Sometimes you never got an inkling until it was too late.'

In its July 1955 issue, *Confidential* ran the headline, 'The Wife Clark Gable Forgot'. He appeared on the cover looking every inch the movie star – next to his picture was a shot of a downtrodden Josephine Dillon. Robert Harrison had forked out $3,000 for a tour of her home, a run-down two-roomed house in North Hollywood. The accompanying feature did not specify the location, though it did print Clark's address for the benefit of those fans and reporters who had not pestered him thus far. The gist of the piece was to inform the world how mercenary he had become since finding fame, courtesy of this unfortunate woman. What it did not add was that *he* had bought the property for Dillon some years before, was also paying for its upkeep, but that Dillon had deliberately allowed the place to fall into a state of disrepair in the hope of shaming him some day.

Clark's agent, George Chasin, advised him to sue the magazine, but he was forced to adopt the same stance of many of Harrison's other victims. Though most of his exclusives were hugely, if not entirely fabricated, Clark knew there was always the danger that Harrison or one of his cronies might some day hit the jackpot. He, along with Rock Hudson, James Dean, and a good many others were terrified of their gay affairs being made public. Therefore he allowed Dillon to have her say, in the hope that Harrison would leave him alone and pick on someone else.

In fact, the double-dealing Harrison had no intention of running an exposé on *any* suspected homosexual star. Ben Maddox, along with the actor who was living with Rock Hudson, were at the same time as Josephine Dillon offered large amounts of money for their stories, but only so that Harrison could inform the studios and entice them into paying him even more *not* to publish. It was all very well, he knew, to run detailed stories about thieves, gangsters, bluebeards and stars who were promiscuous with members of the opposite sex, but homosexuals were part of an alien group of individuals whose activities were taboo. Seven years after the Kinsey Report revealed that one in ten American men actually *enjoyed* having sex with other men and concluded that this should not be considered abnormal, few of even *Confidential*'s liberated regulars would have wanted to acknowledge their existence by reading about them.

James Dean played Harrison at his own game, announcing to all and sundry, 'I've had my cock sucked by five of the biggest names in Hollywood, all of them guys!' And within weeks of being menaced by the magazine, both Clark and Rock Hudson would marry, though Clark does not appear to have rushed into matrimony for any other reason than he was in love. Robert Harrison would get his come-uppance in 1957, in the so-called 'Trial of 100 Stars' spearheaded by Dorothy Dandridge and Liberace. Collectively they would sue him out of business, though by then Clark would be past caring what the scandalmongers had to say about him.

Clark and Kay were married in Minden, Nevada, on 11 July 1955: Al Menasco and Kay's sister, Elizabeth, were witnesses. The honeymoon took place at Menasco's estate in California's Napa Valley. Then began the process of Kay attempting to compromise while fitting into Clark's home environment. Behind her was Carole's ghost, the yardstick against which every subsequent woman in his life had been measured. Carole's foibles and imperfections had died with her, and it was a case of would-be successors contenting themselves with walking in the shadow of her sun. Then there was the danger of treading on eggshells, trying not to make the same mistakes as the dreaded Sylvia. 'When I married that one, I must have been pissed out of my head,' Clark told a British reporter, adding that within a week of Sylvia's departure, Carole's room had been restored to its former shrine.

Kay reminded Clark of Carole, physically, and on account of her lively spirit and colourful vocabulary. She also occasionally called him 'Pa', but that is as far as it went. When they married, he volunteered to sell the ranch so that she would not be constantly reminded of her predecessor. She refused to let him do this, demanding just one concession: she asked that Carole's gun collection be taken off display and that Clark's gun-room be kept locked so that the children would not get their hands on them.

Changes were effected to both of their lives. There were fewer parties at Elcino and social outings were restricted to official showbusiness or studio events. They never stayed out late, protesting they had to get back to the family. And Clark, whose libido had remained sky-high since he learned what it was for, told friends that from now on he would never look at another woman. This he would find impossible, of course. Some outsiders regarded the revised existence as a little *too* idyllic. In an interview with *The American Weekly*, Kay described a typical day in the life of the Gables to a gullible young female reporter. The family always rose early, she said, and once the children had been collected for school, Clark would disappear outside to help his groundsmen with whatever manual tasks were scheduled for that day – even the toughest jobs were not a problem for him. Lunch would be eaten next to the pool, and in the afternoon Clark and his agent would discuss business matters while she worked her way through the house re-arranging the flowers. Later, they would sip cocktails while watching the children eat their dinner, and afterwards Kay would pick up her needlepoint and maybe embroider some meaningful little motif on her husband's favourite slippers. Sometimes the whole family would gather around the *colour* television – or play bingo. On special occasions, Clark would set up the projector and they would watch one of his old movies: he had copies of them all except for *Gone With The Wind*. Then, when the children had been put to bed, they would drink champagne until the early hours and reminisce over times long gone.

In September 1955, the press reported that Kay was pregnant – some hinting that conception had taken place *before* her marriage, which was true. Yet no sooner had Hedda, Louella et al. begun sharpening their claws for the attack than Kay was hospitalised with a viral infection which caused her to miscarry. To help her recover, Clark took her on an extended cruise, then embarked on his next project. Tired, he said, of accepting second-rate scripts that were guaranteed to end up as box-office flops, he formed his own production company, Russ-Field Gabco, with Jane Russell and her husband Bob Waterfield.

Russell and Waterfield had acquired the rights to Margaret Fitt's Western story, *The Last Man In Wagon Round*. This was deemed an unsuitable title for a Gable film, so as a tribute to Clark's standing in the Hollywood community it was changed to the even less appropriate *The King And Four Queens*. Cynics in the know might have thought this alluded to the Haines-LaRocque-Brown-Maddox episodes in his life that he was desperately trying to forget, particularly with *Confidential* reporters snooping around the set.

The 'queens' of course were a quartet of attractive females: Jean Willes, Barbara Nichols, Sara Shane and Eleanor Parker. These are the only inhabitants, along with their stalwart mother-in-law, in a ghost town where a stash of gold is hidden by the four bandit brothers they were married to and now believed to be dead. Only one of the ladies knows the exact location, and as Clark is after the gold he seduces them one by one until he gets his answer – then he marries Eleanor Parker and we are led to believe they live happily ever after.

Clark was disappointed when Jane Russell declined to play the feisty matriarch, offering the role to Jo Van Fleet – the previous year, in her first screen role (aged just 35), she had portrayed James Dean's mother in *East Of Eden* and won an Oscar. Jimmy visited her on the set, taking time off from *Giant*, which he was filming with Elizabeth Taylor and Rock Hudson. Then, on Saturday 1 October, director Raoul Walsh sent everyone home early and production closed down for the day: news had come in of 24-year-old Jimmy's death, the previous evening in a car crash near Salinas.

Acting-wise, Van Fleet was superior to everyone, Clark included, in *The King And Four Queens*. When it was brought to his attention that some of the critics who had seen the rushes were forecasting she had every chance of being Oscar-nominated, he decided to do something about it. Contractually permitted the last say over editing, he had Van Fleet's most powerful scenes cut from the finished print. The critics exacted their revenge by slating his performance. *Time* dismissed the film as 'a tawdry Western', while Bosley Crowther of the *New York Times* mocked Clark's former status by writing it off as 'a dreary comedown for Hollywood royalty'. Soon after its release, the Russ-Field Gabco partnership was dissolved.

It was out of the frying pan and into the fire so far as Clark's next venture was concerned. Warner Brothers assigned him to *Band Of Angels,* a Civil War drama filmed on location in Baton Rouge, Louisiana, with Raoul Walsh at the helm for the third and last time. Jack Warner boasted this would be Clark's finest film since *Gone With The Wind* and confidently hired Max Steiner to write the score. The production was also hastily assembled to compete against MGM's $6 million civil war epic, *Raintree County,* starring Montgomery Clift and Elizabeth Taylor, scheduled for release at the end of the year.

In fact, many consider this to be the *worst* film Gable ever made. He played plantation owner and former slave-trader Hamish Bond, who rescues octoroon (one-eighth Negro blood) slave Amantha Starr, and against convention falls in love with her. Clark wanted the part to be given to an unspecified black actress, but, where Raoul Walsh and Jack Warner were concerned, interacial relationships were still deemed undesirable, so it went to Yvonne de Carlo. The film was rush-released several months ahead of *Raintree County* – and bombed spectacularly. 'Here is a movie *so* bad that it has to be seen to be disbelieved,' observed *Newsweek.*

In June 1956, Kay Gable suddenly fell ill and doctors at the Cedars of Lebanon diagnosed angina pectoris. This kept her out of action until the October, though even then she was still not well enough to accompany Clark to the première of *Giant,* at Grauman's Chinese Theater. Incredibly (if not ridiculously), during the early stages of production director George Stevens had considered casting Clark in the central role of Texan millionaire Bick Benedict, eventually played by Rock Hudson, 24 years his junior. Clark was filmed escorting Joan Crawford into the theatre and once more the hacks began speculating. Joan had married Pepsi-Cola chairman Alfred Steele in May 1955, who would later be revealed as the great love of her life *after* Gable – but she and Clark had never stopped having feelings for one another. Neither went home to their respective partners that night.

# Chapter Ten

# SAFE IN THE ARMS OF MA

Clark's next film would prove his best since *Mogambo*, an exercise in casting caution to the wind by teaming Hollywood's former romantic hero and still loveable lecher with its perennial virgin, Doris Day. Paramount's *Teacher's Pet*, produced by William Perlberg and George Seaton, and directed by the latter was scripted by husband and wife team Michael and Fay Kanin, who had written *Woman Of The Year* (1941) for Spencer Tracy and Katharine Hepburn. It was a gentle sex-comedy, a precursor to the trilogy Doris later made with Rock Hudson. The format is almost the same: Clark the worldly cad assumes another identity to seduce the gullible Doris, who finds him at first reprehensible, then starts to fall in love with him so that by the time his true identity is revealed, she is willing to forgive him anything. There is also the stooge who provides the protagonists with a friendly shoulder to lean upon. In the Day-Hudson films this would be Tony Randall, here it is Gig Young, who was subsequently nominated for an Oscar.

The idea worked well. Clark and Doris were perfectly matched – she getting laughs with her dotty antics, he for his quirky facial expressions and quick-fire delivery. The film was a smash hit, leaving fans of both stars clamouring for more. Clark (for the first and last time in his career) even agreed to plug it at that year's Oscars' ceremony, broadcast live on television in March. He and Doris had been asked to present the award for Best Scriptwriter. The title-track, written by Roy Webb and Joe Lubin and recorded by Doris, stormed into the American charts.

Far from looking ropy as in his last few films, though this was shot in monochrome to reduce the risk, Clark comes across as cosy and affable as the roguish Jim Gannon, the editor of the *New York Chronicle*, whose tough exterior is not completely impenetrable. He adopts a fatherly attitude towards errand boy-cub reporter Barney Kovac (Nick Adams), allowing the boy to write the occasional piece that he guides him through in his spare time. Yet, like any caring father, Jim agrees with the boy's mother that he needs an education, respecting her request to fire him because he knows this is for the best.

Such is Jim's reputation for fairness and for writing good stories that Erica Stone (Doris Day), the eminent lecturer in journalism, wants him as guest speaker at one of her university classes. The two have never met, and he is very much against the idea – not only does he dislike female teachers, he firmly believes the journalist can only learn his trade through experience, not books. He sends her a letter explaining in no uncertain terms why he finds such lessons a waste of time. When his boss *orders* him to go, he assumes the guise of Jim Gallagher, feigning that the only knowledge he has of the trade comes from a reporter friend with whom he plays poker on weekends.

Upon seeing how pretty she is, Jim falls for Erica and repeats what his 'friend' told him: 'He said you'd be a frustrated old biddy who'd read all the text books and never written a line – how someone like that's like betting on a three-legged horse!' Then he squirms when she reads out his letter to her students. Erica gives him his first assignment. He pens a piece about a street killing, purloined from another reporter, which impresses and moves her – the best work any student has ever handed in, she says, and compares what he has written with a recent newspaper headline: 'BLOOD-CRAZED SEX MANIAC STRIKES AGAIN' the kind of reporting she hates:

ERICA: Journalism is so much more then blood and sex . . .
JIM: You liked my story about that murder. That's blood, isn't it?
ERICA: Now, wait a minute. I didn't say that I disapproved of blood. It's just that . . .
JIM: How do you feel about sex?

ERICA: Why, I'm all for it" I [shocked by what she has said] . . .
Goodbye, Mr Gallagher!

Jim is hooked, and unable to concentrate on his work. When he
should be jotting down notes, he is doodling her picture on his pad.
Then jealousy raises its head when he hears Erica talking on the
phone to a mysterious Dr Hugo Pine (Gig Young) and learns that
these two have been spending a lot of time together. Confident he
has more to offer her than the (he assumes) boring, elderly academic,
he grabs her and kisses her so passionately that her knees buckle –
exactly how Doris Day is said to have reacted when kissed for the first
time by Clark Gable.

Cut to the Bongo Club, where Jim is with his bimbo girlfriend,
Peggy (Mamie Van Doren), the resident chanteuse and poor man's
Mae West, whose novelty number, 'The Girl Who Invented Rock 'n'
Roll', doesn't match up to the hype it received at the time. Erica is
also here with Pine, and because he is youngish and good-looking,
Jim realises he has competition: the pair spike each other's drinks but
become friends when Jim learns that Pine is only collaborating with
Erica on a book. The scene where Gig Young and Clark are fixing
drinks is, however, sad, and would have benefited a retake: Clark is
clearly suffering from the shakes, slopping his drink and dropping the
ice.

Now that the way is open for him to pursue her, Jim tells Pine of
the effect Erica has had on him: 'Before, I had contempt for eggheads
like her. I was an obstinate, prejudiced, inconsiderate, wholehearted
louse, but at least I was something. Now that I've come to respect
your kind I'm just a big, understanding, remorseful slob – a complete
zero!' There is, however, a temporary rupture in their relationship
when Erica visits the newspaper office and finds out who Jim really
is. He, likewise, has discovered that her father was a Pulitzer Prize-
winning newspaperman, though this does not prevent him from
opining that Mr Stone's kind of old-fashioned, non-commercial
journalism stinks! Later, Erica goes through some of her father's
features and realises Jim was right. The film ends, maybe a little
disappointingly, not with them in each other's arms, but with Jim

agreeing to guest lecture to Erica's students, which is what she wanted in the first place.

There are said to have been on-set problems between Doris Day and Mamie Van Doren, and between Clark and Nick Adams. Van Doren, probably peeved that Doris's reprisal of her 'showstopper number' in *Teacher's Pet* (while she and Clark are in Erica's apartment) was considerably better and sexier than hers, later claimed that Doris behaved unpleasantly towards her on the set. This is hard to believe: when one reads contemporary reports of the goings-on at Day's other films, particularly her trilogy with Rock Hudson, one wonders how the cameraman managed to shoot a frame without cracking up on account of the hilarity and practical jokes. 'Doris failed in take after take to smile radiantly while watching me dance,' Van Doren bellyached to Doris's biographer, Eric Braun, obviously very sure of herself and missing the point completely – the fact that in the film the two women are supposed to be *rivals* for Jim Gannon's affections.

The dilemma with Nick Adams – or rather Clark's reluctance to work with him – stemmed from Gable's homophobia, and the young actor's position among Hollywood's so-called 'open-secret' closeted gay community – the fact that Adams appeared to be aware of all its murky secrets, past and present. Nick Adams (1931–68) had been James Dean's last lover, and after his death had an affair with Elvis Presley which 'Colonel' Tom Parker, Elvis's cash-obsessed manager shelled out a fortune to prevent being revealed in a *Confidential* exposé. Boastful, predatory and promiscuous, Adams supplied Dean lookalike male whores to big-name actors, Hollywood businessmen and studio personnel – including some of those working on *Teacher's Pet*, and he was also involved with one of the actors in the cast. Clark was terrified that Adams, who knew William Haines, might have been filled in about his gay past. Though it does not show in their scenes together, away from the set he was so nasty to Adams that the younger actor wanted to leave the production.

Doris Day, though almost certainly she would not have been told the real reason for this, was asked to persuade him to stay. Soon afterwards, she invited Adams to join the cast of *Pillow Talk*, the first of her films with Rock Hudson. He also made *Come September* with Hudson and Gina Lollobrigida. In February 1968, having become a household name by way of the TV series, *Saints And Sinners*, Nick Adams was found dead of a drugs overdose – and Elvis Presley would suffer a nervous breakdown.

*Teacher's Pet* was made back-to-back with *Run Silent, Run Deep*, generally regarded as the best submarine movie ever made. It was promoted by United Artists as a cross between *Mutiny On The Bounty* – on account of the fierce rivalry between the two major characters – and *Moby Dick*, because of the Gable character's paranoid obsession with tracking down the Japanese destroyer which sank the last submarine he commanded. The film was the brainchild of established Hollywood beefcake star Burt Lancaster (1913–94). Clark played Richardson, the commander and sole survivor of a World War II submarine in the dreaded Bongo Straits by a Japanese Akikaze destroyer. Such is his desire to blow this to bits that when he gets his next commission aboard the *Nerka*, he drills his men, Bligh-style, risking all their lives to return to the Straits, against the orders of his superiors, to pursue his quarry. Lancaster is his lieutenant, Bledsoe, who feels that *he* should have been put in charge of the craft, yet after almost inciting the crew towards mutiny he becomes just as preoccupied with sinking the destroyer as Richardson.

This change of attitude, however, was not in Edward Beach's original story: he and scriptwriter John Gay were all for Bledsoe seizing control of the submarine, but Clark protested that the critics, confusing the actor with the part, would interpret this as a sign of his own weakness. 'Washed-up' or not, Gable would never accept himself as anything less than the *übermensch* hero, so the scriptwriter provided him with a terminal illness which, as this worsens, compels him to allow Bledsoe to take over – but only under his personal supervision.

Though the interiors were filmed aboard real submarines on a Universal backlot, the ocean and aerial locations were shot at the same San Diego US Navy base where Clark had made *Hell Divers*. Fireworks were anticipated between Gable and Burt Lancaster, another actor with a king-sized ego – and, complicating matters, one third of the Hecht-Hill-Lancaster production company (with Harold Hecht and James Hill), who were financing the project. In fact, the two got along remarkably well. Lancaster had always looked up to Clark, and despite being advised that the ageing star was probably past his best, disagreed to the tune of the $500,000 he offered him to do the film – *and* to insist that Clark's name appear above his in the credits. Also, it was only the third Gable film (the others being *The White Sister* and *Parnell*) where fans got to watch him die at the end – surviving just long enough to give the final command to sink his enemy.

In the June, 22-year-old Judy Lewis married television director Joseph Tinney, at the Roman Catholic Church of the Good Shepherd – having just learned who her father really was. Speaking on the BBC's *Living Famously*, she explained how, two weeks before the ceremony, she had almost called the whole thing off: 'I told my fiancé, "I can't marry you because I don't know who I am!"' She added how Tinney had known the truth all along (though she did not say how he had known), and that her priest had advised her against confronting Loretta, declaring she would never open up. She did, but not until 1966. 'Total strangers knew the story,' Judy concluded, 'I was the only one who didn't.' As a matter of courtesy, Clark and Kay were invited to the wedding, but declined. He did not even send his daughter a card.

Meanwhile, on the strength of *Teacher's Pet*, he was offered another Perlberg-Seaton comedy, *But Not For Me* – directed by Walter Lang, the husband of Carole's best friend, Fieldsie. The two men had fallen out over some trifle soon after Carole's death, and the film (a remake of *Accent On Youth*, a hit for Sylvia Sidney in 1935), is supposed to have been Lang offering Clark a long overdue olive branch. His co-stars were Lilli Palmer, Lee J. Cobb – and 27-year-old Carroll Baker, who a few years earlier had shocked Middle America with her portrayal of the mentally retarded teenage sex kitten in *Lolita*. The story was a familiar one: a middle-aged man (Clark) ditches his wife (Palmer) for a younger model (Baker), then realises the error of his ways and goes back to her. The critics made much of the age gap between the two stars. *Life* magazine was generous in describing Clark as 'still the indestructible all-round charmer, even at fifty-seven' – others were not so sensitive when reminding readers of his double chin, sagging jowls, lived in face and paunch.

When shooting wrapped, Gable took a well-earned break: he and Kay spent several weeks in Palm Springs, mostly at the Bermuda Dunes Golf Club. They so fell in love with the area that they bought a house nearby, and again there was talk of selling the ranch. But it *was* only talk: as much as he loved and doted on Kay, Clark was not yet ready to let go of Carole's spirit. It is now known that he suffered a mild heart attack while golfing at the Bermuda Dunes – almost certainly not his first – and that it was dismissed by himself and Kay as nothing more serious than heartburn. The doctors who treated him, not for the first time, warned him to lay off the cigarettes and booze, and to take things easy for a while. As usual, Clark pleased himself. He had just been contracted to play opposite a sex goddess even younger and more voluptuous than Carroll Baker – 24-year-old Italian beauty, Sophia Loren.

*It Happened In Naples* had originally been scripted for British star Gracie Fields, then the Isle of Capri's most celebrated resident. For several years, visitors to her Canzone del Mare complex, who stopped off at Naples to catch the boat across to the island, had complained of being pestered by the *scugnizzi* – the local name for the city's astonishing 50,000 homeless children under the age of 16. Translated literally as 'spinning tops' on account of the way they operated, these were little more than a decidedly rough army of thugs, thieves, rent-boys and con-merchants. Gracie, along with a local priest, had come to the conclusion that all they needed was somewhere comfortable to sleep and food in their bellies: the two had opened several refuges. As such the film's producer, Jack Rose, and writer-director Mel Shavelson had created especially for Gracie the role of the eccentric, middle-aged Englishwoman who befriends one of these unfortunate urchins. She, however, had turned it down, claiming the *scugnizzi* needed helping, not exploiting. Shavelson therefore changed the gender and nationality of the part, and offered it to Clark.

Even so, the film was fashioned more around Sophia Loren than him. Born Sofia Scicolone in Rome in 1934, but raised near Naples, this illegitimate daughter of an aspiring actress and a Neapolitan peasant had, after several bit-parts, played the lead in *Aida* in 1953, with her voice dubbed by Renata Tebaldi. Her big break had come the following year in Vittorio De Sica's *L'Oro di Napoli*. Five years on, back on home turf, Loren insisted on surrounding herself with as many old colleagues as possible – extras, bit-parts, technicians and De Sica himself – to thank them for helping her back then. Besides Clark, the only non-Italians involved with the production in a major capacity were Jack Rose, Mel Shavelson, and cameraman Robert Surtees, who had worked on *Mogambo* and recently completed *Ben Hur*.

Neither was there any question of Clark romancing his leading lady. Kay and her children had accompanied him to Europe, ostensibly for a three-month vacation that had taken in London, Amsterdam and Salzburg, where they celebrated their fourth wedding anniversary. Now the children and their nanny were ensconced at a rented villa near Anzio, on the outskirts of Rome. Kay, however, as if suspecting he could never be trusted, never left Clark's side for a moment. Sophia Loren, too, was happily married. In 1957 she had wed her Svengali producer Carlo Ponti, 24 years her senior. It was he who persuaded her to learn to speak English as a result of which she had been cast alongside Cary Grant and Frank Sinatra in *The Pride And The Passion* and, in 1958, opposite Grant once more in *Houseboat*.

Shot in the autumn of 1959, *It Happened In Naples* is said to have inspired Michel Simon's later *Le Vieux Homme et l'Enfant*, the story of the anti-Semitic farmer who befriends a Jewish boy in Occupied France. Simon's gruff voice and weather-beaten face complimented every role he played in an illustrious career, and the same may be said for Clark here. The portly appearance and undisguised facial lines perfectly suit the avuncular duties he feels he has to perform as Mike Hamilton, the war veteran. Hamilton returns to Naples to reclaim Fernando (Marietto), the illegitimate son of his recently deceased brother and his common-law wife, and takes him back with him to Philadelphia, where Mike believes he will have a better life and education than in a Neapolitan slum.

It is a pretty noisy affair, but the locations are sublime, more so when the scenario shifts to Capri, where Fernando lives with his Aunt Lucia (Loren). The boy is a little horror, who smokes, drinks wine and fleeces the tourists, while Lucia performs in a local café-concert. Throughout the film we get to see the Gable of old, who menaced but excited Crawford, Shearer et al., save that to his disadvantage he also comes across as yet another know-it-all American tourist – growling at waiters, complaining loudly about the food and transport, and flashing his money around as if this will solve every problem known to man.

Naturally Mike falls in love with Lucia, but this time the tables are turned when *she* seduces *him*. They skinny-dip (or rather their silhouetted stand-ins do) in the Blue Grotto, but it all turns out to be a front on her part, in the hope that the subsequent court hearing will allow her to keep the boy – and it does. Feeling guilty, however, she hands him over to Mike – who changes his mind at the railway station in Naples, realising (at the same time as Lucia realises she really does love Mike) that Fernando belongs with his own people, rich or poor. As such the ending is unsatisfactory because we never learn if the lovers have been reunited.

Making the film was a nightmare for Sophia Loren, who with Carlo Ponti had been served a writ by the Italian authorities, who claimed their Mexican marriage was illegal. Though Ponti had divorced his first wife, Giuliana Fiastri, several years earlier, as divorce was not recognised by the Vatican, he was facing a bigamy charge and Loren was branded in some circles as a scarlet woman when she was nothing of the kind. Eventually, the Ponti-Loren marriage would be annulled: in 1965 he became a French citizen, acquired a divorce from Fiastri from there and 're-married' Loren. In the meantime, with the couple living in exile on the French Riviera to evade arrest, Loren had been secreted into Italy to make the film. And when Clark learned that she would be spending her 25th birthday alone, he worked behind the scenes – paying to have Ponti flown into Naples, under an alias, then ferried across to Capri, where a surprise party had been arranged at Gracie Fields' complex. The evening ended with Gracie serenading the gathering with

'Summertime In Venice', which she was to have sung in the film.

Clark, Kay and the children stayed on at the Anzio villa until the end of November. He told reporters that all he wanted to do for the foreseeable future was play golf and relax with his family as far away as possible from the pressures of Hollywood. Then he changed his mind and for several weeks pored over scripts sent out to him, including one which would sadly turn out to be his swan song: Arthur Miller's *The Misfits*.

The original story had been published in *Esquire* under the title, *The Mustangs*, but changed at the screenplay stage: 'misfit' was rodeo slang for a horse too small or too weak for riding or farm work. In Miller's case it also applied to the actors he had in mind for the film version's protagonists – Clark Gable, Montgomery Clift, Eli Wallach and Marilyn Monroe. Additionally, the story was based on fact. While in Nevada establishing legal residency to divorce his first wife and marry Monroe, Miller had bumped into a trio of washed-up cowboys reduced to earning their crust roping wild horses and selling them for pet food. Miller, whose debut screenplay this was, had given Clark an alter-ego: tough, hard-drinking, over-the-hill redneck Gay Langland, who has been through the mill and whose life takes on a new meaning when he meets a beautiful, but unstable, much-younger woman. Obviously there were comparisons to be made with Clark's own life: the trauma of Carole Lombard's death and the feeling of emptiness this had left in its wake, the living disaster that had been Sylvia, the slump in his career and its subsequent resurrection, his happy marriage to Kay.

Such a scenario, today, would not have seen the light of day, with its references to the senseless slaughter of wild animals. Neither would a man as paranoid about his sexuality as Clark have played a character named Gay. Back in 1960, however, when society was less finicky about animal cruelty and the word 'gay' had a totally different meaning, his only concern while deliberating over whether to accept the role was the physical and mental condition of his co-stars. Indeed, as soon as details of the film were announced, journalists began to lay bets on which of the three main stars would crack up – or die – first.

Thirty-nine-year-old Monty Clift had never completely recovered from the car crash, four years earlier, which had almost cost him his life. En route from a party at Elizabeth Taylor's Benedict Canyon home, he had driven into a telegraph pole, smashing his face against the dashboard. Elizabeth had saved his life by shoving her fingers down his throat to remove two dislodged front teeth and surgeons had almost totally reconstructed one side of his face. Life for Monty, even before the accident, had been a saga of drink and prescription drugs – his way of facing up to the demons brought about not just by his homosexuality, but astonishingly for one of the most handsome actors of his generation, a pathological loathing of his own body – particularly his overtly hirsute upper half. He was also suffering from cataracts and in danger of losing his sight, a point exploited by arch-sadist Arthur Miller, who, adding Method to the proceedings by getting Clark to pronounce, when Monty kept bumping into the scenery all the time, 'You got good eyes, old boy!'

Marilyn Monroe, in what would be her last completed film, was an absolute wreck, clinging to her marriage *and* her sanity by the slenderest of threads. Even Clark, according to biographer Warren G. Harris, denounced her as 'a self-indulgent twat', though he would soon revise this opinion once he began working with her. Shooting should have begun on this guaranteed recipe for disaster on 3 March 1960 ahead of the mercilessly hot Nevada summer. The first delay occurred when director John Huston, one of the most uncom-promising in the business, took an instant dislike to Miller's screenplay and ordered a rewrite. Miller complied, but worked on it page by page while the film was shooting, adding to the chaos because the actors never saw their lines until they turned up on the set.

Clark's agent, George Chasin, had drawn up a list of contractual demands with United Artists: a record fee of $750,000, along with 10 per cent of the gross, which Huston could not have cared less about. What irked him and everyone else involved with the production was Gable's insistence on working on a nine-to-five basis and not one minute either way unless the studio paid him overtime at the rate of $48,000 a week, which of course would be obligatory for night scenes.

Overtime would also be paid, his contract demanded, in the event of shooting running over the proposed 16-week schedule.

Once the studio agreed to his terms, Clark was sent for a medical to placate their insurers – which he failed. The doctors told him to give up smoking and drinking, which he did for a little while, and further suggested a crash diet to bring his weight down to its usual 195 pounds. In Italy it had soared to 230 pounds, he claimed, because Sophia Loren encouraged him to eat too much pasta. Two weeks later he was examined again and given the all clear. In the interim period he and George Chasin held discussions with Howard Hawks, a close friend of Monty Clift, who in 1948 had directed Monty and John Wayne in *Red River*. Hawks wanted Clark and Wayne to do *Hatari!*, a *Mogambo*-style travelogue-drama centred around another pair of misfits who trap wild animals in Africa and sell them on to zoos and circuses. Wayne would eventually make the film, but not with Gable.

The next major delay involved Marilyn Monroe, who on account of an Actors Guild strike was unable to finish *Let's Make Love* on time. To be more precise, when the strike ended, *she* walked off the set because Arthur Miller refused to include a part in *The Misfits* for her co-star and lover, Franco-Italian crooner Yves Montand. If Montand could not appear in the new film, she declared, then she had no intention of completing the other one. Eventually she capitulated, but it took her until early July to finish *Let's Make Love* – only to have Montand dump her and return to his forgiving wife, Simone Signoret.

United Artists announced that *The Misfits* would not begin shooting on 18 July – Clark threatened to tear up his contract on account of the delay, then shrugged his shoulders and headed with Kay for Minden, where they had married on 11 July. They celebrated their fifth anniversary there. They travelled on to the location house provided by the studio on the outskirts of Reno where they were joined by her children.

Surprisingly, Clark bonded with Montgomery Clift, in spite of his dislike of Method actors and having been made aware how Monty had mocked him in the past – not his physical appearance, but over what he saw as Gable's 'distinct lack of real acting ability'. In his opinion, Clark Gable had played the same role – himself – for the past 30 years. So too was Clark concerned about working with a homosexual who, like Nick Adams, knew about every gay secret in Hollywood. This, however, was not the cause of their first on-set row, but Monty's tendency to fluff his lines. When he did this once too often during rehearsals and Clark called him a 'sleazy little runt' and cruelly threatened to smash the other side of his face, Monty barked back, 'Why don't you take out your dentures and kiss my ass?' Clark saw the funny side. Their friendship was further cemented when Monty asked a thirsty Gable if he would like a drink from the hip flask he always carried around in his shoulder-bag: this contained a concoction of orange juice, vodka and barbiturates. Marlon Brando had taken a swig from this while they had been making *The Young Lions* and almost passed out. Clark did so and was completely unaffected.

While shooting *The Misfits* he acted as a surrogate father figure towards Monty and protected him from John Huston's bullying. There would be no homophobic attacks or nasty asides, even when Monty's French boyfriend visited the set. The first time Clark called Monty 'fag', and Monty responded that 'it took one to know one', Clark saw the funny side of this too. Age had seemingly taught him tolerance.

Clark met Monty and most of the cast for the first time at the home of producer Frank Taylor. Arthur Miller and Marilyn Monroe were conspicuous by their absence. According to the legend that one finds hard to believe, Clark installed himself in the biggest armchair in Taylor's living room while John Huston, Thelma Ritter, Kevin McCarthy, Eli Wallach and photographer Henri Cartier-Bresson sat cross-legged at his feet – in other words, paying homage to the King.

It may well have been Montgomery Clift who informed Clark of how Marilyn Monroe had for years kept a signed photograph of him in her bedroom, telling friends that Clark Gable was her real father. Monty also confided in him that they had both made the biggest mistake of their careers in agreeing to work with her, albeit that Marilyn had been a non-negotiable part of the Miller package. She was so nervous about shooting her first scene with Clark that on the evening before this took place, she swallowed a fistful of Nembutals and very nearly overdosed – it took her entourage several hours to revive her the next morning. She spent so long being ill in the 'honey wagon' that when she finally emerged, green and shaking, Clark was just about ready to sign off for the day. Then, once he had fought past her entourage (hairdresser, make-up artists, stunt-double, masseur, wardrobe girl, voice-coach, body cosmetician and, most important of all, her black-clad acting coach, Paula Strasberg!) to give her a big hug and tell her not to worry, Marilyn had had an attack of the vapours. That same evening she bleated to reporters who hung around the set day and night, waiting for some exclusive on her crumbling marriage, 'Mr Gable's in love with me!' The ones who had repeated her fabricated claim to be Clark's daughter were prohibited from referring to this snippet in their columns, for fear of 'Daddy Gable' being accused of having incestuous thoughts!

In fact, Clark was not in the least amorously interested in Marilyn. Inasmuch as he had a fetish for cleanliness, she could not have been less fastidious regarding personal hygiene. Like Jean Harlow, she bleached her pubic hair and never wore panties, even during her menstrual cycle. She suffered from what today would be described as a form of irritable bowel syndrome, persistently belching and breaking wind. She rarely bathed, slept in the nude and ate a lot in bed – shoving what was left on her plate under the sheets before going to sleep. Tallulah Bankhead stood next to her at a party in London and later claimed the odour had reminded her of the offal bins at Billingsgate! Neither would Marilyn succeed in her attempts to seduce Monty Clift, though as with Clark the friendship that developed between them proved far more important than it would have done, had sex been involved. All three stars would come to appreciate the fact that they could lean on each other whenever things got to be too much for them, which with this film would be pretty much most of the time.

Throughout shooting, Marilyn would prove never less than an almighty pain in the backside. When she was not several hours late for a scene, she would not turn up at all. If John Huston bawled her out, she would rush to the honey wagon to throw up. She could not remember her lines and most of the time relied on cue cards. In the past, she had become confused shooting scenes out of sequence, therefore Arthur Miller insisted the entire production be filmed in strict chronological order. This would prove particularly arduous for Clark and Monty, whose most physically exerting scenes would have to be shot, with little or no rest between them, towards the end of the schedule when the unit transferred to the hottest part of the Nevada desert.

On 27 August, Marilyn collapsed. The press were told that she was suffering from acute exhaustion – she had actually swallowed a bottle of barbiturates because she had not wanted to wake up after her latest fight with Arthur Miller. The two had argued incessantly about the film since day one. Marilyn had wanted it to be in Technicolor, while Miller sensibly opted for monochrome: the reduced lighting would eradicate some of the stress lines on the actors' faces. She had also wanted a bigger cut of the budget: she and Miller would be sharing $500,000 plus a percentage of the box-office, which she declared was not nearly enough. Marilyn did not care what the studio was paying her husband – *she* wanted the same as Clark. Miller informed her, in the heat of the moment, that this would never happen because if she lived to be 100 she would never be as *good* as Gable, hence the suicide bid. Rushed back to Los Angeles' Westside Hospital, she was out of action until 6 September.

*The Misfits* is a strange film, a scenario which as it unravels becomes increasingly dark and depressing, with far too many autobiographical references for all concerned – a swan song for Clark and Marilyn, which might have been better not seeing the light of day. *He* certainly deserved better than this – though of course no one had any idea that this would be his last film – playing himself this time as a man genuinely washed-up and worn out, trying to prove himself when there was nothing to prove. For three decades, Gable had served the fans faithfully: retrospectively, the world would have been more content to witness his jovial, wisecracking adieu in *It Started In Naples*. Montgomery Clift, though equally reduced to a shadow of his former self, would see his dignity far better preserved:

between now and his death, at 45 in July 1966, he would triumph in Stanley Kramer's *Judgement At Nuremberg*, then in John Huston's *Freud*, before bowing out with *The Defector*. Only Marilyn truly exonerates herself here, but like Clark the cost to her wellbeing would be astronomical.

The action begins in Reno, where former dance teacher Roslyn Taber (Marilyn) has arrived to divorce her husband – Monty's closest friend, Kevin McCarthy, taking up but a few seconds of screen time. We first see her before a mirror trying to memorise the lines she will pronounce before the judge – Arthur Miller's cruel way of reminding his wife that she could not remember hers. Throughout the film she will be the same as she is remembered now – fragile, edgy, possessed of a childlike innocence, yet never for less than a moment spellbinding to watch. World War II pilot-reduced-to-mechanic Guido (Eli Wallach), a real Job's comforter, turns up at Roslyn's lodgings to buy her car and ends up driving Roslyn and landlady Isabel (the magnificent Thelma Ritter) to the courthouse. Later, while celebrating her new-found freedom, she bumps into Guido again: he is with his cowboy buddy, Gay (short for Gaylord), who has already decided he has had enough of this place. Like Clark, Gay soon gets impatient hanging around too many people, and needs to get out into the country, his true home, for some air. Guido suggests that all four of them drive out to his place on the outskirts of town – the house he was in the middle of renovating when his wife died.

The ensuing storyline – of a young woman who heads off with a group of men in search of excitement, initially with no ulterior sexual motive (and therefore less likely to offend moralist audiences) had been covered before. First, with Johnny Mack Brown, Richard Barthelmess and Helen Chandler in *The Last Flight* (1930) and more recently in Hemingway's *The Sun Also Rises* with Errol Flynn, Tyrone Power and Ava Gardner. Roslyn is the city girl that has never smelled the country, save from a perfume bottle, therefore she sees no problem moving into Guido's house when he and Gay ask her to stay. She and Guido dance to the car radio and, referring to his wife she hardly cheers him up by telling him, 'We're all dying, aren't we? All the husbands and wives . . . even me. And we're not telling each other what we know, are we?' When he tries to kiss her, however, she shrugs him off. She is far more interested in Gay because he has treated her with respect and *not* tried to seduce her. 'You just shine in my eyes,' he says, adding that she is the saddest girl he has ever met. Therefore she decides to stay here with him when Guido and Isabel return to Reno, and they bond by way of their intense loneliness.

We do not get to see the lovers in bed: John Huston believed audiences would have been shocked on account of the 25-year age gap. Instead, we see Gay awaken her with a kiss the next morning. For the first time in his life he has cooked breakfast for a woman and he makes a gentle point of reminding her that this is a one-off! The scene was shot several times. Marilyn is completely naked beneath the sheets and Huston was all for going back on his moral stance for including a shot in the finished print where she exposed her breasts. The censor, of course, would not hear of this. This domesticity continues when Roslyn transforms the half-built house into a home (something Marilyn could never have done), even down to sticking up pin-ups of herself behind the cupboard door. Gay tells her about his failed marriage and his two grown-up children, whom he says look up to him and regularly turn up at the rodeo – actually, they are ashamed of what he has become. The two go horse riding: the camera zooms in on Roslyn's shapely derrière and there is the obligatory swimsuit scene when she emerges from the sea. Also, there is the anticipated display of Gable aggression when he yells at her for getting upset when he is about to kill a rabbit for raiding their lettuce-patch. Their idyll is interrupted when Guido shows up in his plane. He has quit his mechanic's job and wants Gay to go 'mustanging' with him to earn some badly needed cash. As they will require another man to help with the lassooing they elect to pick one up at the Dayton rodeo.

Cue for punch-drunk cowboy Perce Howland (Monty) to make his entrance, 45 minutes into the film, and more actor-character blending. Perce has just been left at the roadside after a hitchhike went wrong, and has spent his last $2 calling his mother. 'I haven't been in the hospital since I talked to you,' he tells her, then asks, 'Ma, what would I want to get married for?' He concludes, 'My face is fine.

It's all healed up, just as good as new!' He is supposed to be referring to a recent rodeo mishap, but the critics and fans knew differently: Arthur Miller sadistically opted for more realism by hinting at Monty's homosexuality and his 1956 car accident. And the tone of the telephone conversation suggests that, like Gay's own family, Perce's care little for his welfare.

Perce enters the rodeo, first riding a horse and then a bull, which throws him once he has mastered it. Gay rushes into the arena and saves him from serious injury. Perce only suffers a cut nose and mild concussion, but Roslyn is nevertheless distraught:

ROSLYN: But what if he'd died? That'd be terrible . . .
GAY: But honey, we've all gotta go some time, reason or no reason. Dying's as natural as living. A man who's too afraid to die is too afraid to live!

Fanciful journalists later drew the conclusion that after shooting this scene, Marilyn had gone home, pondered over Clark's words, and decided to end it all. This is untrue: the suicide attempt, as previously explained, had taken place after a bust-up with Arthur Miller.

Henceforth the four protagonists proceed to fall to pieces. Guido appears unsure who he loves the most – Roslyn or Gay – and becomes increasingly resentful towards them both. Eli Wallach took exception to the fact that his character may have been bisexual, complained to John Huston and shooting was held up for two days while Arthur Miller was asked to clarify the situation by rewriting some of Guido's dialogue. He refused, and Huston told the press, 'Who cares if he's homosexual or not, so long as he's *something*?'

Perce gets hooked on the morphine prescribed for his injury – no problem for Monty, Method actor, who had a quantity of the drug, along with dozens of others, in the large doctor's bag he kept in his car. 'Here's to my buddy – old, elderly Gay,' he pronounces when the quartet hit the bar to celebrate his success in the rodeo, bringing the response from Roslyn (added to the script by Marilyn herself), 'Gay's not old!' Then comes the famous scene, shot on 8 September in a rare (for Marilyn) single take, where she and Perce go outside and she sits nursing his head on her lap, two dreadfully mixed-up, lost souls. 'Don't say anything,' she murmurs, summing up both their lives. 'Just be still. I don't know where I belong... maybe this is just the next thing that happens. Maybe you're not supposed to remember anybody's promises.'

Perce has finally blurted out that he loves her, when Gay interrupts them. His children are here, he says, over the moon to see him, and he wants his friends to meet them. Again, he is kidding himself. Like Ria Langham's offspring (which was in effect what Arthur Miller was saying), they want nothing to do with him and when he returns to the bar they are gone. In a drunken rage of emotion he climbs onto the roof of a car, breaks down completely and rolls onto the hood before hitting the pavement. This remains Clark's most impassioned scene *ever*, and no matter how many times one watches it, it still brings a lump to the throat. Later, after Roslyn gets back to the house and he has almost recovered from his breakdown, he confesses, and with her in mind as its mother, says, 'If I had a *new* kid, I'd know just how to be with him, just how to do.' Ironically, Kay had just announced that she was pregnant, giving the exclusive to Louella Parsons. Their closest friends, including John Huston and Monty Clift, had known for several weeks, but kept the news to themselves on account of Kay's age (44) and the fact that she had been terrified of putting a jinx on herself and miscarrying as before.

Back to the film, and the next morning the friends head for the mountains, which meant the production unit uprooting from the scorching, 110-degrees desert to a dry lake, 4,000 feet above sea-level, 50 miles from Reno. Here, the silt-dust formed choking clouds every time the wind blew and some of the technicians went down with chest infections. Additionally, the timekeeping went haywire. Clark would arrive on set at 8.45 precisely, but because Marilyn had set a precedent by turning up several hours late every single day, the rest of the cast followed suit, figuring no scenes could be filmed in any case without her. Even John Huston stumbled in the worse for wear most afternoons after losing a fortune at one of the Reno casinos – then took it out on the actors. Clark spent much of his wasted time reading, chatting to the technicians, or taking them for a spin around the desert in his new Mercedes.

A Louis B. Mayer or Jack Warner would have fired Marilyn on the spot and not cared two hoots whether or not she carried out one of her many threats to kill herself unless she got it all her own way. She had become, however, the mollycoddled child, fiercely defended by Clark, nursed back to near as possible normality by Monty after each vomiting episode or fit of pique – and the main source of interest for the scores of journalists who manned the set day and night. For United Artists to have got rid of her now would have spelled financial disaster, so everyone soldiered on, putting on brave faces and trying to make the best of a dire situation.

In the desert, tempers flare as the men realise the futility of their mission: it was bad enough expecting to rope just the 15 mustangs Perce claims he has seen, but actually there are only six. The roping scenes, where the horses are lassooed and tied to tyres so they cannot run far before collapsing from exhaustion, are very unsettling to watch. Again, such scenes would not be accepted today. Monty, adding a touch of Method, rejected a stunt-double and refused to wear gloves – the rope burns he ends up with are for real. Clark too insisted on doing his own stunts and John Huston was suitably dissatisfied with the first takes that he ordered them time and time again just for the sheer hell of watching everyone suffer, with Marilyn/Roslyn reacting back then to the blatant cruelty as most people would today.

She first hits out at Guido, whose wartime exploits have left him so hard-bitten that he did nothing to save his dying wife. 'You could blow up the world and all you'd feel sorry for is yourself!' she cries. Then Gay attacks her for being over-sensitive in offering to *pay* for the horses' freedom: his theory is that nothing can live unless something dies – though after watching her fit of hysterics – 'Killers! Murderers!' she screams – he realises she is right, and he and Perce cut the horses loose, save for the feisty stallion. This he pursues, getting dragged through the dust until he brings it under control – Clark's final display of asserting his manhood in front of a woman he loves. 'I just gotta find another way to live, if there is one,' laments Gay, before

Guido leaves in a huff, and Perce mutters a tearful farewell. Then Gay and Roslyn jump into his truck and head for wherever, assuring us that these two psychologically bruised misfits may have a future together. 'How do you find your way back in the dark?' she asks him, not just referring to the night, but to their state of mind and wellbeing after a lifetime of emotional abuse, bringing the optimistic response, 'Just head for that big star straight on. The highway's under it. It'll take us right home!'

These were the very last words Clark Gable would pronounce on the big screen. On 17 October, he and Monty Clift drove to the Christmas Tree Inn, on the outskirts of Reno, where John Huston threw a party for Monty's fortieth birthday. Here, Monty proved there was at least one man in the world capable of drinking Clark under the table. The next day the unit returned to Los Angeles to complete the interiors. And here, on 4 November, coinciding with the announcement that *The Misfits* had gone $500,000 over budget largely on account of Marilyn's indisposition, the final scene with Clark was shot again.

The next morning, Saturday, Clark, John Huston and producer Frank Taylor sat through the rushes. Taylor later recalled how Clark told him, 'I now have two things to be proud of in my career – *Gone With The Wind*, and this one.' There seems little doubt that Taylor was according himself a moment of glory that, with Gable no longer around to back the statement up, would remain undisputed. There had been many proud moments in his life, but *The Misfits* was not one of them – on the contrary, the film would result in him paying the ultimate sacrifice. Huston was displeased with the scene where the characters meet up at the Dayton rodeo and persuaded Arthur Miller to rewrite five pages of script. Monty, Eli Wallach and Marilyn may have been willing to shoot the scene again, but Clark had had enough.

That same evening, he complained of feeling unwell. He told Kay he thought he was coming down with the flu and went to bed early. The following afternoon he was changing a tyre on his jeep when he doubled up with severe chest pains – now known to have been another heart attack. Dismissing this as nothing more serious than indigestion, he again retired early. The next morning, Monday, around 7.30am, he suffered another heart attack and this time Kay summoned his doctor, Fred Cerini, who for some reason rang through to the local Fire Department for oxygen and *then* called an ambulance. He and Kay would be subsequently accused of neglect.

Clark was admitted to the Presbyterian Hospital, where doctors confirmed he had suffered at least one major coronary thrombosis. He was hooked up to a heart monitor, given anti-coagulants and Kay was told that the next 48 hours would prove crucial towards his pulling through. During this period, she slept on a trucklebed in his room. Gable received thousands of cards, letters and telegrams from well-wishers – one, it was rumoured, from President Eisenhower, delivered to the hospital on the evening of 7 November after one of Clark's friends telephoned the White House with news of his illness. The telegram is reputed to have read, 'Be a good boy, Clark, and do as the doctors tell you. Ike.' Like the conversation with Frank Taylor, it is but part of the Gable myth: there had been no telephone call, Clark and the President had not been on first-name terms; there was no telegram. The first Eisenhower heard of Clark's illness had been that morning, while going through the newspapers with his secretary – *before* he had been admitted to hospital. Eisenhower's secretary dispatched a half-formal letter to Elcino during the afternoon and this had been taken to the hospital. Even so, though there would be no further comment from the White House, the gesture would almost certainly have been appreciated.

Dear Mr Gable. I have learned from the paper this morning that you have suffered a mild coronary thrombosis. I trust that your recovery will be rapid and complete . . . I advise you to follow the instructions of your doctors meticulously. I have found this fairly easy to do, except for the one item on which they seem to place the greatest stress, which is 'don't worry and never get angry'. However, I am learning – and in recent weeks I have had lots of opportunities to practice! With all the best, Dwight D. Eisenhower.

One week into his hospitalisation, Clark's specialist instructed he be taken off the heart monitor and the administrator, B.J. Caldwell, confidently announced that he was over the worst. Howard Strickling dropped in for a visit, as did former agent Minna Wallis. On the evening of 16 November 1960, Gable was reported by B.J. Caldwell to be sitting up in bed reading. Kay kissed him goodnight just after 10pm – she was no longer using the trucklebed – and returned to her own room to rest. According to the nurse who was tending him, at 10.50pm, quietly and still reading, Clark leaned back against his pillows, yawned and slipped away.

# EPILOGUE

'The King is dead!' proclaimed the *New York Times*, adding somewhat unfairly that though Clark Gable had not been blessed with the acting talents of post-war British stars such as David Niven and Stewart Granger, he *had* possessed a rarer quality – a truly masculine personality. Other obituaries touched on this, as opposed to his achievements, while the women in his life were conspicuously reticent when it came to speaking to the press about his alleged prowess in the bedroom. Adela Rogers St Johns, who we now know had shared his bed, commented on his 'ordinariness' and recalled him once telling her, 'I'm no Adonis, but I'm as American as the telephone poles I used to climb to make a living. Other men see me making love to Harlow, Shearer and Crawford on the screen. They say that if I can do it, so can they, and they go right home and make love to their wives.'

Though Clark had disapproved of Carole Lombard having a military funeral and he had wanted no fuss over his own, the US military deemed otherwise. It no longer mattered that his wartime activities had been little more than an elaborate publicity stunt, all this was left behind on 19 November 1960 for the ceremony at Forest Lawn's Church of the Recessional, where 18 years earlier he had bid farewell to Carole.

The nine pallbearers included Spencer Tracy, Al Menasco, James Stewart, Robert Taylor, Howard Strickling and Eddie Mannix. Among the celebrities were Keenan Wynn, Ann Sothern, Frank Capra, Van Johnson, Mervyn LeRoy, Robert Stack – and Jack Oakie, who treated the occasion like a première, pausing to sign autographs and getting mobbed by fans. 'Such a pity they didn't bury him instead!' Joan Crawford is reputed to have said. Only two of Gable's leading ladies were present: Marion Davies and Norma Shearer, who told reporters, 'Now he is on the right side of eternity. Bless him.' Myrna Loy, Claudette Colbert, Rosalind Russell and Lana Turner offered no excuses for not attending. Marilyn Monroe was reported as being too distressed to leave her bedroom but sent a wreath from herself and her soon to be ex-husband – she would obtain a Mexican divorce from Arthur Miller on 20 January 1961, the day John F. Kennedy was inaugurated president. Loretta Young and Judy Lewis did not attend for obvious reasons – Judy's daughter, Maria, had celebrated her first birthday on the day Clark died.

Joan Crawford, who had continued her love affair with Clark almost until the end, wished to avoid Kay at all costs. She held her at least partly responsible for his death – for having him examined by the studio doctor rather than getting him to the hospital when he had his first heart attack. But if she only privately criticised her for neglecting him, she (*along* with Kay) publicly condemned Marilyn for keeping him waiting for hours in the Nevada desert while shooting *The Misfits*. She would mourn her greatest love for over a year, shunning all offers of work until working on what would be her last truly great film, *Whatever Happened To Baby Jane?* (1962).

Clark had requested that his casket should remain closed after his death and that not even Kay should be permitted to see him. He had also asked for no eulogies. The 15-minute service was conducted by Johnson West, an Episcopalian chaplain with the Air Force. There were a few short readings from the Bible, including Psalms 46 and 121 – and instead of hymns, a medley of Strauss waltzes, regarded by some as Clark having a last laugh at Hollywood from beyond the grave. Because renovations were taking place within the Great Mausoleum, his casket was returned to cold storage. Four days later, attended by Kay and a handful of close friends, he was interred in the vault he had purchased back in 1942, between Carole and her mother.

*The Misfits* was released on 1 February 1961, what would have been Clark's 60th birthday – a deliberate ploy by United Artists to cash in on the publicity and to hopefully acquire for him (and more box-office revenue for themselves) the movie industry's very first posthumous Oscar. Warner Brothers had already tried this tactic with James Dean after *Giant*, and failed. Though the film did well enough at the box-office Clark's recent demise did not sway the selection committee.

The actual value of his estate was never revealed, but is estimated to have been in the region of $5 million including the Encino ranch and the property in Bermuda Dunes. His will, redrafted in September 1955, two months after he married Kay, was unusually benevolent towards Josephine Dillon, considering the problems she had caused him since their divorce. The house in North Hollywood, which she had purposely allowed to fall into disrepair for the benefit of the *Confidential* feature, was to be hers for life. Despite failing health, Dillon continued teaching and died in a sanatorium in 1971, aged 87. The remainder of his estate was bequeathed to Kay, and a special clause had been added to his will – owing to the inordinate number of affairs he had had and any possible progeny coming forward – that all paternity-suit claimants should be wholly disregarded. He had obviously been thinking about Judy Lewis.

On 20 March 1961, Kay was delivered of a blond-haired, blue-eyed baby boy by Caesarian section. He was baptised John Clark and *because* he did not resemble Clark – lacking the large ears and melon-smile inherited by Judy, and taking into consideration that his mother was no saint – there have always been rumours that he was not Gable's child at all. Having learned how Marilyn Monroe was still feeling guilty over Clark's death – no real surprise since Kay had been the first to accuse her of killing him – Kay decided to make amends. Marilyn had recently been discharged from the Payne Whitney Clinic, having been sectioned by a psychiatrist. Kay went to see her, apologised and Marilyn was guest of honour at John Clark's christening.

After attending Los Angeles' Buckley School, John Clark finished his education in Switzerland, then returned to the United States to open a car-repair business. He would briefly submit to the acting bug: in 1990, married with two small children, he starred alongside James

Brolin and Rory Calhoun in a Western, *Bad Jim*. The promoters considered it so bad it was denied a cinema release and went straight to video – confirming the fact that there would only ever be *one* Gable. Indeed, along with many other Hollywood progeny (one instinctively thinks of the daughters of Marlene Dietrich and Joan Crawford whose tell-all books failed majestically to sully their legend) John Clark Gable's one moment of fame may well have been when he offered what could be considered the supreme insult to his father. He sold his Oscar for *It Happened One Night* for $600,000 to Steven Spielberg. However, to be fair, he then made amends, and deserves credit for, part-funding the Clark Gable Foundation in Cadiz, Ohio, turning the house in Charleston where he was born into a museum and shrine to his memory.

Kay Gable was romantically linked with numerous men after Clark's death, but refrained from remarrying, claiming no man could ever replace Gable. This might well have been true, but the likeliest reason for her remaining single may perhaps have had more to do with her wishing to hang on to her wealth – though she was extremely generous towards the charities she supported. Whether their marriage would have survived, had Clark lived longer, is also open to question given their track records. In 1973, Kay sold the Encino ranch for $1 million: its 20 acres would subsequently be redeveloped into a luxury-housing complex named the Clark Gable Estates in his memory. Kay died in May 1983, aged 66, leaving her fortune to her son. She was entombed in the crypt next to Clark, enabling him to lie between his two favourite wives, something that would doubtless have amused him.

The *New York Times* observed in its obituary, 'Clark Gable was as certain as the sunrise. He was consistently and stubbornly all man.' That he was, and will forever remain definitive and inimitable goes without saying – proof of this lay in the positively putrid biopic, *Gable And Lombard* (1976), with James Brolin and Jill Clayburgh, voted one of the worst films of all time by the *Golden Turkey Awards*.

Seven years after Gable's passing, Joan Crawford, the greatest love of his life after Carole Lombard, would be bleeped when speaking to

David Frost on his television show. When asked by Frost what Clark's special attraction had been, Joan looked him in the eye and replied, 'Balls – he had them!'

# FILMOGRAPHY

Clark Gable appeared as an extra in several silent and early sound productions. In some of these he was left out of the final print: even when he does appear, such as in crowd scenes, he is difficult to spot. Among these early ventures were *White Man, Forbidden Paradise, The Merry Widow, Ben Hur, Déclassée, The Pacemakers* (serial), released 1925–6. Released 1926–8 were *The Johnstown Flood, North Star, The Plastic* Age and *Fighting Blood* (serial). His feature films are listed below.

### THE PAINTED DESERT　　　　　　　　　　RKO/PATHE, 1931
Director: Howard Higgin. Screenplay: Howard Higgin/Tom Buckingham. With William Boyd, Helen Twelvetrees, J. Farrell MacDonald, William Farnum, Charles Sellon.
Clark Gable was fifth billing. 77 minutes.

### THE EASIEST WAY　　　　　　　　　　　MGM, 1931
Director: Jack Conway. Screenplay: Edith Ellis, based on the stage play by Eugene Walter. With Constance Bennett, Robert Montgomery, Adolphe Menjou, Marjorie Rambeau, Anita Page, Clara Bandick.
Clark Gable was fifth billing. 86 minutes.

### DANCE, FOOLS, DANCE　　　　　　　　　MGM, 1931
Director: Harry Beaumont. Screenplay: Richard Schayer/Aurania Rouverol. With Joan Crawford, Lester Vail, William Bakewell, William Holden,* Cliff Edwards, Hale Hamilton.

Clark Gable was second billing. 80 minutes.
*not *the* William Holden

## THE SECRET SIX                         MGM, 1931
Director: George Hill. Screenplay: Francis Marion Crawford. With Wallace Beery, Johnny Mack Brown, Jean Harlow, Lewis Stone, Marjorie Rambeau, Ralph Bellamy, Paul Hurst and John Miljan.
Clark Gable was third billing. 83 minutes.

## THE FINGER POINTS              FIRST NATIONAL, 1931
Director: John Francis Dillon. Screenplay: Robert Lord, based on a story by J. Monk Saunders and W.R. Burnett. With Richard Barthelmess, Fay Wray, Robert Elliott and Regis Toomey.
Clark Gable was third billing. 86 minutes.

## LAUGHING SINNERS                        MGM, 1931
Director: Harry Beaumont. Screenplay: Bess Meredyth, based on the stage play *Torch Song* by Kenyon Nicholson. Photography: Charles Rosher. With Joan Crawford, Neil Hamilton, Marjorie Rambeau, Guy Kibbee, Roscoe Karnes and George F. Marion.
Clark Gable, replacing Johnny Mack Brown, was second billing. 70 minutes.

## A FREE SOUL                              MGM, 1931
Director: Clarence Brown. Srceenplay: John Meehan, based on the screenplay by Adela Rogers St Johns. With Norma Shearer, Leslie Howard, Lionel Barrymore, Lucy Beaumont and James Gleason.
Clark Gable was fourth billing. 91 minutes.

## NIGHT NURSE                   WARNER BROTHERS, 1931
Director: William Wellman. Screenplay: Oliver Garrett/Charles Kenyon, based on the novel by Dora Macy. With Barbara Stanwyck, Joan Blondell, Charles Winninger, Ben Lyon and Vera Lewis.
Clark Gable was fifth billing. 70 minutes.

## SPORTING BLOOD                                    MGM, 1931

Director: Charles Brabin. Screenplay: Willard Mack/Wanda Tuchock, based on the novel *Horseflesh* by Frederick Hazlitt Brennan. Photography: Hal Rosson. With Madge Evans, Ernest Torrence, Marie Prevost, Lew Cody, J. Farrell MacDonald and Harry Holman.
Clark Gable was top billing. 80 minutes.

## SUSAN LENOX – HER FALL AND RISE          MGM, 1931

Director: Robert Z. Leonard. Screenplay: Wanda Tuchock/Zelda Spears/Edith Fitzgerald, based on the novel by David Graham Philipps. Photography: William Daniels. With Greta Garbo, Jean Hersholt, John Miljan, Alan Hale, Russell Simpson, Hilda Vaughan and Cecil Cunningham.
Clark Gable was second billing. 83 minutes.

## POSSESSED                                        MGM, 1931

Director: Clarence Brown. Screenplay: Lenore Coffee, based on the stage play *The Mirage* by Edgar Selwyn. Photography: Oliver T. Marsh. With Joan Crawford, Wallace Ford, Skeets Gallagher, John Miljan, Frank Conroy, Clara Blandick and Marjorie White.
Clark Gable was second billing. 75 minutes.

## HELL DIVERS                                      MGM, 1931

Director: George Hill. Screenplay: Harvey Gates/Malcolm Stuart Boylan, based on a story by Lt Commander Frank Wead. With Wallace Beery, Conrad Nagel, Marie Prevost, Cliff Edwards, Marjorie Rambeau, Dorothy Jordan and John Miljan.
Clark Gable was second billing. 98 minutes.

## POLLY OF THE CIRCUS                              MGM, 1932

Director: Alfred Santell. Screenplay: Carey Wilson/Laurence Johnson, based on the stage play by Margaret Mayo. Photography: George Barnes. With Marion Davies, C. Aubrey Smith, David Landau, Ruth Selwyn, Raymond Hatton and Ray Milland.
Clark Gable was second billing. 71 minutes.

## RED DUST                                          MGM, 1932
Director: Victor Fleming. Screenplay: John Lee Mahin, based on the
stage play by Wilson Collison. Photography: Hal Rosson. With Jean
Harlow, Mary Astor, Gene Raymond, Donald Crisp and Tully
Marshall.
Clark Gable was top billing. 83 minutes.

## STRANGE INTERLUDE                                 MGM, 1932
Director: Robert Z Leonard. Screenplay: Bess Meredyth/C. Gardner
Sullivan, based on the stage play by Eugene O'Neill. Photography:
Lee Garmes. With Norma Shearer, Ralph Morgan, Robert Young,
Alexander Kirkland, Maureen O'Sullivan and May Robson.
Clark Gable was second billing. 108 minutes.

## NO MAN OF HER OWN                            PARAMOUNT, 1932
Director: Wesley Ruggles. Screenplay: Maurine Watkins/Milton H.
Gropper, based on a story by Edmund Goulding and Benjamin
Glazer. With Carole Lombard, Dorothy Mackaill, Grant Mitchell,
George Barbier, Elizabeth Patterson, Tommy Conlon and J. Farrell
MacDonald.
Clark Gable was top billing. 84 minutes.

## THE WHITE SISTER                                  MGM, 1933
Director: Victor Fleming. Screenplay: Donald Ogden Stewart, based
on the novel by Francis Marion Crawford and the stage play by
Walter Hackett. Photography: William Daniels. With Helen Hayes,
Lewis Stone, Louise Closser Hale, Edward Arnold and May Robson.
Clark Gable was second billing. 107 minutes.

## HOLD YOUR MAN                                     MGM, 1933
Director: Sam Wood. Screenplay: Anita Loos/Howard Emmett
Rogers, from Loos' story. Photography: Hal Rosson. With Jean
Harlow, Stuart Erwin, Muriel Kirkland, Dorothy Burgess, Garry
Owen and Elizabeth Patterson.
Clark Gable was second billing. 88 minutes.

## NIGHT FLIGHT

MGM, 1933

Director: Clarence Brown. Screenplay: Oliver Garrett, based on the novel by Antoine de Saint-Exupéry. Photography: Oliver T. Marsh/Charles Marshall/Elmar Dyer. With John Barrymore, Helen Hayes, Lionel Barrymore, Robert Montgomery, Myrna Loy and William Gargan.

Clark Gable was third billing. 82 minutes.

## DANCING LADY

MGM, 1933

Director: Robert Z. Leonard. Screenplay: Allan Rivkin/Zelda Spears/P.J. Wolfson, based on a story by James Warner Bellah. Photography: Oliver T. Marsh. Costumes: Adrian. With Joan Crawford, Franchot Tone, Fred Astaire, May Robson, Ted Healy & His Three Stooges and Nelson Eddy.

Clark Gable was second billing. 93 minutes.

## IT HAPPENED ONE NIGHT

COLUMBIA, 1934

Director: Frank Capra. Screenplay: Robert Riskin, based on the story, *Night Bus* by Samuel Hopkins Adams. Photography: Joe Walker. With Claudette Colbert, Roscoe Karns, Walter Connolly, Alan Hale, Jameson Thomas and Ward Bond.

Clark Gable was top billing. 105 minutes.

## MEN IN WHITE

MGM, 1934

Director: Richard Boleslawski. Screenplay: Waldemar Young, based on the stage play by Sidney Kingsley. Photography: George Folsey. With Myrna Loy, Elizabeth Allan, Jean Hersholt, C. Henry Gordon, Wallace Ford, Russell Hardie and Otto Kruger.

Clark Gable was top billing. 78 minutes.

## MANHATTAN MELODRAMA

MGM, 1934

Director: W.S. Van Dyke. Screenplay: Oliver Garrett/Joe Mankiewicz, based on a story by Arthur Caesar. Photography: James Wong Howe. With William Powell, Myrna Loy, Mickey Rooney, Leo Carrillo, Nat Pendleton, George Sidney, Isabel Jewell and Muriel Evans.

Clark Gable was top billing. 93 minutes.

## CHAINED                                    MGM, 1934
Director: Clarence Brown. Screenplay: John Lee Mahin, based on a story by Edgar Selwyn. Photography: George Folsey. With Joan Crawford, Stuart Erwin, Otto Kruger, Una O'Connor and Akim Tamiroff.
Clark Gable was second billing. 73 minutes.

## FORSAKING ALL OTHERS                        MGM, 1934
Director: W.S. Van Dyke. Screenplay: Joe Manckiewicz, based on the stage play by E.B. Roberts and F.M. Cavett. Photography: George Folsey/Gregg Toland. Costumes: Adrian. With Joan Crawford, Robert Montgomery, Charles Butterworth, Rosalind Russell and Billie Burke.
Clark Gable was second billing. 81 minutes.

## AFTER OFFICE HOURS                          MGM, 1935
Director: Robert Z. Leonard. Screenplay: Herman Mankiewicz, based on a story by Laurence Stallings/Dale Van Every. Photography: Charles Rosher. With Constance Bennett, Billie Burke, Stuart Erwin, Harvey Stephens, Katherine Alexander and Hale Hamilton.
Clark Gable was second billing. 75 minutes.

## CALL OF THE WILD        TWENTIETH CENTURY-FOX, 1935
Director: William Wellman. Screenplay: Gene Fowler/Leonard Praskins, based on the novel by Jack London. Photography: Charles Rosher. With Loretta Young, Jack Oakie, Frank Conroy, Reginald Owen, Katherine DeMille, Sidney Toler, Herman Bing and James Burke.
Clark Gable was top billing. 93 minutes.

## CHINA SEAS                                  MGM, 1935
Director: Tay Garnett. Screenplay: Jules Furthman/James McGuiness, based on the novel by Crosbie Garstin. Photography: Ray June. With Jean Harlow, Wallace Beery, Rosalind Russell, Lewis Stone, C. Aubrey Smith, Donald Meek, Hattie McDaniel and Dudley Digges.
Clark Gable was top billing. 89 minutes.

## MUTINY ON THE BOUNTY    MGM, 1935

Director: Frank Lloyd. Screenplay: Talbot Jennings/Jules Furthman/Carey Wilson, based on the trilogy (*Mutiny On The Bounty, Men Against The Sea, Pitcairn Island*) by Charles Nordhoff and James Norman Hall. Photography: Arthur Edeson. With Charles Laughton, Franchot Tone, Eddie Quillan, Herbert Mundin, Donald Crisp and Movita Castenada.

Clark Gable was second billing. 130 minutes.

## WIFE vs SECRETARY    MGM, 1936

Director: Clarence Brown. Screenplay: Norman Krasna/Alice Duer Miller/John Lee Mahin, based on the novel by Faith Baldwin. Photography: Ray June. With Jean Harlow, Myrna Loy, James Stewart, May Robson, Hobart Cavanagh, Gloria Holden, Gilbert Emery and Margaret Irving.

Clark Gable was top billing. 86 minutes.

## SAN FRANCISCO    MGM, 1936

Director: W.S. Van Dyke. Screenplay: Anita Loos, based on the story by Robert Hopkins. Photography: Oliver T. Marsh. With Jeanette MacDonald, Spencer Tracy, Jack Holt, Ted Healy, Shirley Ross, Margaret Irving, William Ricciardi and Harold Huber.

Clark Gable was top billing. 113 minutes.

## CAIN AND MABEL    WARNER BROTHERS, 1936

Director: Lloyd Bacon. Screenplay: Laird Doyle, based on a story by H.C. Witwer. Photography: George Barnes. With Marion Davies, Allen Jenkins, Roscoe Karns, Walter Catlett, E.E. Clive and Ruth Donnelly.

Clark Gable was second billing. 89 minutes.

## LOVE ON THE RUN    MGM, 1936

Director: W.S. Van Dyke. Screenplay: John Lee Mahin/Manuel Seff/Gladys Hurlbut, based on the story by Alan Green/Julian Brodie. Photography: Oliver T. Marsh. Costumes: Adrian. With Joan Crawford, Franchot Tone, Reginald Owen, Mona Barrie, Ivan

Lebedeff and William Desmarest.
Clark Gable was second billing. 8 minutes.

### PARNELL                                    MGM, 1937

Director: John M Stahl. Screenplay: John Van Druten/S.N.
Behrman, based on the stage play by Elsie Schauffer. Photography:
Karl Freund. With Myrna Loy, Edna May Oliver, Edmund Gwenn,
Donald Meek, Alan Marshall, Billie Burke, Montagu Love and
George Zucco.
Clark Gable was top billing. 96 minutes.

### SARATOGA                                   MGM, 1937

Director: Jack Conway. Screenplay: Anita Loos/Robert Hopkins.
Photography: Ray June. With Jean Harlow (doubled by Mary Dees),
Lionel Barrymore, Frank Morgan, Walter Pidgeon, Hattie McDaniel,
Una Merkel, Cliff Edwards, Jonathan Hale and George Zucco.
Clark Gable was top billing. 100 minutes.

### TEST PILOT                                 MGM, 1938

Director: Victor Fleming. Screenplay: Vincent Lawrence/Waldemar
Young, based on a story by Lt-Commander Frank Wead.
Photographer: Ray June. With Myrna Loy, Spencer Tracy, Lionel
Barrymore, Marjorie Main, Samuel S. Hinds, Virginia Grey and
Gloria Holden.
Clark Gable was top billing. 117 minutes.

### TOO HOT TO HANDLE                          MGM, 1938

Director: Jack Conway. Screenplay: John Lee Mahin/Laurence
Stallings, based on a story by Len Hammond. Photography: Hal Rosson.
With Myrna Loy, Walter Pidgeon, Walter Connelly, Leo Carrillo,
Virginia Weidler, Johnny Hines, Marjorie Main and Willie Fung.
Clark Gable was top billing. 105 minutes.

### IDIOT'S DELIGHT                            MGM, 1939

Director: Clarence Brown. Screenplay: Robert E. Sherwood, based
on his stage play. Photography: William Daniels. With Norma

Shearer, Edward Arnold, Charles Coburn, Burgess Meredith, Joseph Schildkraut, Laura Hope Crews, Skeets Gallagher, Fritz Feld and Virginia Grey.

Clark Gable was second billing. 102 minutes.

### GONE WITH THE WIND                                   MGM, 1939
Directors: Victor Fleming/George Cukor/Sam Wood. Screenplay: Sidney Howard, based on the novel by Margaret Mitchell. Photography: Ernest Haller/Lee Garmes. Music: Max Steiner. With Vivien Leigh, Leslie Howard, Olivia de Havilland, Hattie McDaniel, Thomas Mitchell, Butterfly McQueen, Ann Rutherford, Evelyn Keyes, Ona Munson, Victor Jory, Laura Hope Crews, Barbara O'Neill, Harry Davenport, Isabelle Jewell, Ward Bond, Cammie King and many more.

Clark Gable was top billing. 223 minutes.

### STRANGE CARGO                                        MGM, 1940
Director: Frank Borzage. Screenplay: Lawrence Hazard, based on the novel *Not Too Narrow, Not Too Deep* by Richard Sale. Photography: Robert Planck. Music: Franz Waxman. With Joan Crawford, Ian Hunter, Peter Lorre, Paul Lukas, Albert Dekker, Eduardo Ciannelli and John Arledge.

Clark Gable was second billing. 110 minutes.

### BOOM TOWN                                            MGM, 1940
Director: Jack Conway. Screenplay: John Lee Mahin, based on a story by James Edward Grant. Photography: Hal Rosson. With Claudette Colbert, Spencer Tracy, Hedy Lamarr, Lionel Atwill, Frank Morgan, Chill Wills, Marion Martin, Richard Lane, Minna Martin and Curt Bois.

Clark Gable was top billing. 114 minutes.

### COMRADE X                                            MGM, 1940
Director: King Vidor. Screenplay: Ben Hecht/Charles Lederer, based on the story by Walter Reisch. Photography: Joseph Ruttenberg. With Hedy Lamarr, Eve Arden, Oscar Homolka, Felix

Bressart, Vladimir Sokoloff, Sig Ruman, Likhail Rasumy and Edgar Barrier.
Clark Gable was top billing. 90 minutes.

## THEY MET IN BOMBAY                    MGM, 1941
Director: Clarence Brown. Screenplay: Anita Loos/Edwin Justus Mayer/Leon Gordon. Photography: William Daniels. With Rosalind Russell, Peter Lorre, Jessie Ralph, Reginald Owen, Matthew Boulton, Eduardo Ciannelli, Luis Albertini, Jay Novello and Rosina Galli.
Clark Gable was top billing. 83 minutes.

## HONKY TONK                           MGM, 1941
Director: Jack Conway. Screenplay: Marguerite Roberts/John Sanford. Photography: Hal Rosson. With Lana Turner, Frank Morgan, Claire Trevor, Marjorie Main, Albert Dekker, Chill Wills and Veda Ann Borg.
Clark Gable was top billing. 103 minutes.

## SOMEWHERE I'LL FIND YOU              MGM, 1942
Director: Wesley Ruggles. Screenplay: Marguerite Roberts, based on a story by Charles Hoffman. Photography: Hal Rosson. With Lana Turner, Robert Sterling, Reginald Owen, Patricia Dane, Lee Patrick, Charles Dingle and Van Johnson.
Clark Gable was top billing. 106 minutes.

## ADVENTURE                           MGM, 1945
Director: Victor Fleming. Screenplay: Frederich Hazlitt Brennan/Vincent Lawrence, based on the novel, *This Strange Adventure*, by Clyde Brion Davis. Photography: Joseph Ruttenberg. With Greer Garson, Joan Blondell, Thomas Mitchell, Tom Tully, Richard Haydn and Harry Davenport.
Clark Gable was top billing. 122 minutes.

## THE HUCKSTERS                       MGM, 1947
Director: Jack Conway. Screenplay: Luther Davis, based on the novel by Frederic Wakeman. Photography: Hal Rosson. With

Deborah Kerr, Sydney Greenstreet, Ava Gardner, Adolphe Menjou, Edward Arnold, Keenan Wynn, Gloria Holden and Aubrey Mather. Clark Gable was top billing. 114 minutes.

## HOMECOMING                                          MGM, 1948
Director: Mervyn LeRoy. Screenplay: Paul Osborn, based on the novel *The Homecoming of Ulysses* by Sidney Kingsley. Photography: Hal Rosson. With Lana Turner, Anne Baxter, John Hodiak, Gladys Cooper, Cameron Mitchell, Ray Collins and Marshall Thompson. Clark Gable was top billing. 113 minutes.

## COMMAND DECISION                                    MGM, 1948
Director: Sam Wood. Screenplay: William Laidlaw/George Froeschel, based on the stage play by William Wister Haines. Photography: Hal Rosson. With Walter Pidgeon, Van Johnson, Brian Donlevy, John Hodiak, Charles Bickford, Edward Arnold, John McIntire and Marshall Thompson. Clark Gable was top billing. 110 minutes.

## ANY NUMBER CAN PLAY                                 MGM, 1949
Director: Mervyn LeRoy. Screenplay: Richard Brooks, based on the novel by Edward Harris Heth. Photography: Hal Rosson. With Alexis Smith, Audrey Totter, Mary Astor, Lewis Stone, Barry Sullivan, Marjorie Rambeau, Edgar Buchanan and Leon Ames. Clark Gable was top billing. 110 minutes.

## KEY TO THE CITY                                     MGM, 1950
Director: George Sidney. Screenplay: Robert Riley Crutcher, based on a story by Albert Beich. Photography: Hal Rosson. With Loretta Young, Frank Morgan, James Gleason, Raymond Burr, Marilyn Maxwell, Lewis Stone, Raymond Walburn, Pamela Britton and Zamah Cunningham. Clark Gable was top billing. 96 minutes.

## TO PLEASE A LADY                                    MGM, 1950
Director: Clarence Brown. Screenplay: Barre Lyndon/Marge

Decker. Photography: Hal Rosson. With Barbara Stanwyck, Adolphe Menjou, Will Geer, Roland Winters, Lela Bliss, Emory Parnell and Lew Smith.

Clark Gable was top billing. 91 minutes.

### ACROSS THE WIDE MISSOURI                                    MGM, 1951

Director: William Wellman. Screenplay: Talbot Jennings, based on a story by himself and Frank Cavett. Photography: William Mellor. With Ricardo Montalban, Adolphe Menjou, John Hodiak, Maria Elena Marques, Jack Holt, J. Carroll Nash, Alan Napier and Richard Anderson.

Clark Gable was top billing. 78 minutes.

### LONE STAR                                                   MGM, 1952

Director: Vincent Sherman. Screenplay: Howard Estabrook/Borden Chase, based on Chase's story. Photography: Hal Rosson. With Ava Gardner, Broderick Crawford, Beulah Bondi, Lionel Barrymore, James Burke, Ed Begley, William Farnum, Moroni Olsen and William Conrad.

Clark Gable was top billing. 93 minutes.

### NEVER LET ME GO                                             MGM, 1953

Director: Delmer Daves. Screenplay: Ronald Millar/George Froeschel, based on the novel *Came The Dawn* by Roger Bax. Photography: Robert Krasker. With Gene Tierney, Richard Haydn, Kenneth More, Bernard Miles, Belita, Karel Stepanek, Theodore Bickel and Anna Valentina.

Clark Gable was top billing. 69 minutes.

### MOGAMBO                                                     MGM, 1953

Director: John Ford. Screenplay: John Lee Mahin, based on the stage play *Red Dust* by Wilson Collison, and Mahin's screenplay for the earlier film. Photography: Robert Surtees/Freddy Young. With Ava Gardner, Grace Kelly, Donald Sinden, Laurence Naismith, Philip Stainton, Dennis O'Dea and Eric Pohlmann.

Clark Gable was top billing. 113 minutes.

## BETRAYED                                    MGM, 1954

Director: Gottfried Reinhardt. Screenplay: Ronald Millar/George Froeschel. Photography: Freddy Young. With Lana Turner, Victor Mature, Louis Calhern, Wilfrid Hyde-White, O.E. Hasse, Ian Carmichael, Nora Swinburne, Roland Culver, Leslie Weston and Niall MacGinnis.
Clark Gable was top billing. 103 minutes.

## SOLDIER OF FORTUNE   TWENTIETH CENTURY-FOX, 1955

Director: Edward Dmytryk. Screenplay: Ernest K. Gann, based on his novel. Photography: Leo Tover. With Susan Hayward, Gene Barry, Michael Rennie, Alexander D'Arcy, Russell Collins and Tom Tully.
Clark Gable was top billing. 94 minutes.

## THE TALL MEN         TWENTIETH CENTURY-FOX, 1955

Director: Raoul Walsh. Screenplay: Sydney Boehm/Frank Nugent, based on the novel by Clay Fisher. Photography: Leo Tover. With Jane Russell, Robert Ryan, Cameron Mitchell, Juan Garcia, Harry Shannon, Emile Meyer, Mae Marsh, Doris Kemper, Tom Fadden, Argentina Brunetti.
Clark Gable was top billing. 120 minutes.

## THE KING AND FOUR QUEENS    UNITED ARTISTS, 1956

Director: Raoul Walsh. Screenplay: Margaret Fitts/Richard Alan Simmons, based on a story by Fitts. Photography: Lucien Ballard. With Eleanor Parker, Jo Van Fleet, Barbara Nichols, Jean Willes, Jay C. Flippen, Arthur Shields and Sara Shane.
Clark Gable was top billing. 86 minutes.

## BAND OF ANGELS              WARNER BROTHERS, 1957

Director: Raoul Walsh. Screenplay: John Twist/Ivan Goff/Ben Roberts, based on the novel by Robert Penn Warren. Photography: Lucien Ballard. With Yvonne de Carlo, Sidney Poitier, Efrem Zimbalist Jr, Patric Knowles, Torin Thatcher, Rex Reason.
Clark Gable was top billing. 125 minutes.

## RUN SILENT, RUN DEEP                UNITED ARTISTS, 1958
Director: Robert Wise. Screenplay: John Gay, based on a novel by Commander Edward Beach. Photography: Russ Harlen. With Burt Lancaster, Jack Warden, Brad Dexter, Nick Cravat, Mary LaRoche, Joe Maross, Eddie Foy III, Don Rickles, Ken Lynch and John Bryant.
Clark Gable was top billing. 93 minutes.

## TEACHER'S PET                PARAMOUNT, 1958
Director: George Seaton. Screenplay: Fay and Michael Kanin. Photography: Haskell & Bloggs. With Doris Day, Nick Adams, Mamie Van Doren, Gig Young, Peter Baldwin, Marion Ross, Jack Albertson and Vivian Nathan.
Clark Gable was top billing. 119 minutes.

## BUT NOT FOR ME                PARAMOUNT, 1959
Director: Walter Lang. Screenplay: John Michael Hayes, based on the stage play, *Accent On Youth* by Samson Raphaelson. Photography: Robert Burks. With Carroll Baker, Lilli Palmer, Lee J. Cobb, Thomas Gomez, Barry Coe, Tommy Duggan, Charles Lane and Wendell Holmes.
Clark Gable was top billing. 104 minutes.

## IT STARTED IN NAPLES                PARAMOUNT, 1960
Director: Melville Shavelson. Screenplay: Melvyn Shavelson/Suso Cecchi d'Amico/Jack Rose, based on a story by Michael Pertwee and Jack Davies. Photography: Robert Surtees. With Sophia Loren, Marietto, Vittorio de Sica, Paolo Carlini, Claudio Ermelli and Giovanni Filidoro.
Clark Gable was top billing. 99 minutes.

## THE MISFITS                UNITED ARTISTS, 1961
Director: John Huston. Screenplay: Arthur Miller. Photography: Russell Metty. With Marilyn Monroe, Montgomery Clift, Thelma Ritter, Eli Wallach, Estelle Winwood, James Barton, Kevin McCarthy, Dennis Shaw, Philip Mitchell, Walter Ramage and Lew Smith.
Clark Gable was top billing. 124 minutes.

Additionally, he made guest appearances in the following productions:

**1932**
*Jackie Cooper's Christmas*

**1934**
*Hollywood On Parade Number 6*
*Hollywood On Parade Number 13*

**1935**
*Starlight Days At The Lido*

**1944**
*Hollywood In Uniform*
*Be Careful!* (Narrator only)
*Wings Up!* (Narrator only)

**1951**
*The Screen Actor*
*Calloway Went Thataway!*

**1953**
*Memories In Uniform*

# Documentaries

**CAROLE LOMBARD & CLARK GABLE** (1987, 26 minutes)
An episode of BBC Worldwide's acclaimed *Great Romances* series, produced by Jonathan Martin, scripted by Robin Cross and narrated by Robert Powell.

This features brief biographical details of the two stars, clips from their early films, home-movie footage in colour of one of their hunting trips, a silent press-conference after their wedding (to blank out Carole's cursing!) and actual out-takes from two of her films, where she lets rip. There is also footage of the final war-bonds rally and the plane-wreck. 'The years with Lombard had been the happiest of Clark Gable's life,' Powell concludes, before adding, 'Lombard had died for love, pure and simple.'

**GABLE ON FILM: A BIOGRAPHY** (2000, 30 minutes).
Released by Delta Entertainment as a bonus to their restored DVD release of *The Painted Desert*. Produced by Roy Shakked, scripted by Tim Bartel and narrated by Barry Stigler. A misnomer on both counts, but a worthy addition to the Gable fan's collection because it contains rare theatrical trailers: *Lone Star* (theatrical release, with Gable voiceover), *China Seas, Mutiny On The Bounty, To Please A Lady, Run Silent, Run Deep* and *The Misfits*.

**LIVING FAMOUSLY: CLARK GABLE** (2003, 58 minutes). An episode of the BBC television series directed by Steve Greenwood and narrated by Caroline Quentin. It could have been better researched and the producer stretches things (with the exceptions of

Judy Lewis and Barry Norman) with an unrelated guest list. What does a daytime television fashion expert have to do with Clark Gable, and do we really need to see middle-aged Scarlett O'Hara lookalikes who confess to dreaming of being in Clark's arms? Even so, it is the best of a pretty paltry bunch, though there are several howlers. Gable was *not* registered as a girl on his birth certificate, nor did he knock on Josephine Dillon's door while working as a travelling salesman! Additionally, aside from the publicised event while shooting *Call Of The Wild*, he was not in the habit of frequenting brothels – women always served themselves to him on a plate. And he most definitely did not have a 'hidden penthouse' tucked away in Hollywood for 'clandestine' meetings with Carole Lombard. Barry Norman does his best to salvage the production by repeating Gable's own take on how he wanted to be remembered: 'He was lucky, and he knew it!' Then fellow critic Derek Malcolm camps the whole thing up by opining, 'If he went up to heaven and God asked him what he'd like to be remembered for, he'd have to say *Gone With The Wind*!'

# Bibliography:
## Primary And Secondary Sources

Albert, Katherine, 'What's Wrong With Hollywood Love?' *Modern Screen*, undated.
— 'What They Said About Joan Crawford': *Photoplay*, 8/31
Alpert, Hollis, *The Barrymores*, Dial Press, 1964
Anger, Kenneth, *Hollywood Babylon I & II*, Arrow, 1986
Baskette, Kirtley: 'Hollywood's Unmarried Husbands & Wives 1, *Photoplay*, 1/39
Bret, David, *Tallulah Bankhead*, Robson Books, 1996
— *Joan Crawford*, Robson Books, 2006
— Interviews with Marlene Dietrich and Douglas Fairbanks Jr, David Bret, 1993
Camp, Dan, 'Career Comes First With Loretta', *Motion Picture*, undated.
Chrisman, J Eugene, 'Norma Takes A Dare', *Screen Book*, undated.
Crawford, Joan, *Portrait of Joan* (with Jane Kesner Armore), Doubleday, 1962.
Eames, John Douglas, *The MGM Story*, Octopus, 1979.
Essoe, Gabe, *The Films of Clark Gable*, Citadel, 1972
Eyman, Scott, *Lion of Hollywood: The Life & Legend of Louis B Mayer*, Robson Books, 2005.
Gardner, Ava, *Ava, My Story*, Bantam, 1990.
Greif, Martin, *The Gay Book of Days*, W H Allen, 1985.
Hall, Gladys, 'Gable: Why I Stay Married/ What's The Matter With Lombard?', *Modern Screen*, undated.

Harris, Warren G, *Clark Gable*, Aurum, 2002

— *Gable & Lombard*, Simon & Schuster, 1974.

Hopper, Hedda, *The Whole Truth and Nothing But*, Doubleday, 1963.

LaGuardia, Robert, *Monty, A Biography of Montgomery Clift*, Arbor House, 1977.

Lambert, Gavin, *Norma Shearer*, Knopf, 1990.

Lee, Sonia, 'Jean Harlow, From Extra To Star', *Screen Book*, undated.

Lewis, Judy, *Uncommon Knowledge*, Pocket Books, 1994.

Maddox, Ben, 'What About Clark Gable Now?', *Screenland*, undated, part-spiked.

— Jean Harlow, The One Star Who Has No Enemies', *Screenland*, undated, part-spiked.

— 'Jean Harlow Carries On', *Screen Book*, undated.

— 'Why Girls Say "Yes!"', *Silver Screen*, undated, part-spiked.

Mann, William J, *William Haines: Wisecracker*, Penguin NY, 1988.

Manners, Dorothy, 'The Girl Without A Past', *Photoplay*, 10/35

Medved, Harry & Michael, *The Golden Turkey Awards*, Angus & Robertson, 1980.

Mooring, W H, 'Prescription for Joan Crawford', *Film Weekly*, 4/39.

Newquist, Roy, *Conversations with Joan Crawford*, Citadel, 1980.

Niven, David, *Bring On The Empty Horses*, Putnam, 1975.

Norman, Barry, *The Hollywood Greats*, Hodder & Stoughton, 1979.

Parsons, Louella, *Tell It To Louella*, Putnam, 1961

Porter, Darwin, *The Secret Life of Humphrey Bogart*, Georgia Literary Association, 2003

Quinlan, David, *Quinlan's Film Stars/ Character Actors*, Batsford, 1981 & 1986.

Quirk, Laurence J, *Fasten Your Seat Belts: The Passionate Life of Bette Davis*, Robson Books, 1990.

— The Films of Joan Crawford, Citadel, 1968.

Ramsey, Walter, 'Franchot Tone, Gentleman Rebel', *Photoplay*, undated.

Rooney, Mickey, *Life Is Too Short*, Hutchinson, 1988.

Stenn, David, *Bombshell, The Life & Death of Jean Harlow*,

Lightning Bug, 1993.

Swindell, Larry, *Screwball, The Life of Carole Lombard*, Morrow, 1975.

Thomas, Bob, *Thalberg, Life & Legend*, Doubleday, 1969.

Tornabene, Lyn, *Clark Gable: Long Live The King*, Putnam, 1976.

Turner, Lana, Lana: *The Lady, The Legend, The Truth*, Dutton, 1982.

Wallace, Irving, with Wallace, Amy; Wallace, Sylvia & Wallechinsky, David, *The Secret Sex Lives of Famous People*, Chancellor Press, 1993.

Wayne, Jane Ellen, *Golden Girls of MGM*, Robson Books, 2003

— *Golden Guys of MGM*, Robson Books, 2003.

— *Crawford's Men*, Robson Books, 1988.

— Ava Gardner, *Her Life & Loves*, Robson Books, 1990.

Wilson, Ivy Crane, *Hollywood Album*, Sampson Low & Marston, 1953.

# INDEX